Now Is Too Late^2

Survival in an Era of Instant News

GERALD R. BARON

EDENSVEIL

Published by Edens Veil Media

Please direct any comments, questions, or suggestions regarding this book to:

Edens Veil Media
1319 Cornwall Ave., Suite 200
Bellingham, WA 98225
(360) 671-8708
(360) 647-5351 fax
www.nowistoolate2.com

ISBN 0-615-13203-0
Printed in the United States of America
Second Edition

Table of Contents

Summer Solstice, 2006

Acknowledgements

Writing a book is a journey, as is building a business and living your life. As one looks back on any journey, usually there are a number of people you can point to and say, "I would not be here if it were not for them."

As I reflect back briefly on the journey that is this book, the business that it involves and my very rich life, there are far too many people who fit in that category for me to mention here. Yet, it would be wrong to decide because of that to mention none. And while there are no such clear divisions in life, I have broken my expression of appreciation into groupings of those who assisted most with this book, with the arduous task of building a company now known as AudienceCentral, and of maneuvering through this life.

Book

There are a great many clients who gave me the opportunity to learn, and colleagues with whom I had the privilege of working alongside. I cannot even begin to mention all of them, and attempting to do so would be to risk disappointment and questions. But to all of you, and you know who are, I say thank you for contributing your ideas, experiences and character with me. Thank you for giving me the opportunity to learn and forgive me for taking credit in this book for the lessons you taught me.

There are those who contributed directly to this work, however. They include Chris Haley, Tim O'Leary, Neil Chapman, Steve Brinn, Norm Stanley, Judith Moorad, Mark Koslicki, Chuck Martin, Steve Hortegas and many others. They are all included in this book, but only they will be able to identify themselves.

My highly respected colleague Jonathan Bernstein was of immense help in many ways, including editing the new chapters in this edition – not to mention all the ideas and experience I have gained from working closely with him. Bob Elmer, former employee and now fulltime novelist, was helpful not just in teaching me more about writing, but also in providing a model of dedication. Carol Spano was a great help in keeping track of all the edits and versions and Jessica Evans did the final editing and helped assemble all the pieces for this edition. Brian Sibley and Ryan Pemberton picked up where Jessica left off, due to her taking a new position. Scott Friesen did the compelling cover design for this edition as well as the much improved page design. Rob Takemura of Applied Digital Imaging was a great help in preparing the issue for print.

Business

Much of what is conveyed in this book has been learned in the process of building a new technology business aimed at helping leaders communicate effectively in this instant news world. Consequently, it is very difficult if not impossible, to separate those who contributed most directly to the success of that business and whatever is valuable in this book. While this list is far from exhaustive, these people stand out for their many contributions.

AudienceCentral's CEO Paul Grey has done a remarkable job building a company with very limited resources, which in many ways, is now a powerhouse. He also took the time to edit each revised chapter. Mike New is an inspiration and encourager with great vision and passion. There were a few people who were strong supporters from the very beginning of this journey, and who encouraged with funds as well as words; to them I will be forever grateful. They include Bill Palmer, Steve Brinn, John Gargett, Bill Kidd, Glenn Butler, Bob Warshawer, Butch Edison, Tim Clossey, and Paul Hansen.

Creating new technology is rarely possible alone. PIER, as a product, would not be here were it not first of all for Kjell Ostlund, the original programmer (and his sidekick Jesse Pollack), Todd Quessenberry who enhanced and modified it, and Barney Boisvert, whose incredible talents made it a actual, stable product; I stand in awe.

Marc Mullen was the first employee of this new venture. We date the birth of the company to his arrival. Everyone who knows AudienceCentral knows that it would not be here without this remarkable man who teaches all those who have the great pleasure to work with him, as well as for him, what dedicated, humble service means. And I couldn't be happier that one of his protégés, who is blossoming under the opportunity and leadership, is my own son, Geoffrey. My gratitude also goes to Jamie Imus for his enthusiasm and commitment, to Brian Rockwell and Dan Timmins out on the front lines, and to Lach Mullen for bringing more of that Mullen grace and goodness to the office. Carol Spano was mentioned already in relation to the book, but she is very much a backbone without whom it seems we all would collapse.

Although not directly involved in the building of AudienceCentral, my colleagues and associates at Baron & Company have contributed far more than they are credited with, in part by allowing me the freedom to wander occasionally from my responsibilities. Particular thanks go in this regard to Jason Glover, Jason Lee, and Scott Friesen and Diane Williams who form the creative team. My thanks also to Alexandrea Spaulding who provided valued leadership during my wandering, and to Steve Hortegas who has since then taken a very different path, but who was immensely helpful in keeping the ship afloat while I was distracted by writing and starting this venture. Gabe Rodriguez, Brian Rollo and Dan Mason, who now head the Internet application area – what will be next guys?

Most of all in this connection I need to thank Marilyn Vermeulen. Marilyn has been my bookkeeper and close support for most of the past twenty-five years in business. It may surprise many who know her to think that she could be so supportive of someone who can never walk a straight path, but she has. And knowing I had to face her furrowed brow and wry smile when I came looking for money to spend on some new crazy idea, has kept me out of trouble on many occasions. Thank you Marilyn, for your faithfulness and dedication.

Life

This book, and the experiences recorded in it, is but one part of a very rich and full life. All those who are in my life contribute to its contents, and many have also had to suffer through my enthusiasms about this project and the work I love. It is a good time to thank them as well.

First, Sid and Margaret Baron who gave me life, gave me a model to life my life by, taught me about faith, courage and commitment, and gave me three great brothers and two sisters, I thank you. Jim, Ron, Alan, Kaye and Julie and your families, thank you for your love, forgiveness and acceptance. I also want to thank my wife Lynne's family, the Bosman clan, for your quiet strength and joy.

At great risk of missing someone important, I also want to thank my good friends Bill Palmer, Mike Roberts, Alan Brim and Frank Imhof. A hunting trip or two with Frank, and I've had many, will teach most of what you need to know about crisis management.

I've saved my own family for last, for good reason. They are the joy of my life, my reason for waking up. Their support, affection and good humor has sustained me and motivates me to be the best I can be. To Chris and Deborah Baron, Geoff and Amy Baron, Gabe and Ashley Rodriguez, my grateful thanks. Lynne and I have been gifted with the greatest joy it seems anyone can experience in this life with the coming of grandchildren Emily and Ethan Baron and Baron Rodriguez. Thanks children, and keep them coming!

Finally, it is impossible to adequately thank my wife Lynne. She has been my friend, companion, lover and helpmate for almost 33 years as I write this. It's been a marvelous and surprising journey and there cannot be anyone I would rather have traveled it with than Lynne. Her great gifts of knowing and appreciating beauty have added immeasurably to my life, and her wonderful warmth and friendliness have not only compensated for my opposite tendencies, but have brought numerous friends into our life together. Thank you Lynne, and I look forward to the rest of the journey.

The final word is to offer thanks to my Creator and Lord who taught and teaches the depth of loving sacrifice, which stands at the heart of all true and good action. To You, all glory.

Foreword to the Second Edition

As a former drama student, I believe that life is a story and all good books, including non-fiction, have at their heart a compelling story. A story contains a beginning, middle and end. It has characters you care about, action that defines character, and a setting that contains and reflects the action.

As you will read, the story here begins in 1999. Although well into a career in marketing and public relations, an event on an early summer day began a sequence of events and activities that have culminated in the book you hold in your hand. And somehow, I had an inkling at the time. During those intense days, I remember telling my wife that I thought life would never be quite the same.

Entrepreneurs and creators are, at heart, dissatisfied people. They see things as they are and see that they could be changed. They then see how they can be changed, and given the right mix of support and commitment, they set about making those changes. That was true of my experience in helping to manage public information in a high profile and devastating tragedy. The world had changed, I saw, but the people, processes and tools that we were using to try to meet the demands of a changed world were lagging far behind.

After a technology solution was developed, I found there was a more intractable problem than simply not having the appropriate technology. Those who needed to make decisions about how to manage public information in extreme circumstances did not understand how the world had changed. I couldn't fix that problem with technology, I concluded. But perhaps I could with a book.

The first edition was drafted in late 2001, shortly after the attack on our country. That experience highlighted a great many things relevant to this topic. Other events also brought the role of the media and the changing expectations of audiences to the forefront. When I sat down to write this second edition in early 2006, I was surprised to see how much has changed in the world of public information. There is undoubtedly an increased awareness of the need for speed and direct communication in our instant news world, but the rules are being rewritten before we even get a chance to learn the new ones. The old world, dominated by network broadcast news and major print journalism, is rapidly giving way to the world of global, internet-connected citizen journalism. In this world, the once powerful, such as CBS's Dan Rather, can find themselves overcome almost overnight by the new powerhouses – the bloggers who amass tens of thousands of readers while sipping coffee at Starbucks. We see the ancient respected founts of knowledge such as the Encyclopedia Britannica overwhelmed in mere months by a free form, largely unmanaged and unmanageable source of knowledge and opinion known as Wikipedia.

I was talking with one executive of a non-profit organization who had been through numerous crises in his thirty-year career of organization management and who was now dealing with a "perfect storm" sort of crisis. The difference between the earlier crisis and this one? Speed. With email, global networks of people and organizations, information and false information spreads at ever increasing speeds.

At heart, this book deals with two issues: technology and what it is doing to our expectations about communication. Understanding the rapidly changing world of public information and how reputations are made and lost is critically important to almost any leader of any organization subject to public and stakeholder opinion. My goal in this is simple. It is the same as my goal in helping clients through future-threatening crises. I want to help good people accomplish good things. If this succeeds in helping you prepare for what can happen, I will have accomplished my goal.

I encourage you to contact me with your questions, comments, arguments or (even) praise. You can reach me at ***www.nowistoolate2.com***

I.
Discovering the New World of Instant News

Mid-June in the far upper corner of the Pacific Northwest is a time of anticipation. The long spells of dreary rain begin to give way to the piercingly bright blue of summer and, when the sun does emerge, the days are long with the sun setting shortly before 9 p.m.

June 10, 1999, was one of those promising days. Two 10-year-old boys were playing in the park right below their homes. Not like most city parks, this park is a typical Northwest rainforest, though right near the heart of a city of more than 70,000 people. Trails cut narrow swaths through a dense and dark forest. Whatcom Creek runs through the center of the park and, immediately after it exits the park, it flows right through downtown Bellingham. Past the big car dealership, past a number of office buildings, right below the jail windows, right past City Hall, and past the Whatcom County Courthouse. The stream starts at Lake Whatcom, a 12-mile lake at the eastern edge of the city. After plunging down a beautiful falls with a drop of about 30 feet, the 50-foot wide creek meanders through the towering firs and hemlocks, finally exiting into Bellingham Bay right near the Georgia Pacific pulp and chemical plant.

The near-downtown stream was a favorite of fishermen as well. Around 4 p.m., an 18-year-old, who had just graduated from a local high school the week before, was enjoying early summer by fly-fishing on the creek. He was about a half-mile upstream from where the boys were playing.

What happened next began a series of events that changed my understanding of what was happening in the world, much as Sept. 11, 2001, changed the understanding of many others around the world.

Returning from a speaking engagement in Spokane, a six-hour drive east along Interstate Highway 90 from Bellingham, I received a phone call near 5 p.m. My wife was frantic. "What was that?" she shouted in my ear. My wife is a remarkably calm and strong woman. Hearing the fear and uncertainty in her voice immediately put me on high alert.

"What do you mean, 'What was that'?" I asked.

"It looks like half the town has blown up!" she said.

From her point of view, it was not an exaggeration. She was observing from the front yard of our house a mile and a half long wall of black smoke that would quickly tower to 30,000 feet. I asked if it was Mount Baker. The nearly 11,000-foot mountain was a semi-active volcano and after Mt. St. Helens, everyone in our region is aware of the risk of sudden volcanic activity. She didn't know. She had to check on the kids and so she was gone off the phone.

My kids – there were three of them. That was my concern, and mental inventory. One was safely in college in Chicago. My second son was in an apartment about a half-mile north of us – right in the direction of the plume. My daughter was safely at home.

"Turn on the radio," I snapped at my young employee who was driving the car. We tried to get a Seattle station that might have some news, but we were on the edge of their coverage area. Not long after the aborted phone call, we picked up a breaking news story on the radio. A pipeline explosion in downtown Bellingham. A huge plume of black smoke. No more details.

There are four oil refineries in our area. It's a natural place given the enclosed waters of northern Puget Sound and the proximity to the Alaska North Slope oil fields. The millions of gallons of fuel produced by these four refineries flowed primarily through a fuel products pipeline. All the jet fuel used by the busy SeaTac airport came directly from the refineries to the airport via pipeline.

The pipeline was built in 1965 and ran from the Cherry Point area about 10 miles northwest of Bellingham where two refineries were located, around through what was then the outskirts of Bellingham, south toward Mount Vernon, where the lines from the two refineries near Anacortes connected with the main pipeline at a point called Bayview.

I had become quite familiar with one of those Anacortes refineries because it had become a major client. The refinery had experienced a devastating accident with six fatalities and I was assisting with rebuilding community relationships and with ongoing media coverage.

Shortly after hearing from the scratchy radio about some enormous explosion just a mile or so from my house, and trying to keep myself calm while I repeatedly tried to get my wife on her cell phone which was now continually busy, I received another call. It was from Houston. On the phone was a communication manager who was the contact point for my work with the refinery. He calmly informed me that the "Away Team," a group of professionals designated to deal with major incidences for their company and related companies, was on the way to Bellingham.

"Why?" I asked.

"Because it's our pipeline," he said. Actually, my client was the managing partner in an ownership structure that included one other major oil company with a refinery in the area and a transportation company.

Until getting that call, I was a member of the audience, affected by the events and with a high demand for information. So high was my demand that I was presumptuous enough to call the manager of the local radio station on the phone to get more information since I was still too far away to get the local radio signal. But with that phone call from Houston, my position changed. I was no longer an audience member, impatient for any bit of information, I became a part of the team that tried to meet that demand – a team that faced innumerable obstacles to getting the right information to the right people when they wanted it. The realities of the new world of instant news were about to make themselves very clear.

The two 10-year-olds were good friends. Both were active in sports, particularly baseball. They played together a lot and a favorite place was the creek, which dropped down a deep gully behind their homes. Something must have seemed strange to them that day. A strong smell, an overpowering smell like gasoline. As strong as it was, it didn't deter them from playing near the stream with a barbecue lighter they carried with them.

Upstream from them, a little below the city's water treatment facility, stood the 18-year-old fly fisherman. He too must have noticed the smell. Quickly it became overpowering. As he started to try to get away from it, it overwhelmed him and before he could climb out of the fast flowing stream, now flowing not just with water but with some of the 277,000 gallons of gasoline spilling from a 27-inch wide gash in the underground pipeline, he fell into the gasoline and water mixture and drowned.

Fumes were now rising from the stream into the canopy of heavy trees that covered both sides of the stream and the steep sides of the canyon through which it flowed. The barbecue lighter, just an interesting toy to the boys, now lit off the gasoline choking the stream and a rolling explosion began in two directions at once. It thundered downstream to the point where it meets the Interstate Highway 5 Bridge, which crosses the creek just before entering downtown. It also rolled a half-mile upstream, flashing up Hannah Creek, a small tributary, until it reached the point of the leak just yards below the city's water treatment facility.

The boys, with horrific burns over 90 percent of their bodies, managed to climb up the steep bank to be met by horrified friends and family members. They were rushed to the local hospital, then to a regional burn center in Seattle, but their lives ended early the next day.

In the scale of events, this may not rank up with major earth shattering news events such as Sept. 11, or even major industrial disasters, such as Exxon Valdez or Bhopal. But to Bellingham citizens, and particularly to those directly affected by this event, it marks a milestone by which time, history, and lives are measured. "Where were you June 10?" makes as much sense in our town as it does asking where you were

Nov. 22, Dec. 7 or Sept. 11. Almost all people of the area have their stories about where they were, what they were doing and how they heard. How they first heard, and how they got subsequent information that was important to them, is the relevant question that we are dealing with here.

We could take any event like this and look how the information about it would flow in various times and cultures. For most of human history, information about life changing events would be personal and direct. You tell me what you know and I tell the next person or perhaps a group of people. That is definitely not mass media. The first thing that might be considered close to mass media was the town crier. As villages and towns emerged, news, and even commercial announcements, were made by a person with a loud voice calling out from a tower. With this method, you could get the word out to perhaps a small village or at least a larger group. A small village might stretch the definition of mass audience, but the crier was definitely a medium – an intermediary who carried the message from the person or event serving as the source to an audience presumably hungry for the story.

Gutenberg's machine led to the ever faster and cheaper production of the written word. Newspapers emerged and made it possible for a great many people to get essentially the same information relatively quickly. Mass media was born. It took on a greater immediacy with radio, and achieved an even greater impact when immediacy was combined with the real-time images of television.

For the past 300 years, we have been living in a world of expanding public information dominated by the media: a "media world." In a media world, information comes directly or indirectly. Direct information is still very much limited to personal observation or talking directly to someone else by phone or personal, face-to-face conversation. Indirect, or information via media, is provided by those who control the means of distribution – the printing presses or broadcast transmitters. This is the way things have worked for a long time, and most people have been pretty content to have things work this way. However, things are no longer quite so simple, because now there is a new way of communicating that blends the personal with the impersonal, and at the same time destroys the monopoly that media have held on mass public information. The Internet provides the immediacy, visual impact and information content of the best of other media, but it delivers that content directly to the individual member of the audience. This immediacy, directness and depth result in profound changes in expectations. The adoption of the Internet is but one of several significant technological and cultural changes that has altered how the world gets its information. This change represents new risks and new opportunities for businesses and organizations that may find themselves, willingly or not, in the news.

When the ground beneath us moves, when sea changes occur, the reaction is not necessarily immediate. On June 10, 1999, I was living in the instant news world but didn't realize or comprehend it. As a result, my behavior and actions, as well as those of my colleagues working hard on the information response to the pipeline tragedy, were a response to a world that had changed. Only in looking back on the things we did well and those things that could have been improved did I begin to more thoroughly understand that we are living in a fundamentally different era.

The Gatling gun – a rudimentary machine gun – was introduced during the U.S. Civil War. Close formation charges against overwhelming artillery or machine gun firepower made absolutely no sense. But tactics do not change readily. The tried and true methods are often relied upon until clearly and unquestionably proven to be no longer useful. The battle of English longbow archers against the massed glory of French knights is another example. Agincourt would have been an easy victory for the French if they had more thoroughly understood how the strong arms and powerful bows of the English peasantry could defeat their formerly undefeatable armor.

Providing public information is not exactly a war, although for those on the front lines, it can feel uncannily like a genuine battle. The consequences can be quite serious – for the reputation of the company or organization as well as for the impact on a great many lives. The devastating hurricanes of 2005, Katrina and Rita, provide clear examples of the critical nature of public communication, both for public safety and for the reputation of people and organizations involved in responding to these events. After Sept. 11, we are more aware that providing the right amount of accurate public information at the right time is a fundamentally strategic issue as far as national security and national welfare are concerned. The point here is that tactics need to change when there has been a fundamental shift in the ground rules. The ground rules of public information have changed forever. The way the media gathers, prepares and distributes the news has changed. Perhaps more importantly, the role of the media as the sole provider of mass public information is no more. We shall not return to the days when soldiers marching in lockstep toward a well-entrenched enemy, who has the firepower to wipe them all out, is the strategy of choice. And we shall never return to the days when corporate and organization executives and their communication staffs and experts can operate under the old paradigms of a mediated, news-cycle world and expect to protect their reputations.

That the media continues to be a primary means of public information is beyond question. But the traditional media are changing as well, in part to meet the new challenges represented by the Internet. The changes in traditional media, combined with the use of the Internet as a direct means of public information, require substantial change in policies, people and technology for those concerned about reputation protection in this modern news era.

Information Response

Early morning on June 11, 1999, the basement of the Whatcom County Courthouse was being quickly turned into a response command post. The Bellingham Fire Department was in command during the immediate response, and they were closely monitoring the progress of fumes throughout the city's sewer system during the night. As the afternoon turned into uneasy night in the small city, most residents were unaware that a citywide evacuation was actively considered but eventually determined to be unnecessary.

The sheriff's search and rescue team began conducting a thorough search of the "hot zone" while the ground near the rupture site still flamed. It was then they discovered the body of the 18-year-old fly fisherman. At that time it was unknown if there were more fatalities or injuries.

Responders began arriving from all over. Soon there were more than 40 response agencies and over 300 people crowding into the small offices and corridors of the courthouse basement. An information team was loosely organized and we began to develop the information needed for the press of media standing outside the door of the command center and calling by phone. While the response commanders got themselves organized, Bill Boyd, the Bellingham Fire Department spokesperson continued to speak for the response. Company officials along with the response commanders decided to hold a press conference at 11 a.m. on the morning of the 11th. The top company official on-scene, the vice president in charge of operations for the pipeline, would be the one to face the cameras and reporters.

Earlier, a Sheriff's Department helicopter was attempting to land near the city water treatment plant about an hour after the explosion occurred. As it was seeking a clear place to land, another helicopter swooped in and landed. The Sheriff's Department helicopter landed nearby and, furious with the intrusion, the sheriff deputy strode up to the people exiting the other chopper. It was the executive team arriving from the pipeline company's offices in Renton, near Seattle. The deputy recalled later how the copter's passengers emerged, tears streaming down their faces, and his intention to issue his complaint disappeared. He realized, as he recounted later, there was tragedy all around that day. The company had operated for 34 years without so much as a serious injury, now this.

At 11:00 a.m., the company executive stood before the press in front of a large mahogany dais where the Bellingham City Council meets. Satellite trucks lined the street outside City Hall. Perhaps two-dozen reporters waited inside with about six television crews. He started out, "This is the blackest day in our history..." It was a quotation that provided the headline for the next day's local daily. He hadn't slept during the night; he was clearly visibly shaken and shocked. The press conference did not go well. The Fire Department and Bellingham Police officials gave solid summaries specific to the search and rescue efforts, the damage to the creek, the extent of the fire and explosion and the current state of the hot zone. The executive received questions about cause, about what the company could have done to prevent it, whether or not the company was accepting responsibility and why in the world was the pipeline crossing a creek that flowed right into downtown.

An enduring image I have of that day is the lead public relations manager for the company with his arms around his friend, the company vice president, as they walked from the City Hall following the difficult press conference back to the Emergency Operation Center, or command post, in the basement of County Courthouse. The PR manager had been brought out of retirement to help with the response, and through his long history and extensive contacts in the oil industry, had gotten this manager his job a number of years earlier. The two were old friends, now brought together again under circumstances that probably seemed unimaginable when, years earlier, they celebrated this executive landing his new job. And even at this low point, they likely could not imagine that these tragic events would lead to six months in prison for the pipeline company manager.

For the next three weeks, the EOC (Emergency Operation Center), as it came to be called, was the center of my life. Fortunately, I was in my own hometown and so could go home at night after a long day in the EOC, unlike my compatriots who called one of the local hotels home. A routine slowly emerged:

- Collect the facts by attending the Unified Command briefings or going around to the key players in the Fire Department, sheriff's office or Department of Emergency Management to find out what was going on.
- Assemble the facts into the next version of the Fact Sheet being prepared to issue to the media. Get signoff from the commanders on the Fact Sheet.
- Coordinate with the various agencies such as Department of Ecology, Environmental Protection Agency, police, fire and sheriff's office for the next press conference.
- And always, without stop, attempt to stem the tide of reporters calling by phone, collecting outside the door, and attempting to catch anyone who might emerge from the relative safety of the over-crowded EOC.

As the long, long days emerged into weeks, the focus expanded to include the various people in the community who wanted to know what was going on and who had a right to know what was going on. Phone calls, meetings, broadcast faxes, mailings and public meetings were all used to get information out about the response, the unfolding story of the horrific damage to the park and the environment and the very limited information emerging about how this sort of thing could have happened.

It was in reflecting back on the experience of dealing with the pipeline incident, along with several other situations of high public interest, that the realization grew that we are living in a very different world. The new era of instant news was creating very different expectations from the news media and the audiences – expectations about speed and directness of information. Reviewing the coverage in the newspapers and television reports demonstrated something I had been increasingly aware of: news is often designed to fit a pre-determined formula. It's a formula not dictated by the information but by the media's understanding of the audience's need to be entertained. It is a blending of information and entertainment that results in public information being packaged in a way that resembles melodrama, complete with white hats and black hats. It seems to intentionally ignore the complexities of real life and real events. In the new era of instant news, information demands are growing exponentially and audiences are quickly developing whole new expectations regarding events or facts that affect their lives.

In many respects, while the communication team did an admirable job, we were living in an era that had passed by. We had entered a post-media world, but were operating as if it was still a media world. We were in the early stages of an instant news world but we operated in a time frame and with measured steps that reflected a much slower news environment. The subsequent viewpoint expressed by some in the community that the public information effort was bungled, was not an indictment against the effort made, but more a reflection that change had occurred. The team members, who came from government agencies, from the companies involved, from public relations and communications firms, did a credible and professional job. But like the massed columns advancing in the U.S. Civil War, or the inglorious charge of the French mounted knights, we were fighting a battle with outmoded tactics and technologies. This was only clear, however, after the battle was long over.

A Non-Instant News Response

Not everyone is afforded the luxury of a wake-up call that a new day has dawned. My wake-up call came on reflection of what was done well and what could be improved. The evidence of an instant news world was all around, but not clearly visible or understandable until realizing the ways in which we missed the mark. At the time, it appeared there were no choices or options. Later, however, those options became more visible and with them, an understanding that an entirely new way of thinking about providing public information was needed.

Listed below are some of the key elements that were identified as indicators that change was needed.

1) No "Golden Hour" response
2) Inadequate internal communication
3) Antiquated information distribution
4) "Scratchpad" method of database development
5) Handcuffed without email
6) Separate Web team to update site
7) Behind the curve on media response
8) The "media first" mistake
9) The approval process slow down
10) No inquiry and response tracking
11) No way to easily update new reporters

1. No "Golden Hour" Response

While definitions may vary, most crisis communication experts consider the first hour of response the "Golden Hour." Why focus on this first hour? Because in most breaking news events, the initial reports will emerge in this first hour and the story will begin to be told and written. As the old saying goes, "You only have one chance to make a first impression." Every subsequent news story will either follow the line of the initial story or will contradict it. Every reporter is influenced by the initial information emerging and the initial public reports, as is every member of the audience. The information that is available, the way it is prioritized and presented, who it comes from, who it does NOT come from, the context of the information, the history of similar events – all these are critical items normally included in the first reports emerging from an incident.

In the pipeline incident, there was no effectively coordinated "Golden Hour" response. The initial reports coming from a company spokesperson operating on contract from a location nowhere near the scene later turned out to be completely inaccurate. The company had little to no visibility until 11a.m. the next morning at a press conference. The inability to very quickly "push" information to the media and other stakeholders about the company, its background and history and whatever information about the incident that was known at that time, did not bode well for the ongoing information response. Since this event, in working with a wide variety of company executives and communication managers, it has become clear that this inability to meet new information demands was not unique, but is very common. While some companies and industries with high risk of major public events have extensive preparations in place, many do not. Many communicators seem to believe that a communication team has hours or even days to put the infrastructure in place, organize the information process and get to work. But numerous events such as Sept. 11, Enron-Andersen, the devastating 2005 hurricanes and other stories, demonstrate that the communicator's understanding of doing it "now" means they will probably be too late.

2. Inadequate Internal Communication

In a real news-making event, the communication team has a great many responsibilities. Effective internal communication is certainly one of them but it is frequently inadequately managed because of the overwhelming demand for information from reporters and external stakeholders. It is natural for those trained in public relations to think first about responding to the media, but failing to communicate effectively internally impacts the effectiveness of the actual response, sometimes dramatically. Sept. 11 demonstrated to many executives that they were unprepared to quickly reach employees at their workplaces or homes, particularly in a major news event when telephone service was impaired. One of the main lessons coming from the failed response of federal, local and state organizations in Hurricane Katrina was that internal communication was disastrously ineffective.

Internal communication means effectively gathering the needed bits and pieces of information, as well as being the source of reliable information for internal audiences. Those audiences include corporate management, employees, other company communication team members, the immediate response team, and other agencies or organizations involved in the response. The reality is that many of these people who need to have the latest and most accurate information about what is going on are not likely to be on scene. It looks like an impossible situation – and without the proper planning, policies and technologies it really is impossible. Communication teams, who believe they are prepared to deal with media response, quickly become overwhelmed in a situation in which one of their most critical needs is keeping internal audiences, who are not on-scene, fully up-to-date with what is happening.

In the emergency center following the pipeline accident, the communication team on-scene was focused on preparing and distributing information to the media. This was the task the team understood it was assembled for. All other efforts were secondary, ad hoc and uncoordinated. The impacts of this can be very significant; one of them being the confidence or lack of confidence in the entire response team by the corporate and agency leaders who are not on-scene. If the organization leaders who are not on-scene don't have high-quality and timely information about what is going on, they cannot evaluate the effectiveness of the response. They need this information to determine whether or not additional resources are needed and whether or not to begin second-guessing the decisions of those who are extremely busy managing the response.

3. Antiquated Information Distribution

Technology has revolutionized business and government in the past many years. Unfortunately, there's a good chance if you find yourself in a command post responsible for managing an overwhelming crush of reporters and information-hungry stakeholders, your most important tools may be random scratch pads, barely workable phones and perhaps a single fax machine. You will likely find yourself in an alien and overcrowded setting, thinking longingly of your well-equipped office with its high-speed connection, computer, information resources, contact databases, and everything else you need to do your job.

At the very time when the dot-com explosion was dominating the business scene, the pipeline accident communication team did not have so much as a fax machine to support the communication effort. There were a few computers scattered around the EOC. The process of getting them adequately connected to working printers was enough of a challenge. Internet connection was not a reality until several days into the event, and then it was strictly through dialup connections. A few employees took laptops with them, but without a real network; data was transferred by floppies. In the basement of the County Courthouse, cell phones were mostly unusable.

The information process as it evolved was fairly simple. Someone would handwrite a draft of an updated information release and get it to the computer that was connected to the printer – an excruciatingly slow printer. The printed draft would be taken to the Unified Commanders and others who had direct knowledge of the latest information for their review and approval. The changes would be noted and a clean draft would be re-entered and printed, then back for approval. When it was approved, usually three to four drafts later, it was rushed to my office about six blocks from the EOC. There, one of my employees would stand by the fax machine and send it out to the rapidly growing list of fax numbers of reporters who were eagerly waiting for the latest dispatch from the incident's "joint information center." In the early days, the situation was very dynamic, so you can imagine how out-of-date the information was when it finally reached the desk of the last reporter on the fax list.

4) "Scratchpad" Method of Database Development

In an event of significant public interest, a large number of people are going to want, and expect, the latest information. The most important of these are the family members, close friends and associates of anyone who may be hurt or killed in the incident. The list quickly grows to neighbors closest to the event, to employees, to company leaders, to local elected officials, to people from the various agencies responding to the event, to prominent people in the community who hold their place because others consider them continually "in the know" and to – oh, yes, reporters: local reporters, regional reporters, national and international, industry reporters, stringers, publishers, broadcast executives and on and on.

As mentioned earlier, our method of distribution was to answer questions on the phone and to send our updated fact sheet to an outside office where someone stood for an ever increasing amount of time faxing it out and manually adding to the rapidly growing fax list. In a few days, it took two hours to send the broadcast fax. Now, if you were on the tail end of the two hours, and you were a reporter, you would probably not rely on the faxed fact sheet. When you got the new one, you'd probably call in and see what was new since the fax broadcast had started.

The growing list was developed very simply. Anyone of perhaps 10 or more people in the EOC assigned to take media or community calls would answer the phone, and if a reporter asked to be put on the fax distribution list, or wanted a call back for a later answer, the responder would take down the name, phone or fax number on any old piece of paper lying around. If it was to be added to the fax list, it would usually make its way to me and I would take it back to the office along with the next update. From there, my administrative assistant, Carol, would load it into the fax machine. There was no way of knowing whether the question was answered, whether the person got the information they needed, and no way for the communication leaders or information officers to know who had called, for what reason and whether a response had been properly offered. Management of the message was definitely by walking around.

5) Handcuffed Without Email

Connection junkies that we are, when separated from our cell phones, our text pagers and certainly our email, we become almost panic stricken. In the pipeline incident's EOC, most cell phones had very weak to no coverage and because Internet connections were almost nonexistent, email was out of the question. In "old world" crisis communications planning, the information center is designed to be a place where all those participating in the information function can gather together. Reality is not so neat. There are a number of people critical to the information function who cannot be physically present, but who need to participate in the information process – company and agency leaders, lawyers, experts with critical information, responders on-scene, etc. Take some of the routine methods of communication away, and everything tends to slow down and lose efficiency. Take email away, and replace it with phones that need to be shared with many others, all of whom have an urgent need for communicating, and you have frustration and inefficiency.

We have all become accustomed to working at our comfortable workstations. We have the tools at hand that we rely on to get things done. But in a crisis incident with a defined command center and information center, we find ourselves removed from that comfortable and efficient world. When the demands for efficient and accurate work are higher than they can possibly be in our normal routines, we are asked to do without the very things we rely on for quality communication. There was perhaps no greater lesson than this coming out of Hurricane Katrina. True disaster planning takes into consideration that all of your resources, including your EOC, your vehicles, your telephones, computers and Internet connections, may all be washed away. But you must still, respond and respond effectively.

There can only be two solutions to this very significant challenge – either we find a way to work from our well established work stations, or the tools we use to communicate, including email, PDA's, wireless phones, etc., must be completely accessible at the information center, regardless of where it is located. Joint information center locations must either be extremely well equipped with all the tools you would have access to in your office, or we must adopt the concept of a "virtual joint information center" in which a team can operate effectively regardless of location.

6) Separate Web Team to Update Site

It is quickly becoming commonplace that in any situation involving significant public interest, a Web site must play a key role. The effectiveness of a Web site as a critical information tool is dependent on the degree to which the communication manager or managers have direct and immediate control. Since 1999, there have been tremendous advances in the technologies that enable Web content to be managed "on the fly" by non-programmers or non-html writers – in other words, the rest of us. The widespread use of content management systems as well as the introduction of the Web-based virtual communication center has made it possible to free crisis Web sites from IT control and put control in the hands of communicators.

All things considered, in mid-1999, during the early stages of the response, we were fortunate to a have a Web presence for the event. It featured photos taken by the HAZMAT trained photographer authorized to take photos to be shared by all news organizations. No one was allowed into the "hot zone" without such training on operating in environments where hazardous materials are present. This resulted in the only photos or videos used coming from helicopter shots or those provided by the Fire Department authorized photographer. In addition to the photos, the Web site had all the latest fact sheets and these were usually posted within an hour or two of being approved.

But, the Web site used for the incident, provided only a fraction of the potential benefit for the information response. It was managed by one person, which meant it was limited by her availability and her work schedule. She was a county employee taking orders from the County Department of Emergency Management director. While this represented few significant problems, it became clear that as far as the Web was concerned, it was this person who managed information flow. The Web address was that of the county and it was almost impossible for anyone to remember. Since it was the county's property and under their control, information items of interest to reporters or an interested public on things such as the company's safety record, background information on the company, general pipeline safety information and the like were not considered for posting. There was also no way for the Web site to capture names and emails of visitors seeking updates, nor was there any ability to manage interactive communication, including receiving and responding to visitor inquiries – an ability that is far more critical today than it was in mid-1999.

As a result, after the emergency response began to evolve into a more long-term restoration effort, we developed a Web site for the company. Previously, the company did not even have a Web presence, being one of those companies not normally in the public eye, and whose managers considered it an advantage to "fly under the radar." Why bring yourself to attention when everything is going along swimmingly? So, a Web site was built to provide the kind of company information of interest to the public, the emerging activists as well as the media. Only now, the information focused on this one large event that would likely define the company in the minds of the public for all time.

7) Behind the Curve on Media Response

Few executives, or even communication professionals, can adequately prepare for the crush of eager, insistent reporters that automatically comes when the company or organization finds itself in the maelstrom. The media training, experienced by many people who may find themselves under the hot lights or behind the micro recorders, is valuable but rarely comes close to putting the stress on people like the real thing. This is particularly true when the person who steps in front of the camera knows that the questions may be intentionally aggressive, and the media may have already tried the company or organization in their own private courtroom and have delivered a guilty verdict.

As in most real situations, the press conferences were only the tip of the iceberg in the pipeline incident. It started out with the reporters trying to get the latest information from anyone who would talk to them. Then it changed to phone calls, often times over and over and over from the same reporter. And then new reporters would call, from the same publication or broadcaster, who needed to be taken through the entire sequence of events one more time. It is not unusual for the same reporter to call repeatedly to the information center with the same question looking for different responders to provide different answers. Then it evolves into private and individual interviews by phone or in person with reporters intent on getting scoops or pursuing their special angles.

Each stage of the process involved a different type of reporting and, as a result, should have received a different kind of media response. But despite the best efforts of everyone involved, in hindsight we were continually one stage behind the reporters. When they shifted to a new game, we were still playing the old one. Not able to take a strong step forward in information management, the information center continued in a highly reactive mode rather than taking the opportunity to anticipate and keep pace.

It was my strong sense at the time that we were doing a good job of handling the crush. It is true, the team worked well together, responded as efficiently and effectively as possible given the constraints we had. In retrospect, with the advantage of hindsight and particularly from the company's standpoint, I later understood we were continually playing catch up. Aside from the effort to reach out early to the community influencers, there was little effort to "get ahead of the curve" and take proactive steps to directly communicate key information and anticipate the direction of coverage and public interest. It is a situation that perhaps many people would consider normal or acceptable, but as will later become clear, getting behind the media curve is frequently deadly in this new era of instant and direct communication.

8) The "Media First" Mistake

How can putting the media first be a mistake to a communications professional, particularly a "public information officer?" Simply because there are a number of stakeholders who expect and believe they have a right to the absolute latest and most up- to-date information. Provide them unadulterated and truthful information before, or at least simultaneous with the media, and you gain appreciation and support. Give it to them through the media, and you are considered "unresponsive" or "uncaring."

Some of these people have been mentioned already. They include anyone with a close connection to the individuals who may have been personally and directly affected by the incident – family members, neighbors, co-workers and relatives. They also include local elected officials, community leaders and agency managers, such as the heads of state environmental regulatory agencies or the head of the local Red Cross. With an incident of sufficient scope, these people include the governor, U.S. senators, and state-elected officials. When you start making a list, particularly when you think about these things in advance of an incident, you understand that there are quite a few people who have a reasonable expectation of getting direct and immediate information about what is going on. But you only have a small crew to work with and there are numerous reporters out there. Besides, the critical stakeholders are rarely outside your door or phoning incessantly demanding information.

As in most situations like this, the communication team in this incident was involved primarily in meeting the needs of the media. One of the best things we did, from the company perspective, was fax a letter from the president of the company to a list of local elected officials and community leaders within a couple days of the incident occurring. This direct, personal and relatively immediate information was very well received. It was in observing the value that was placed on this limited direct communication that helped me understand that most of the opportunities for such communication were passed up because they were impossible in our situation. Direct communication to those critical stakeholders would seem impossible to most in situations like that. Yet, in this new era of instant communication, stakeholders do not see it as impossible. That means they have an expectation that either you will meet or you won't. The new understanding going into such situations is that the media is one group among a number of groups of equals, which is a big change.

At the very time the information center was hard at work communicating with the media, a local activist group was communicating directly through a growing network of contacts. The environmental disaster, in addition to the human tragedy, awakened passions in many in the community. These were passions that were easily inflamed by the direct communication being conducted by the activist group who spotted in this situation an opportunity to provide leadership in a new cause: pipeline safety. The momentum built by this group proved to be a potent force in the weeks and months ahead and demonstrated that those involved in such incidents need to have and use the same direct communication methods of those who wish to take advantage of such situations to pursue their own agendas.

9) The Approval Process Slow Down

"Now, now, now!" Reporters and all those others looking for information aren't content with "later" and "tomorrow." While urgency has always been a critical element of effective reporting, "now" takes on a more urgent meaning with the advent of 24-hour instant news coverage. After the best available information was collected and "word-smithed" into a new statement for the press, it needed to be "vetted" for approval. The final authority in a situation managed under the Incident Command System is the Unified Command. The Incident Command System, as we will see later, provides a highly structured and effective approach to crisis management. At the top are the Unified Commanders, unified in title at least. In this case, the Unified Command was comprised of leaders from state, federal and local agencies as well as a company incident commander. The Unified Commanders all needed to review and approve any public information prior to release. Getting their approval is one critical task, but the main issue was gaining the approval of attorneys. Even in the earliest days of the response, company attorneys were there, participating as part of the "away team." The proximity of a company attorney in the EOC made approvals relatively easy; things got much more difficult when multiple attorneys in different cities also needed to review information prior to release.

In the pipeline incident, the entire public information process, and particularly the approval process, was made considerably more challenging because of criminal investigations. Within a half-hour after the explosion occurred, the company was informed by the U.S. District Attorney's office in Seattle that a criminal investigation had been launched. By law, the company was obligated to inform all its employees who could be subjects of the investigation that they should seek their own counsel and that the company, again as provided by state law, would not provide attorneys for them, but would pay for the attorneys they chose. Soon, in addition to the company attorney or his or her replacements in Houston needing to approve public statements, a variety of executive attorneys who were located from Seattle to Anchorage, Alaska, needed to review information before it could be released.

Some of the most difficult situations involving timing of press reports were a result of the time-lag involved in getting approval from communication team members, including attorneys, who were not physically present at the information center. This difficulty, an exceptionally common problem in fast-paced information management, is a primary reason why today's instant news environment requires a thorough change in policies and communication technology.

10) No Inquiry and Response Tracking

"Who was *that*?" we'd ask the communication team member who was handling a call from a particularly aggressive caller. That is how information about the inquiries coming in was shared. There was no way of keeping track of who was calling, what information they wanted, who provided the information to them, what was said, or even whether or not their questions had been answered or all promised responses had been fulfilled.

In a JIC situation, responders include staff from many of the agencies involved in the response. A public relations person from the company involved may find himself or herself sitting next to a public information specialist from the Coast

Guard, the state environmental agency, or the EPA. The ability to respond well and work together as a team is dependent on forming some level of group cohesion. Operating well together means talking to each other about the calls that are coming in, sharing information, asking questions and learning from everyone else's experience.

This highly informal process would be greatly assisted and strengthened by better inquiry tracking. Some communication plans require responders to fill out two-part forms logging each inquiry, the time it arrived, who responded, what was said, when the response was completed, etc. This is very helpful and significantly improves quality control, but, as we will see, it only solves part of the problem. It is useful to those who are physically part of the response team in one place at one time, but does nothing for those members of the team who aren't actually there.

11) No Way to Easily Update New Reporters

It is common to think that when a major news-making event occurs, you "can't throw enough bodies at it." The problem with that thinking is the more bodies you throw at the response, the more difficult it is to operate with efficiency and control. The real answer isn't simply increasing the number of people to handle the response; the answer is in controlling the work that the team needs to do and ensuring that the few are highly efficient. One of the ways to control the work and enhance efficiency is to understand what creates much of the work.

While a crisis communication team may receive hundreds of phone calls in a few hours or days, this does not mean there are hundreds of reporters. Most calls come from the same media outlets calling repeatedly. There are two reasons for this. One reason is that the reporters want to make certain they are continually updated. It became a standing joke in the EOC when one of the more persistent and sneaky reporters made his hourly phone call. "It's Bernie (not his real name). He wants to know if there's anything new." He was constantly looking for an edge on the other reporters and felt by keeping up a continual effort and talking to a different responder each time he could finagle some information that would provide a scoop.

The second cause of the high volume of phone calls was the fact that reporters work on shifts, too. They didn't necessarily consider it their job to brief the reporters taking the next shift on the background of the accident and the latest information. That became the job of the hard pressed information staff. Here's where the lack of control over the Web site really hurt because it could have been used considerably more effectively to provide background information. A technique used in this response, which help considerably, was using a "rolling fact sheet." As new information emerged, the updated information was added to the previous version of the fact sheet so over a period of time reporters could see the progression of information and therefore get a better picture of the chronology of the event.

Despite this process, it became clear that an effective information response required a much more efficient means of updating reporters new to the story as well as satisfying those looking for the latest info in a way that discouraged them from making their routine "anything new?" calls to the EOC. If reporters knew that the very best place for them to be was at their computers watching their email in-basket, and that no one was going to get any newer or better information than that which came to them via email, it would cut down on the number of calls coming into the command center to a great extent. The more repetitive and unnecessary work eliminated, the higher quality the response will be from the limited resources available.

A New Approach Needed

While there were important lessons to be learned from this, and from every incident involving the news media, the most important lessons go far beyond techniques, tactics and strategies. There are three critical elements of a communication response to a public issue or news worthy incident: people, policies and technology. Interdependent and intertwining, each element needs to be effective and aimed at the single objective of protecting or building the organization's public trust through accurate, timely information.

As a member of the public looking at a news story, we do not typically see the people hard at work behind the scenes. But they are people with all the dynamics of personality, turf battles, personal agendas, ambitions and fears. One of the people I knew during the pipeline incident EOC was a woman who was a competitor in the local public relations business. Clearly, she didn't like me. She was a volunteer with the local Department of Emergency Management and was helping out with the information process in the early stages. It was obvious in a very short while that she deeply resented my even being in the EOC. On more than one occasion when I was performing my duties she would aggressively challenge me, "Who authorized you to do that?" Instead of getting into an unnecessary turf battle that had nothing to do with the response, I just shrugged my shoulders and walked away. Fortunately, she was gone in a day or two.

There were a considerable number of personal battles going on. A public relations staff member for one organization felt another one was intruding on her territory, and in the midst of the craziness of trying to respond to the information demands, organization leaders had to make decisions about who should go and who should stay. They made the wrong decision, and in doing so, seriously weakened the team's effectiveness. Contract workers maneuvered and positioned to increase their roles and thereby lengthen their tours of duty. Sometimes the inherent distrust between corporate people and staff of government agencies showed itself, and too often – not just in this instance, but in several others I personally observed – the tendency of some government agency people to engage in power games became painfully obvious and obstructed the work at hand.

Not only do personalities and personal agendas affect how the response is handled, but individual work styles and comfort levels do as well. This is particularly true when technology that goes beyond pen and paper is employed. Even in this age, there are more than a few who say, "I'm comfortable with writing everything down on paper," and simply cannot cope with any other way. This also applies to non-technology issues. How media calls are handled and how the interaction works between team members depends to a considerable degree on the individuals who suddenly find themselves thrown together in an extremely high stress situation.

Policies also determine outcomes. Has the company determined that its goal is to be the first and best source for information? One of the most important factors is whether or not there are written policies for handling a number of crucial decisions. Similarly, if there are written polices but they are not available to those who need to make decisions, they might as well not be written. In this particular incident, I was not aware of any written policies or crisis communications plan. Policies emerged, no doubt, and those policies began to set the course for public information strategies and decisions. But they were policies based on the personal experience and approach of the person who emerged as the designated manager of the public information and public affairs efforts. As specific issues are explored, such as involvement of the legal team, timing issues and dealing with mounting criticism, you will see how these policies were articulated and how they resulted in some of the perception and reputation difficulties that emerged.

We have already discussed the impact of technology on the response. That clearly is one of the central themes of this book. As we delve into that in greater detail, the relationship between people, policies and technology cannot be forgotten. That was one of the most important things learned in the weeks and months following June 10, 1999.

2.
Toward A Post-Media World

Citizen journalism. Blogosphere. Wikis. Podcasting.

These are just a few of the terms that have entered our conversation in the past few years. Every one of these terms is an indicator that we are on a path away from a media-dominated world.

It is unimaginable to most readers of this book that at one time, not so long ago, we had one radio station. KDKA started in Pittsburgh in 1920 and soon fed its content to the nation through a chain of six transmitters. Readers may also be surprised to learn that it was only a few years ago that only a handful of national magazines existed to serve the nation's magazine readers. It may be less surprising to recall that only in the last decade have the three major broadcast news organizations lost 60 percent of their audiences.

We have come to take it as a given that news and information about the world will come to us via traditional media. Traditional media is expensive; the cost of entry is high. This is one reason why it holds such power. Few can afford the investment needed to build the transmitters, printing presses and the entire infrastructure needed to deliver information quickly to thousands and millions of viewers or readers. The power of the media to control public opinion and influence the events of history is most clearly demonstrated by the fact that despotic governments have two main concerns: control the military and control the media. Company and organization leaders are very well aware of the fact that media have tremendous influence over the future of their enterprises. Positive coverage in the press or on national television can catapult a small company to instant success, while negative stories can bring even the most well-established and respected giants to sad endings in short order.

Traditional media are highly competitive. Audiences are the product they deliver to their customers, the advertisers. Audiences want, and demand ever faster, more vivid, more exciting, more relevant information. Those in the news business employ the technologies, strategies and infrastructure needed to meet this accelerating demand; hence, the era of instant news. But there is a vital element of the new era of instant news that is threatening the dominance of traditional media as the primary conveyors of public information. The Internet has quickly become a vital tool for the news organizations as well as an important means of distribution. But unlike the printing presses and transmitters, the news organizations do not control the Internet: they do not make the rules; they do not manage the application and use of the Internet. It has proven wild, uncontrollable and resistant to almost all efforts to corral its use and misuse.

The Internet provides audiences with access to vital information at the speed of light. It provides a depth of information to the average viewer that was previously not possible. The Internet allows publication of information in all forms – audio, video, text – at a cost that is unmatched by any other major media. It also provides the audience with one of the things they want most: control.

More than offering the audience what it wants, the Internet has a lot to offer broadcasters or publishers. All major traditional media have embraced the Internet as a critical adjunct to their broadcasting and publishing efforts. But much more than that, the Internet offers the ability to publish or broadcast to virtually anyone with a computer and a connection. The sources of news are multiplying. People with messages to send, with agendas to pursue and with vital information to offer, have discovered they too have control.

Traditional Media and the Global Experience

An argument can be made that Internet use for public information on Sept.11, 2001, demonstrated that we are moving into an era of instant news dominated by this powerful new medium, no doubt many will argue the point. After all, Sept. 11 is when virtually the entire world shared the unutterable shock of watching two of the greatest symbols of American prestige crash to the ground, taking with them the lives of more than 5,000 innocents. They shared this experience via global television. The global village became real in a way shared with few other events in human history. The overwhelming sense of shock, horror and sadness was felt in real time, around the globe, as people of many nations and cultures flocked around the nearest available television to stare numbly at the fireballs and clouds of dust. Those who found reason to exult in the collapse of these proud symbols of American economic, political and military power also shared the experience. The pictures of exultation in the streets of Palestinian villages brought home to many in the complacent West the visceral power of hatred and wrath.

Good friends of ours were travelling in Europe at the time. After visiting the cemetery of forefathers in a small town in Switzerland, they heard of the events happening in New York and Washington D.C. No television in their room, they found a lobby where CNN was broadcast. There they shared not only with strangers from Switzerland, but all of us back home, the same emotions of fear and disbelief. When we discussed this with them a week or so later, it was if we had both been at the scene together because we did indeed see it together. The same images, the same sounds, the same information and the same emotions – just separated by 7,000 miles of land and water.

In the days before the attack, approximately 160 million people were online around the world according to the Internet traffic analysis firm comScore Networks. On Sept. 11, 2001, that number declined by almost 30 million. Analysts suggest this decline was because many were spending time with traditional media. Proof, it seems, that Sept. 11 was a high point of the media world, not the post-media world. But we must look a little deeper to see to what degree the Internet as means of interpersonal communication as well as a means of gaining immediate public information had already penetrated the hold the traditional media had on information.

Use of the Internet on Sept. 11

A young woman from our community was working at the Pentagon on the morning of Sept. 11. Like many others, the Internet had become a way of working for her and, in some respects, a way of living. Someone in the hall said something about a plane hitting the World Trade Center. She immediately went to her normal news sites. She couldn't get on. There was no access to any of the common news Web sites she normally reviewed. Before she had the time to seek alternative sources, her world went dark as the third hijacked airliner crashed into her building just a few offices away. She escaped through the darkness and confusion.

Her experience of turning to the Internet was not unique and neither was her experience, that day, of finding most news site inaccessible. The Internet is used every day for a wide variety of purposes: hobbies, entertainment, commerce, socializing, research, etc. Gathering information about important events is only one use. But on Sept. 11, that changed. The millions of people normally using the Internet for all kinds of reasons suddenly rushed to the news sites and any other site that could give them the information they were seeking relating to this event. In fact, although the number of Internet users on Sept. 11 declined, according to comScore Networks, the number of site visits jumped 240 percent, from 1 billion to 3.4 billion. The number of page downloads jumped 272 percent, from 5.7 billion to 21.2 billion. And the number of minutes spent online jumped 245 percent, from 8.2 billion to 28.3 billion.

There is no question at all that TV was the primary means by which Americans, as well as the rest of world, gained information about the terrorist attacks. 79 percent of Americans said television was their primary information source and Internet users reported an even higher dependence on television: 80 percent. One chat room contributor even suggested that computers should be turned off that day: "This is definitely a case where online sources are going to lag well behind TV. It's on all the major channels. I think all Americans should be let out of work/school to watch; it's major history. What I mean is that this is one of those times to abandon your computer and go turn on a TV. Any TV."

The fact that so many did exactly that, and yet the news sites, and government and company sites involved became overburdened, is the significant point here. During normal times, about 22 percent of the 100 million plus American Internet users gain some news via the Internet every day. According to an AOL/RoperASW Cyberstudy poll, more than 75 percent of Americans who use the Internet use it regularly to gain news. French online users are considerably more news hungry at 96 percent. On Sept.11, 60 percent of American Internet users went in search of news related to the event: 57 percent of male Internet users and 43 percent of female Internet users. Two factors contributed to that: a flood of international visitors hitting US-based news and information sites and the sharp decline in non-news use of the Internet. Dollar sales on the Internet dropped 58 percent that day and most other non-news uses saw similar drops. Interestingly, by Sept. 20, most of these non-news uses of the Internet were back up to their pre-Sept. 11 numbers and even showed increases in some areas.

The traffic in Internet news sites skyrocketed. CNN.com, for example, had almost 12 million unique visitors, nearly a seven times increase over their normal traffic at that time. CBS.com increased over eight times to almost two million unique visitors. Most news Web sites experienced significant traffic increases, with the sites known for immediacy receiving the greatest increases.

The young woman in the Pentagon who had come to rely on news sites to help keep her informed of what was going on in the world found those sites unusable on the morning of Sept. 11. It was not just because millions of people were hitting these sites; their use of them was particularly burdensome. Fifteen percent of American Internet users got audio or video streamed to their desktops from these sites on that day, and 7 percent requested the automatic email alerts that would keep them plied with up-to-the-minute information. Given this kind of use, it is not surprising that a great many people who turned to the Internet for information simply couldn't get it.

Keynote, which measures Internet performance and availability, reported that the major news sites were largely unavailable between 9 a.m. and 10 a.m. Eastern Daylight Time on Sept. 11. CNN.com, NYTimes.com and ABCNews.com all showed 0 percent availability. USAToday.com (less hard hit than the others) showed 18.2 percent availability and MSNBC.com showed 22 percent availability. In order to improve access, CNN reduced the size of its homepage from a normal of 255 kilobytes to just 20 kilobytes. When these numbers are looked at in comparison with the large hit rate and the number of viewers accessing audio and video streaming media, the question arises: how many more people would have been logged on if the performance had not been so degraded?

One indication is how many people gave up going to news and other informational sites they were seeking. Forty-three percent of Internet users said they had trouble getting to the sites they wanted. Forty percent of those kept trying and eventually got there, 39 percent went to alternative sites and 20 percent of those reporting trouble simply gave up on using the Internet to get the information they wanted. It is easy using this information to calculate a potential audience for CNN.com on Sept. 11 of over 15 million. And that was in 2001, when the use of the Internet for immediate news was still a relatively new phenomenon.

But the news sites were not the only ones to be hit hard. This is particularly significant since our interest here is directed at companies; organizations and agencies that may some day find themselves at the center of strong public inquiry. The New York/New Jersey Port Authority Web site (panynj.com) had an over 7,000 percent increase in unique site visitors. The Red Cross disaster relief portal had a 2,300 percent increase and fbi.gov had a 1,300 percent increase. What was the impact on performance? Normal site access time for the FBI site is under one second. On Sept. 11, it jumped to 180 seconds – three minutes. How many people in today's broadband environment are going to wait three minutes for a page to download? Not many. So the question again arises, how many more would have used these sites at these critical times if the performance had been better? And what did those users of the Port or Red Cross or FBI sites feel when they expected that they would be able to get the help they needed from their government agencies or the organizations who were supposed to be there to help them at all times?

What about those who turned to American Airlines or United Airlines? After I returned to my office from SeaTac airport where I was just boarding a flight to LA when the announcement came that all flights were cancelled, I personally tracked the performance of the United and American Web sites. It took a few hours to get back to my office and United already had a statement on their Web site expressing their concerns for the victims and explaining how to get information. American Airlines was inaccessible for some time, then provided a convoluted method of getting at information, and it wasn't until well into the afternoon before a similar statement of concern showed on their site.

It can certainly be argued that no one responsible for planning online resources for these news organizations, government organizations or involved companies could be blamed for not anticipating an event of the scope of Sept. 11. And yet, the warning signs for overwhelming information demand were there. On Jan. 31, 2000, Alaska Airlines flight 261 went down off the coast of California and 1.2 million people hit the company Web site in just 13 hours. When the USS Cole was bombed in August 2000, in a preview of the September event, more than 5 million visitors logged onto the US Navy Web site. And, according to Keynote, the Bridgestone/Firestone Web site crashed when the tire recall was announced on August 9, 2000. The same thing occurred when more than 200,000 people per hour tried to keep up with the 2000 presidential voting action by visiting the Florida state department of elections Web site: it too crashed.

In the global village, a company's Web site is a front door. If big news occurs, the residents of the global village will not wait for the newspaper to be printed. They will not even turn on their car radios and wait for the news, or get the latest from the 6 p.m. evening news. When news hits about your company or organization, those in the village will come knocking on your front door – potentially by the millions. The question is, will there be any one there to answer? Or will they find the door closed and inaccessible with a sign saying, "We don't want to talk"?

The Personalization of Media

The TV audience on Sept. 11 was enormous: certainly in the hundreds of millions and probably in the billions. Television delivered on its promise like few other times in history. All the technology, planning and investment made by news organizations around the world proved its value in delivering the vital information demanded by millions and millions of viewers and readers. The global village was very much alive and sharing the emotions of shock, grief, fear and anger. But in this grand moment of traditional media triumph, the newcomer was demonstrating that the future just might belong to instant, personal, digital communication.

The Internet was used not only to get generalized information on the latest about the attacks. The other, more personal and direct uses of the Internet on Sept. 11, most clearly demonstrate the unique qualities of this new medium and its advantages over traditional media. An analogy could be made between the rail system and the automobile. At the turn of the last century, the railroads were the undisputed master of transportation on the continent. An upstart alternative, the automobile was in its infancy. But the automobile and its variants such as the truck in the early 1900's could hardly be envisioned to replace the well established rail system. Cars and trucks couldn't carry virtually unlimited numbers of passengers and freight over long distances at the cost that rail could offer. Automotive transportation did, however, offer some important advantages that proved to be significant enough to overcome the great economic advantages of rail. It was personal, flexible and came in an almost infinite variety of packages: buses, pickup trucks, long haul trucks, motorcycles, limousines, sports cars, etc.

The clear advantages of the Internet as a means of highly personalized communication can also be seen in the use of this new tool on Sept. 11. The Internet is a remarkably flexible and diverse tool. While 50 percent of users on Sept. 11 used the Internet to get news about the attacks, 69 percent used the Internet to gain information related to the attacks. For example, one third of Internet users sought financial information that day; almost one quarter did some research on Osama bin Laden and Afghanistan. Nineteen percent used the Internet to download pictures of the American flag; 15 percent sought information about victims or survivors; 13 percent checked on flight status of their own or someone else's plane, and 12 percent visited commemorative Web sites while online.

Since we are looking at Internet use on that fateful day as a way of predicting how people will use it in the future, perhaps the most telling uses were more personal. These included receiving comfort, participating in discussions and making direct contact or finding information on what happened to their loved ones. Nearly one third of American Internet users, or about 30 million people, used the Internet as a sort of coffeehouse, bar or family room. They participated in chat rooms, bulletin boards or signed on for a listserv. Only about 5 million posted some comments or observations: most observed. What were they observing? Discussions about what the US should do in retaliation, expressions of sadness and comfort for those directly affected and suggestions for how individuals could deal with their emotions after the attacks.

If we had foresight following Sept. 11, and could predict how the Internet would evolve in society, we would predict its use as a social networking tool even more than as a news media, vehicle for commerce or shortcut to soft porn. Social networking is now the driving force in Internet use and, as of early 2006, it is the focus of attention of much of the corporate world trying to determine the most appropriate strategies for Internet applications.

The telephone was the second most used medium of communication on that singular day. While most Americans phoned family members or friends that day, the use of email was down corresponding to the number of people on the Internet and the focus on news. But for a surprisingly high number of people, the Internet was crucial to finding relatives. About one third of the people in the US that day, who tried to reach friends or relatives by phone, had difficulty because of the extreme traffic on the phone networks. Four to five million Internet users reported that they used the Internet to contact loved ones specifically because of difficulty with the phone. Even though individual site performance was degraded because of heavy traffic, Keynote reports that there was essentially no negative impact on the Internet infrastructure. Unlike other events, such as an accident in a railroad tunnel, which cut some critical fiber lines, Sept. 11 showed the Internet infrastructure was not affected by the dramatic increase in page views and downloads.

In February 2001, residents of the greater Seattle area experienced an earthquake that caused some significant damage in downtown Seattle. In the minutes after the quake, phone lines were largely inaccessible because of heavy traffic. Similarly, cell phones were largely unusable. Email was a critical link for a number of people, including a client in Houston calling to answer media questions about impacts on their refinery located in the area. The Web-based communication technology described in a later chapter became an important means of internal communication when the phone lines were unusable.

The Internet is both a mass medium and a highly personalized medium. It is the power and intimacy of personal conversation melded with the accessibility and wide distribution of television. It can have the dramatic impact of stunning visual images and sounds combined with the most personal and individualized messages. Here is where the automobile analogy starts to break down. The railroads did one thing very well after they were well established: moving people and goods in mass very efficiently along a very specific route and according to a very specific timetable. Automobiles eliminated the specificity of routes and timetables and emphasized flexibility, but could not come near railroads for the efficiency of mass transportation. You might have a vehicle like a bus or truck that could come closer to replicating some of the railroads advantages, but you ended up losing some of the personal, individual and flexible characteristics of the car. The Internet can be both train and car simultaneously. One moment the viewer can receive the latest possible information in audio and video form, placing his or her eyes at the very spot of the action. The next moment, the user can send a prayer request (one third of Internet users used it for prayer on Sept. 11) to a loved one or share highly personal messages that would otherwise be done only by telephone or in person.

It is this quality of the Internet as a public information medium – mass personalization we might call it – which delivers its power and is changing the way news and public information is handled. News in the traditional media is largely linear – particularly TV. In other words, you get what they want to give you on their schedule. "News at 10!" Then there is this totally predictable and uniform stream of information: the top local story, a few major national or international headlines, a more in-depth local story, then weather, then sports, and a wrap-up, all interspersed with commercials at totally predictable intervals. As a viewer, you sit and take what is dished out – highly efficient, completely impersonalized and totally outside of your control.

Newspapers and magazines are also linear but in a different sense. At least they can be scanned. The creators of *USA Today* recognized the significant change in how people gained information when they designed the paper and maximized the opportunities for scanning. With a newspaper, the reader can at least control which stories he or she wants to read and to what degree. It is this flexibility, combined with printed material's portability that has kept broadcast media from becoming even more dominant in our world. However, printed material is linear in the sense that the information it provides is made available to the user on the publisher's timetable, not yours.

Certainly, there's the "Extra Edition." The terrorist attack also revealed the anachronism of "immediate print," at least in our community. *The Bellingham Herald* (our local daily newspaper, then owned by Gannett), which publishes a morning edition, published a mid-afternoon "extra." Certainly the cries of "Extra!

Extra! Read all about it!" on the streets of major US cities in the 1930s or 1940s made all the sense in the world. People just didn't have universal, immediate access to their radios or TVs. On Sept. 11, 2001, I saw a *Bellingham Herald* employee on the street corner waving down busy traffic trying to sell those extra editions. I reached down to my text pager that kept me updated of what was going on as the world was changing almost minute by minute, and chuckled. Printed material by its very nature is required to be linear in terms of publishing. It simply can't meet the immediacy of broadcast or the Internet or text pagers or telephone or personal conversations. When it tries, it is both humorous and sad.

A Multitude of Broadcasters and Publishers

Publishers and broadcasters have had great power and influence. This will continue for some time, no doubt. The mass media are symbols of a capitalist world because there is a strong relationship between capital and control. The person who had the capital to build a water-driven sawmill or a steel mill was the one who had control of the vital resource. When totalitarian states wanted to control the economies of their nations, they nationalized property and capital. When dictators wanted to control the minds of their citizens, they grabbed control of the means of information distribution: the printing presses and transmitters. Control those few things and you can control information. But as Peter Drucker pointed out in his book Post-Capitalist Society, these fundamental underpinnings of our world can and do change. Knowledge, Drucker said, is the new basis for wealth-creation. It is the new wedge between the haves and have-nots. It is the new underpinning of society. Knowledge and the Internet versus capital and mass media. The synchronicity spells a fundamental change in our world.

The public relations industry exists, in part, because companies and organizations that depend on public perception and understanding do not, and cannot, control the means to gain those perceptions. It is a source of high frustration for a great many leaders. One leading business owner in a western state became so frustrated with the media promoting ideas contrary to his understanding of the world, that he used his considerable wealth to buy out one of the daily newspapers in his city. This way he could control what appeared on the editorial pages. He found that owning the second daily paper in a mid-sized city was not a very economical proposition and he ended up selling out to the leading daily. But when he sold, part of the deal was that he, or someone he designated, had access to that paper's editorial page on a scheduled basis. While not every executive will take their desire for control of the media to that degree, most, at one time or another, could relate to the frustration that led to those expensive decisions.

A new response is emerging. If you do not like what the media are reporting about you or your organization, you can be your own publisher. In the post-media world, everyone is, or can be, a broadcaster or publisher. The control the mass media have held over the distribution of information to millions, including you and me, is being eroded. Certainly, the major media are leading the way in the use of the Internet for public information distribution. But they do not control it, own it or make the rules. Individuals or organizations with computers, or simply an Internet appliance, can create audiences, distribute information and facilitate interchange. The executive who was led by frustration to invest millions in a daily paper could have published his views and built his audience for much less with this new medium.

As we entered the 21st century, a new publishing phenomenon emerged. "Blogger" is a term that describes a new form of Internet publisher. The term comes from "Web logger," a heavy Web surfer who created logs of the information and links found on the Web that interested him or her. The post-media world potential of these bloggers was noticed by John Ellis, himself a blogger, writing in the April 2002 issue of *Fast Company*:

"Major news organizations breathed a huge sigh of relief when dotcom mania came crashing down. That meant that the barriers to entry in their markets were re-erected and that their (mostly) monopoly positions were re-secured. Now the bloggers are at the gates, eating into the media's value-added proposition. It's no small threat, because the peer-to-peer technology that underlies it is what the military calls a 'force multiplier.'"

Those were prophetic words. As this update is written in early 2006, there are now well over 10 million bloggers and as many as 1 million update their blogs on a daily basis. The audience is estimated at over 50 million viewers daily. While most blogs attract very few, if any viewers, some have attracted audiences in the millions. The top 200 blogs have over one million page views per month, and the top 20 have over 10 million page views per month. To put this in perspective, imagine for a moment the investment required to attract an audience of over one million viewers per month using traditional media. The investment required of a blogger is a computer, a high-speed connection and the savvy to understand how to build an audience on the Internet.

The point is citizen journalism is here and now. This means that virtually anyone can decide to be their own broadcaster and publisher. But if the media-frustrated executive can assume the role of publisher and broadcaster, the instant news world of the Internet also means that the executive's opponents can do the same. In fact, the early days of the Internet are showing that organizations and individuals who can be described as accusers, activists or attackers are leading corporations and organizations in their understanding of this important new opportunity. This is one of the major trends that make this new instant news era an exceptionally risky one for those concerned about protecting reputations.

It has become very clear that bloggers, as well as the new journalists or encyclopedia writers who submit to Wikipedia, are not under the same editorial processes that professional and respected news organizations use to protect their reputations. When these "truth filter" systems fail, as they did for CBS during the 2004 election, the consequences are extremely severe, even to a seasoned journalist like Dan Rather. But bloggers and Internet publishers do not operate under the same set of expectations. A national news story in late 2005 identified a Wikipedia contributor as having intentionally provided false and damaging information about another individual. Such is the information frontier we live on.

If the perception about you, your company or organization, your products or services, your brand or brands, is important to you, then it is vitally important that you understand how the means of creating those perceptions has changed and is changing. More is at stake here than what is the best way of getting people and packages from one part of the country to the other. The new era of instant news means that the risks to brand value and reputations are higher than ever. But where there are risks, there are also opportunities. Those who choose to understand, prepare, and proactively communicate swiftly and directly will see that the new era offers access and information distribution opportunities not otherwise available.

Marshall McLuhan may have somehow been envisioning the Internet when he wrote nearly 40 years ago:

"Rapidly we approach the final phase of the extensions of man – the technological simulation of consciousness, when the creative process of knowing will be collectively and corporately extended to the whole of human society."

The process of knowing is what communication strategy is all about. What do others who matter know about you, your business, your character, your activities? Many people "know" more about Enron, Andersen and Martha Stewart and their activities and character than they did before the stock crash occurred.

What they know is due primarily to the media, the extensions of humankind. The Internet promises to bring that process of collective knowing to a new and different level. With the Internet, consciousness can, and is, being technologically simulated and it is now possible that much of human society around the globe can participate as one in this process of knowing. Communication strategists and those leaders responsible for building and protecting reputations need to carefully consider the implications.

3.
The New Audience

On Saturday, August 12, 2000, the Russian submarine Kursk experienced a devastating explosion in the Barents Sea. The explosion was heard by an American submarine on maneuvers and registered on a Norwegian-based Richter scale. The event started a tragedy of errors in public communication, which demonstrated the Russian government was clearly not prepared for the openness and speed of the instant news world. Perhaps more surprisingly, it showed the Russian population was prepared for this openness and speed – just a decade after the collapse of the Soviet Union, with its totalitarian control over news media and public information.

The Russian navy first reported on Monday, August 14 that the submarine was experiencing difficulties with flooded torpedo compartments after firing a torpedo. A little later, a top navy admiral reported the submarine had been in a "serious collision." They further reported that rescue efforts were "well under way." Russian President Vladimir Putin was vacationing near the Black Sea and the growing public outcry finally forced him to cut his vacation short – five days after the explosion occurred. In the meantime, the newly freed Russian press were scrambling to find answers and discovering, for perhaps the first time since "*glasnost,*" what it meant to be expected to deliver information to a nation demanding answers. Since real information was not forthcoming from those who were in the know, reporters followed the pattern of Western media by writing lengthy speculative articles and putting talking heads on the television screens who argued about what might be going on and why it happened. CNN.com reported on August 18: "Lacking detailed information on the cause of the accident, newspapers have dedicated page after page to competing theories about why the Oscar-class nuclear submarine sank. News outlets have turned to former submarine officers, submarine designers and diving experts for speculation on what happened and how the rescue effort is proceeding."

While on vacation, Putin had remained quiet and out of sight. Perhaps he decided it was something he should deal with when a local television station showed a meeting between Deputy Prime Minister Ilya Klebanov and family members of the sailors, who many hoped were still alive. The meeting had barely begun when the angry crowd began to heckle him. It was left to Putin to tell the Russian people when he did finally return to Moscow that he had been informed very early after the accident that the chances for a rescue were remote.

An article in *The Wall Street Journal* article summed up the instant news world lessons. The anger of the families was focused on the extremely poor communication, complaining primarily that they needed to find out what was going on from the media. Meanwhile, the news media were complaining, with very great justification, that the information they received was sparse, conflicting and inaccurate.

What makes this an interesting case study for the "now is too late world" is that the families – people with a very strong stake in this incident – had an expectation of information that was not realized. They expected and demanded that their government talk to them directly, give them the straight scoop no matter how painful and not leave them with ill informed speculators via the media. This was Russia in the year 2000! This was a people who have not had much of a concept of a free press in most of their centuries of history. The whole idea of "*glasnost*" or "openness" was a brand new and daring concept just 15 years earlier. Yet, in that short time, and due in large part to their exposure to the freedom and openness of information in the West, these people had built expectations that the Russian government, and even their very enlightened new leader, were not prepared to meet.

The damage to the young and dynamic new president serves as an object lesson for every executive and organizational leader who is not prepared for the new information demands of the instant news world. For many people in the world, this was Putin's introduction to the stage of public opinion. What opinion did they gain of this man? Someone unwilling to interrupt a vacation while his sailors are dying under the ocean and while his people are clamoring for information and answers? He was, in crisis management terms, perceived as unresponsive. Unresponsiveness equals incompetence and irresponsibility in the heightened information expectations of this new world. The Soviet leader who had opened this Pandora's Box of openness, and who had learned his own painful lessons of the consequences of this, reflected the opinion of the world and the Russian people when he publicly criticized the new president. CNN.com reported: "Mikhail Gorbachev, the former Soviet president attacked for his delay in commenting on the Chernobyl disaster 14 years ago, adds his criticisms of President Vladimir Putin to the vocal public outrage over his handling of the Kursk tragedy. Gorbachev says the Russian president's errors were 'mistakes of style' and that Putin's initial response, which came four days after the Kursk tragedy, was 'inadequate.'"

The tragedy of communication failure played out in a similar way in January 2006 in West Virginia when an explosion trapped thirteen miners underground. The rescue team had to go 13,000 feet from the entrance to reach the miners. The garbled message from the rescue team came to the Command Center and those in the Center understood them to say that 12 were alive and one had died. Family members in the Command Center used their cell phones to call family members waiting anxiously outside and there was great jubilation and cries of "Miracle!"

Approximately a half hour later, the Incident Commander received correct information that there was one critically injured survivor and the rescue team had found the 12 miners dead. Knowing of the joy and relief going on in the church nearby, the commanders apparently became frozen in indecision and uncertainty. Three hours went by before they informed the stunned gathering and the entire world that the information had been false and that their worst fears were confirmed.

Whatever anger the family members had toward the mining company for safety issues that might have contributed to the accident were magnified many times over by the miscommunication. Failure to communicate quickly, accurately and with sensitivity will exacerbate any tragedy. Indeed, it is the communication failure that becomes the primary issue, as it appears to demonstrate clearly the character of the individuals responsible.

Relevance and Demand

When events and facts matter to people, it has always been important to get information to them as quickly as possible. Expectations are what have changed. The new instant news world audience, largely because of digital technology and worldwide high-speed networks, has a radically different set of expectations about information than previous audiences.

This certainly is not the only time technology has changed expectations – it is an absolutely predictable response to the introduction of innovations. We never used to expect packages to be delivered across country overnight. Federal Express changed our expectations and, as a result, changed how everyone else in the package delivery business operates, including the US Post Office and United Parcel Service. The Pony Express was a significant improvement in mail delivery – much faster than sending letters around the Horn. But the telegraph changed the expectation about getting information, and it was only a short time later that the Pony Express, so recently seen as exceptionally fast, now was viewed as slow and outdated.

The introduction of the telegraph, coming before the US Civil War, provides an excellent illustration of the dramatic changes currently underway in the news business. Prior to the telegraph, news reporting was highly subjective, and unabashedly so, with most newspapers aligned with a political party or a point of view. Because the telegraph was a scarce commodity, the idea of pooling reports emerged and the Associated Press was created. The idea was that the basic facts would be sent to the various papers where writers would then interpret those facts along party lines, as was common in the newspapers of that day. But some papers printed the AP reports with their bare-bones, information-only style. This led to a "just the facts" style of presentation, which proved highly popular and quickly dominated news reporting. US Civil War news coverage demonstrated the degree to which content and delivery mechanisms are strongly linked, and we see this same linkage now in the new world of instant news driven by technology change.

The demand for information can be extremely intense. It can overwhelm, for a period of time, the basic human needs, including food, sleep and virtually all other pressing physical demands. Witness the families and friends of those lost in the World Trade Center and Pentagon attacks – many spent days wandering, asking, begging, pleading for the slightest bit of information about what happened to their loved ones.

There is a relationship between the relevance of information and the demand for that information. The expectation of being able to supply it in a timely fashion can be simplistically charted:

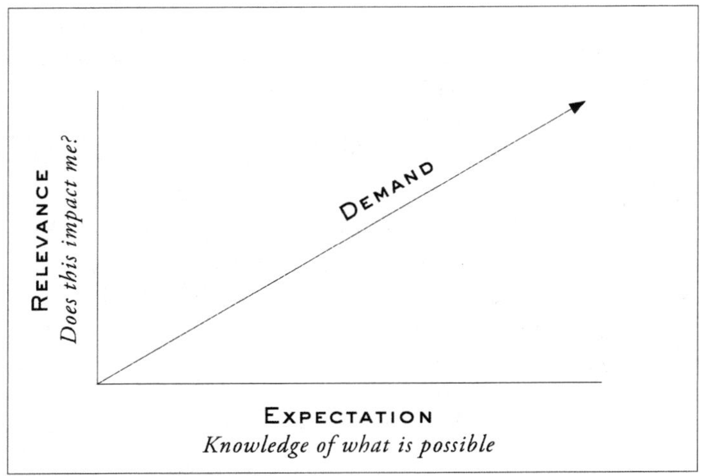

Figure 3.1: *Relationship Between Relevance, Demand and Expectations*

When the information is highly relevant, there is a high demand – the higher the relevance the higher the demand. When this demand is combined with the belief or knowledge that the person or organization has the information, and has the means of supplying it but does not, the frustration level goes up.

Relevance is directly related to what is important in the lives of the individuals desiring the information. Their personal security and well being, along with the security and well being of those closest to them, are of the utmost importance. Relevance and demand for information is very high whenever security is at stake. Security, of course, can mean concern for physical safety, but it can also mean financial security and hopes and plans for the future. The family and friends of those people trapped in the World Trade Center had an extremely high demand for information, as evidenced by their unstoppable efforts to gain whatever bits and pieces of information they could find. The families and friends of the victims of the

Kursk disaster and the West Virginia mine tragedy also had a very high demand for information, particularly when there was still hope for rescue.

But relevance and corresponding demand does not necessarily lead to frustration and anger. That reaction has everything to do with expectations. For example, suppose you hear that there is an accident in your community. You give it a passing thought, but there is little relevance based on that information since there are a number of accidents that occur and very few affect your security and sense of well being. But then you get some more information that indicates it was in your neighborhood. Now you become a little more concerned because the chances of someone you know or care about being involved in the accident have increased. Then you find out that it involved a red Mustang. Your teenage son drives a red Mustang. Now the presumed relevance of the information is high and so is the demand. In fact, the demand is so high that like those relatives and friends of the World Trade Center and Pentagon attacks, you will probably not rest, or eat or even think of anything else until you get the information that you desperately need.

When you hear of the accident in your community, you do not turn on ABC Evening News or CNN. You have no expectation that they will cover some local traffic accident. You also probably do not expect your local television news broadcast, radio station or newspaper to carry the information – most of them being far too slow for your information demands anyway. Where do you turn for information? Assuming no one is home, you may call your local police department or your local hospital. Should you discover they have the information you are seeking but don't provide it to you, your frustration level will go very high. There could be a host of reasons:

> "I'm sorry, we don't have the staff or budget to answer all requests for information about accidents."
>
> "I'm sorry but until our officers return from the field and fill out all their paperwork we simply can't release that information. Policy, you know."
>
> "I'm sorry, but we haven't installed radios or cell phones in our police cars, so at this point we just can't know what is going on."
>
> "I'm sorry, but until we can thoroughly investigate the accident and have all the information verified by our attorneys we can't tell you anything. It's important for us to be accurate and not cause anyone any undue alarm, you know."
>
> "I'm sorry, but it is our policy to provide information about accidents to the media and they will probably have a report on this in about four hours."
>
> "Yes, we have that information, but the person who is assigned to provide it has gone home for the day. Could you call again tomorrow?"

"Hold on just a second, OK, as soon as the person gets off the phone answering a call about a cat up a tree we should be able to get that for you. No wait, there's another call waiting about a stolen hubcap. Man, we're really busy. Sorry about that, but we should be able to get back to you in a couple of hours."

Frustration increases when there is high demand because of its importance to the audience's life and the fact that there is a reasonable expectation that the person has the information and the ability to share it, but is withholding the information. How would a parent confronted with technological, policy or staff excuses perceive the police department? Uncaring? Incompetent? Bureaucratic? Would such perceptions extend to other areas of the department? When a newspaper article was written about their difficulty in capturing a local bank robber, isn't it more likely that the parent who had experienced frustration regarding information determine that this was one more example of a poorly run organization?

When a company or organization is involved in an event that has a direct and immediate bearing on the safety, security and well being of anyone, there is now an expectation of information that is unprecedented. Even a few years ago, a company involved in an industrial accident, for example, was expected to provide information to the media according to their news cycles and directly to the family members involved. There was limited technological capability and, therefore, no expectation to immediately communicate to employees, shareholders, an extended list of friends and families of those involved, community leaders, government officials, regulators or even the media.

Pre-Gorbachev, the people of the Soviet Union had low expectations for information from their government, even when events directly involved them or their loved ones. By the time Putin was president, their expectations were close to matching those in the West and were what can be considered instant news world expectations. Key stakeholders, who can be defined as those individuals whose relevance is high, in the Kursk incident expected direct, immediate and top level communication. Not hearing from Putin was a problem. They couldn't care less that his precious holiday on the Black Sea was interrupted. Not hearing immediately was a problem, and not hearing directly was a huge problem.

Those are some of the key expectations of the post-media world audience and one of the main reasons why it can be called the post-media world. Stakeholders expect:

Communication From the Top People Involved

They do not expect communication about things that affect their lives to be relegated to lower level staff, or even communication professionals.

Immediate Information

If you have information now, they want that information now. Excuses about wanting to wait until there is better information simply do not fly. They will understand the caveats. But they will not understand not being told what you know to be true at that particular point in time.

Credible Information

The audience's demand for accuracy is primarily a demand that the source for the information be trustworthy. Understanding this helps deal with the potential conflict between speed and accuracy. They want to be told what you know now and they want assurance that you can be a trusted source of information. You will be trusted if you provide the information you have, if you demonstrate that you are doing your utmost to meet their information needs and if you correct inaccurate or incomplete information as soon as you have better information. Mostly, you will be trusted when the audience knows that you take their need for fast, accurate information seriously and providing that is a higher priority to you than protecting yourself from any negative consequences of that information.

Direct Information

Stakeholders do not want to be forced to get the information they need in the same way as everyone else who does not share their level of relevance. If relevance is high, so is the demand for direct information. One thing is certain: expectations will increase. These expectations exist largely without factoring in the presence of the Internet and the widespread understanding that the Internet can facilitate speed, accuracy and directness. Events such as the Sept. 11 attacks and the widespread use of the Internet on an informal basis to connect, find information about missing relatives and pass on information about what was going on in the attacks and the response, will no doubt heighten expectations of the new audience.

Instant News Case Studies

The coast of Oregon was the scene of an international news story in 1998: the New Carissa incident. A freighter lost power, eventually becoming beached on the pristine coast of Oregon not far from Portland. The ocean-side communities of this area are heavily dependent on the tourist trade, so the thousands of gallons of fuel oil on board threatened an environmental and economic catastrophe. In the post-event public information debriefing that I was able to attend, I learned one growing expectation that is certain to increase in the instant news world.

Public information team members working for the Coast Guard and as representatives for the company that owned the freighter were inundated for weeks with reporters. The national media arrived in force and demanded a great deal of time and attention. The Coast Guard, which must deal with significant news events on a frequent basis and which has, in general, an excellent reputation for providing timely, accurate and forthright information, was particularly inundated with requests for interviews, tours and additional background information on topics such as "in situ" burning. After the event was over, an important issue was discovered. The local reporters, elected officials and community leaders had felt shunted aside during the days of national and international media attention. As Lt. Chris Haley, Public Information Officer for the US Coast Guard during the incident, said afterward, "After the Connie Chungs had left, we still had to deal with the local reporters and officials. And we needed to deal with them for a long time afterward. We discovered that they felt they had not been properly attended to while the national media was on the scene."

The reality is that local reporters and stakeholders have a stronger vested interest in the events than the national audience. And they are going to be there for the long term. It is natural and understandable that communication officials on scene during an event may give priority to those media whose audiences are vast and whose impact on the reputations of those involved may be enormous. Combine this situation with increasing expectations based on the awareness of new technological capability, and this demand for attention at all levels will only increase. It will simply not be acceptable to a local publisher when you try to explain unequal access by telling her that Tom Brokaw was simply more important. The good that may have been accomplished on the fleeting national level will be lost in the much less fleeting coverage at the local level.

Early in 2001, an accident occurred in a refinery in the UK. A prominent national newspaper in the UK wrote: "… (XYZ Company) had no information on the blast beyond that available from local police and fire brigade sources." What were these media folks expecting? That the company would communicate with them directly? That they should provide them more information than what they were getting from the local police and fire departments? Obviously.

It was not the only information problem this company faced. Major industrial facilities have "fence-line neighbors." These are people who live near enough to the facility to be potentially impacted by accidents or other unpleasant events. They are definitely stakeholders when you define stakeholders as those people whose safety, security and well being are potentially affected by the organization. In talking with the company involved, it was their perception that they were quite busy after the incident providing information to the large number of media who were inquiring about the accident. So much so that not until two weeks after the event did they get around to opening their email. When they did, they found emails from fence-line neighbors asking whether or not they should evacuate their homes. Imagine the response of one of those stakeholders if they had gotten one of these messages in return:

> "Thank you for your inquiry. Your ideas, comments and questions are very important to us. We will respond to this message when we are able."

Or, two weeks after the event: "Thank you for your email. We hope that you were able to get the information you needed about evacuating from the local police. We apologize for not being able to provide this for you, but I'm sure you can understand that we were far too busy answering important calls from reporters to be bothered with your personal safety and well being. Have a nice day."

These people were using instant news world communications and expected a huge, multinational company to do the same. They were expecting direct, immediate, accurate information that affected their safety and well being. What kind of success will the company have now in their community relations efforts trying to convince these very important neighbors that the company is doing everything possible to ensure their safety and security? Who will be on the front lines of any activist activities aimed at driving this facility out of the area? And who will have a powerful story of corporate irresponsibility to tell?

Another major industrial accident involved the deaths of several people enjoying a recreational area. The two people within the company designated to handle the public information were inundated with calls. As they reported later, "We spent 24 hours a day responding to the media. That's all we were doing was responding!" This was a plaintive cry after newspaper reports came out claiming the company was "unresponsive." Why were they unresponsive? Because the reporters from those particular media outlets were not able to get through to these two beleaguered staff people and, as a result, concluded they were "unresponsive." And they were. If a reporter cannot get his or her question answered, no excuse in the world carries any weight. A question not answered in the time required by the media goes down as unresponsive.

The Role of the Internet in Changing Expectations

In the year 2000, members of Congress received over 80 million email messages. That's almost 150,000 emails for each member. Most of those writing emails discovered, as I did, that the only response you can expect from your Congressional representative or senator when you send an email is a totally oblivious automated reply making some promises that it is clear they have no intention of keeping. But, this is somewhat understandable, given the volume.

By early 2006, more than 200 million Americans, two-thirds of the population, were using the Internet regularly. Sixty million use search engines daily. And the vast majority of Internet users utilize it to send email messages. Messages to friends, families, co-workers, customers, pastors, teachers, etc. Messages to their doctor's offices, and to fellow researchers, and to someone in Turkey that they just bought an antique lamp from on eBay. Every imaginable kind of human relationship is represented each and every day in the bits and bytes flying through the fiber and wireless connections. They use this form because it is incredibly fast, inexpensive and increasingly accessible. While those opposed to computers, and their role in our world, view the use of electronic or digital communication as "impersonal," users of it see it as just the opposite. It is very personal, highly individualistic and infinitely flexible as the incredibly wide variety of types of messages display.

The problem is that when we use this technology, we expect a response. And we expect a response that reflects the nature of the medium. Personal, individualized, flexible, direct, immediate, fast, non-intrusive, etc. – mostly fast and personal. That's why getting an automated message three days after you sent an email to a senator's office is simply not acceptable. It may be all they think they can do, but it leaves the impression that either the senator has no concern for your communication, is in a previous technological age, or is simply incompetent and unable to adequately represent you.

There was a time when an American president invited his constituents to write to him directly and he sat down and replied personally to the hundreds of people who took him up on his offer. But President Jefferson has been gone for some time. By offering email addresses to constituents, there is an implied invitation to write in, and with that implied invitation, there is an implied promise of personal, direct and speedy response. That expectation is a long way from being fulfilled.

It is quite natural to assume that companies or organizations much larger and more powerful than you would have access to technology and systems at least equal to that which you use from your home every day. That's why those people in the UK who used email to find out if their homes were safe to spend the night in must have been so disheartened to receive a message (presumably a form one at that) two weeks after the event.

The Web is billed as an instantaneous method of publishing information to potentially millions of viewers. That's why when a company Web site shows absolutely no recognition of earth-shattering events involving that company, it is quite understandable for those who go to that site for information come away with the impression that the company either does not care or is incompetent. The impact of technology on expectations is all around us. We might create a reverse Moore's Law, which described the exponential growth of computer performance. The dissatisfaction with outdated technology and methods will increase exponentially every 18 months, corresponding to the introduction of better, faster, cheaper technologies and methods. Once people understand that technology makes it possible for newsmakers to provide them direct, accurate, up-to-the-minute information about what is important to them, they will demand it. The reality is, more than 200 million Americans who are Internet users are very aware of the capability of this technology to deliver direct, personalized information. They are demanding it.

Characteristics of the New Audience

The new digitally-savvy audience has a high expectation about information caused by their awareness of what the Internet makes possible. These expectations include:

Speed

The first requirement is speed. Internet speed. Light speed. The new audience has little to no tolerance for the fact that it may take time for those responsible for collecting, packaging and distributing the information to do their jobs. The major news media are coming to understand this. TV news programs and newspapers alike tout their Web sites as places to go to get more up to date and more complete information. As we will discuss further, this has destroyed news cycles. News cycles in the instant news world occur every minute, 24/7. A news cycle is how long it takes to get the info and post it on a Web site. Once that is done, the process of using the slower methods of distribution can begin.

While most major media have come to understand this new demand, and have responded to it, newsmakers have only begun to comprehend what this demand for speed means for them. Crisis communications plans written for the media world are simply outdated. The instant news world crisis communications plans require virtually instantaneous communication of even the smallest amount of information available. It violates all the old rules. Such is the nature of change.

Credibility

The new audiences also demand that those providing information to them be completely believable. There is no tolerance for "spin" in the sense of selectively providing information or twisting the facts to leave impressions that are not truly reflective of reality. It certainly appears at first glance that there is a gross contradiction between the demand for speed and the demand for credibility. And if credibility were truly equated with accuracy, that would be true. Accuracy, however, is only part of the picture. Credibility is the whole picture.

In the early reports from the Sept. 11 attacks, there were a great many stories reported on national news that were highly inaccurate. The presidential election crisis of 2000 was caused in part because of national news reporters making significant errors in calling the election for Bush, then Gore, then Bush, etc. But these inaccuracies are for the most part quickly forgotten – providing the party making the error owns up to it. We are remarkably forgiving of mistakes. We are much less forgiving of the hubris that seeks to convince that we are incapable of making mistakes.

A case in point: who is probably the least credible person on the 10 p.m. news team? I would suggest it is the weather reporter. Because I, for one, have never seen a weather reporter stand up and say, "You know on last night's news I predicted a winter storm with 70 mile per hour winds and, frankly folks, I was dead wrong. I apologize and I'm going to work even harder to take this maze of data that I get and give you a forecast that will be more reliable." Similarly, one of the greatest criticisms of newspapers is that they may make a page one error that causes people or organizations a great deal of problems, but the correction is buried someplace on the inside and in such small type that only the most bored newspaper reader would ever come across it.

In an age of extremely high expectations of speed, those providing information need to understand that there is considerable tolerance for error providing the errors are acknowledged, explained and it is clear that there is a strong desire and intention to provide the best and most accurate information then available.

Priority on Communication

The new audience also has little tolerance for the many pressures on company or organizational leaders during a crisis event. When it is their family or loved one involved, when their personal security is at risk, there should be no higher priority for the top people in the company to deal with than the need for information. A company executive may disagree with this perception, but the problem is, as the saying goes, perception is reality. And when a perception grows that the executive involved is too busy to tend to the priorities of those whose perceptions really matter, then it can be a career-ending priority mistake. Putin learned that lesson the hard way. Fortunately, he didn't make that mistake during a presidential election. New York City Mayor Rudolph W. Giuliani may have understood this concept better than anyone in the last few years. While no doubt the demands on him were overwhelming in the hours and weeks following the attacks on his city, there is no question that he made communicating with the citizens of his city – from individuals to the masses – his absolute top priority. As a result, he was not only *Time* magazine's Person of the Year, but has been used as the model for effective leadership in a crisis in the dozens or hundreds of crisis communications seminars and presentations offered after the Sept. 11 event.

One of the greatest challenges for communication professionals today is to convince the leaders of their organization that their own long-term viability and the ability of the organization to operate may very well depend on the priority they place on public communication at a time of crisis.

Direct

Perhaps the most significant and challenging expectation of the new audience is the demand for direct communication. When a voter who has supported an elected representative in the past election with financial contributions sends an email to them, they usually do that expecting a response, a direct response. A response indicating that the elected representative has paid attention to them. It really doesn't matter to them that it may be one of 300 emails the representative received that day.

When a person in a house near a plant containing hazardous chemicals finds smoke from the plant billowing in her direction, she does not expect to wait to hear from the media about whether or not she and her family should evacuate, shelter in place or not be concerned. She doesn't expect to have to wait to hear about it on the 6 p.m. news, and doesn't expect to wait until she opens her paper in the morning. Family members of those in a plane reported down expect to be able to get the information immediately and directly. Employees and investors of a company that finds itself the target of a US Securities and Exchange Commission probe expect answers on their desktops, now.

The new audience is very aware that the technology to provide direct and immediate information to those seeking it is readily available. Should a company, organization or elected representative choose not to use that technology, it sends a signal that communication is not important. It is no longer any excuse to say, "We communicate to the public through the media." It is like saying, "We prefer to use a town crier, if you don't mind."

With the growing use of the Internet for public information, there is a very rapidly growing audience that expects information directly. An airline experiencing a tragic crash will certainly be expected to communicate directly with family members of those on the plane involved. But passengers flying to that destination on tomorrow's flight will also expect and demand direct information. Company leaders around the world expect it; shareholders large and small will expect it. Members of the public with fear of flying and experts with special knowledge of a potential problem involved will all expect direct communication. The fact is, everyone who knows that direct communication is possible because they are Internet users and because they have at least some level of interest in the event, will expect direct communication. This reality, perhaps more than any other, makes the instant news world also a post-media world.

Personalized

Like Federal Express in the package delivery business, Amazon.com and other online retailers created an expectation for direct communication that extends to everyone in the public information business. Amazon tailors its offerings to me. When I sign on, the company shows they know my name, they know what I like and presumably what I don't like. They make suggestions about products I might be interested in based on my previous purchases. They give me helpful hints about products based on other people's purchases. It is, in effect, intelligent technology that creates the benefits of personalized service. No one is fooled for a minute into thinking this is really personalized service – and a great many prefer the personalized service over the super-efficient replica. But, for those who want the advantages of efficiency with at least some degree of pseudo-personalization, this is a huge step forward. This creates a huge problem for providers of public information because when it is known that technology can provide this kind of personalized, customized information, it will be expected and demanded. It is logical for today's information consumers to believe that if Amazon can personalize information to sell them something, an industrial giant can communicate directly and personally when their family's lives, health and safety are involved.

The demand for personalization is expressed on several levels. One is the growing understanding that technology can make providing very specific, very relevant information possible. No need to wade through a lot of extraneous material that may be of interest to someone else. With an understanding of the capabilities of technology, there will be no patience for that. Information must be custom tailored – if not to individuals then at least to groups and sub-groups. Investors have a need for different information than fence-line neighbors. Employees have a different need than national reporters. But personalization also means "personal." As mentioned earlier in the New Carissa incident, local reporters and dignitaries expect to be treated with at least as much respect and deference and time as national reporters or the state governor. A communication plan that does not take into consideration these very high expectations is almost certain to result in reputation damage, even though every other aspect of the communication plan may work to perfection.

The News at my Hip

When I think of the instant news world and the rapidly expanding expectations of hundreds of millions of people around the globe, the picture that comes into my head is not the millions hunched over their computers in spare bedrooms and office cubicles around the world. It is the commuter in her car or riding in his train carrying a text pager that primarily comes to mind.

On Sept. 11, like everyone else, I can remember exactly where I was when I heard the news. I had just received my boarding pass at an Alaska Airlines electronic kiosk. I was at SeaTac airport bound for Los Angeles. I checked the boarding time: 6:45 a.m. PDT. I made a quick trip to the restroom expecting by the time I returned to the boarding area, the flight would already be boarding. Instead, when I returned, I heard the tail end of an announcement from the service counter saying that all flights were temporarily on hold because of terrorist activity. I remembered a very brief announcement on the radio just as I was parking the car about some early reports of an airplane hitting the World Trade Center. Automatically, I turned to the CNN Airport Network News monitors hung from the ceiling in the boarding area. The screen was blank. I reached for my text pager. That's where I learned the news.

While others awaited further word from the service desk, I followed the breaking news on my text pager. From that I deduced that it was not likely that we would be flying soon. Not long after, the announcement came that all flights were cancelled indefinitely and planes that had already pushed back from the gate were being called back and passengers were being de-planed.

With a text pager that offers instant news service, not only is the newspaper a ridiculously slow way of receiving news, even the instantaneous world of broadcast begins to look outdated. People simply don't have a radio or television with them all the time and it is frequently not convenient to park in front of a tube – either computer, TV or combined.

As information technologies further combine so that a wireless phone is indistinguishable from a PDA, which is indistinguishable from an Internet device allowing two-way text or voice communication, which is indistinguishable from the video iPod, which also gives you the latest podcast, the expectations for information delivery will be significantly greater than they are now. Which means the challenge of getting the right information, to the right people, right now will be all that much greater.

4.
How the News is Changing

In the media world, it used to be clear who was in the news business and who was not. News businesses provided news, non-news businesses did not. Reporters worked for companies who were in the business to provide news. News businesses get paid, usually by advertisers, to collect, package and distribute information of interest to news audiences. Non-news businesses or organizations exist for other purposes – perhaps to deliver public service such as environmental protection, or to produce commercial goods such as fertilizer. Providing news for these businesses is simply not their reason for existence. In an instant news world, that distinction is becoming increasingly fuzzy.

One of the most significant trends to come out of the collection of technologies we call the Internet, is the emergence of citizen journalists. "Blogging," from the term "Weblog," which used to describe people who would record and publish what they discovered on the Internet, reflects the ease with which almost anyone who writes today can also publish. As mentioned earlier, some of the bloggers have accumulated audiences in the millions and have influence as great as any of the celebrity journalists that used to be staples of our early evening hours at home. But our focus here will not be on blogging and citizen journalism as much as how changes in the news business have affected any company that might find itself in the news.

In the instant news world, companies and organizations that find themselves at the center of public interest will be expected to collect, package and distribute the news. Why? Because the Internet user with high relevance/demand requires it. The US Navy is in the business of protecting our nation. They do not get paid for providing news. But for the five million people who went to the US Navy Web site after the USS Cole was bombed on Oct. 12, 2000, the fact the Navy was not in the news business was of little interest to them. Those five million people expected the Navy to provide them the information they were seeking about who, what, when, why and how. Some may say this is just information, and not news. The distinction is lost on the stakeholder or news viewer who simply wants to know what happened. Similarly, when an airliner goes down, the airline is expected to provide the news, even though there may be hundreds of reporters and news agencies fighting hard to provide the fastest, most accurate information that is needed to build and keep the audiences needed to keep their advertisers happy.

Government agencies increasingly are finding themselves as news packagers and distributors. Sept. 11 certainly demonstrated the high degree of interest shown in government Web sites relating to the attacks. Government news sites, such as the FBI, slowed to a crawl under the burden of increased traffic. The US Postal Service suddenly found itself a primary news source for information about the anthrax attacks and, in less than a month, saw its Web traffic burst from a few hundred visits a week to nearly 300,000. During Operation Enduring Freedom, the terrorist campaign in Afghanistan, news viewers could go to their TV news programs or the Web sites of commercial news organizations such as CNN.com, FOXNews.com, MSNBC.com, or they could go directly to www.defenselink.mil/news. There, viewers can get the press releases issued by the Department of Defense and see videos of press conferences. They can get the information as it was presented, which can be substantially different from what is conveyed after the information goes through the packaging process. If anyone has seen an actual press conference, or even watched an entire conference via C-SPAN, the difference in meaning between what actually is said at the conference and what is used in the few second sound bite that ends up in the packaged news can be astonishing.

Competition among news providers is expanding. Most companies, organizations, agencies and individuals – those I am referring to as "newsmakers" – would prefer that the news businesses do the job of providing the news. They don't want to get in the business of supplying public information in the sense of profiting from it by attracting advertisers, nor do they want the requirement of providing information to detract them from their reason for existence. But the new audience will not allow them that option. When the information is relevant and demand is high, the burden is put on those people or organizations in a position to provide the fastest, most accurate, most up-to-the-second information. We instinctively understand that the news media are rarely, if ever, the first to know, and they do not necessarily have the most complete knowledge. They are intermediaries. They go in between. They mediate the news. They are media.

There is one federal agency that seems to clearly understand the changing expectations of the audience and they have embraced the changes. That agency is the US Coast Guard. This agency has frequently been lauded in public relations industry news articles for the excellent job they do in providing press information. But they have gone far beyond press information. They consider it their job to provide as much detailed information in the form their audiences want just as soon as they possibly can.

They employ the latest in public information technology – virtual communication centers – as the primary means of distributing public information. During Hurricane Katrina in the fall of 2005, the Coast Guard alone of all government agencies received praise for their response in large part because they never stopped, nor even slowed, their communication. Despite the fact that their 8th District headquarters in downtown New Orleans was underwater along with all the computer equipment, servers and phones, they never skipped a beat. One photo that was displayed on front pages across the nation showed a Coast Guard member writing down names to be rescued using a flashlight. The image was taken by digital camera, uploaded to a laptop, which was on the Internet via cell phone modem. The accompanying story was written and the photo uploaded to a Web server located safely on the West Coast. The information officer posted that photo to the www.uscgstormwatch.com Web site, the Coast Guard site for hurricane information. The article was also emailed to the reporters, family members and others who had signed themselves up on the site to receive ongoing updates. In doing so, the Coast Guard demonstrated how, even during the most challenging of circumstances, reputations are made and maintained in an instant news world.

No doubt there are executives and perhaps even communication leaders for newsmaker organizations who are thinking right now, "We don't have to accept this situation. We have a choice about whether to provide the information directly or go through the news media." The problem with that thinking is the impact on reputation. We have seen the impact on the reputation of the Russian government, and Putin in particular, when he failed to meet expectations about providing direct and accurate information. We have repeated examples in corporate communication history of the devastating impact on brands when companies do not communicate with the speed, directness, credibility or humanity that today's audiences expect. And this is in the very early stages of the post-media world when it is still commonplace to get news from the news packagers. When more news consumers become Internet veterans, when the Internet is freed from the prison of spare bedroom PCs, when universal, full-time, wireless access is commonplace, those companies or organizations who choose to communicate through intermediaries will be viewed as heartless, oblivious, backward, or all three.

For those willing to allow the news media to do the communication job for them, Enron and particularly Arthur Andersen provide uncomfortable object lessons. Andersen's situation was a reputation crisis that became a financial crisis, unlike Enron's, which was a financial crisis that became a reputation crisis. The reputation crisis for Andersen was precipitated primarily by decisions made by some to destroy documents needed in the Enron investigation, but then it was greatly exacerbated by a slow, uncertain, inconsistent and indirect communication response.

There is another aspect to this growing competition among news sources that will cause many newsmakers to rethink a strategy of simply allowing the news businesses to be the source of information about the organization: opponents. The competition for news audiences is not just among news businesses, and not just among news distributors and newsmakers. Add opponents to the picture. These include activists, competitors, disgruntled former or present employees, busybodies or anyone with an agenda that conflicts with yours. All these are now potentially equipped with technology that levels the playing field for gathering and distributing information in a way that wouldn't have happened two decades ago. As you will see in the next chapter, opponents are becoming very aware of the instant news world reality that everyone is a broadcaster. They are grabbing the microphone. They are building audiences and communicating directly. They are not content, for the most part, to allow the media to do their speaking for them. They are becoming the "media" themselves.

News audiences in the instant news world have a dizzying array of options for information about an event relevant to them. Information, or news about the event, can come from traditional news media, traditional media using untraditional channels such as Internet news sites, the company or organization involved in the incident, opponents, politicians weighing in, bloggers, activist groups, disgruntled employees and so on. All will be competing for the fleeting attention and fickle perceptions of the news audience. The outcome of the competition may have significant consequences.

Understanding the News Business

The purpose of this chapter is to better understand how news businesses compete with each other to provide today's audiences with what they want. Understanding the news packagers and distributors better accomplishes two important purposes for newsmakers: it enables the communication team to provide the journalists with what they need in order to do their jobs, and helps newsmakers, cum news packagers, properly package the news in ways today's audiences expect.

It is a strange but powerful testament to the American democratic/market system to have one of its most important democratic institutions a resounding market success. Imagine if the military or regulatory agencies such as the Environmental Protection Agency found a way to effectively do their job and make a profit without taking any tax dollars. Yet, few would argue that the news media, the "fifth estate" as it is sometimes called, is an essential pillar of our open, democratic system. Aside from the minor exception of public broadcasting, it is not supported by tax dollars, but instead generates huge profits and represents a sizeable portion of our national and local economies. That freedom from taxation, and therefore from government ownership, is central to the news media's ability to do its job. In his book The World is Flat, *New York Times* columnist Thomas Friedman concludes that one of the few remaining obstacles keeping China from generating the economic supremacy its leaders desire, is the lack of a free press that hinders corruption.

The news media's diversity, ubiquity and competitive instincts have, for the most part, served America exceedingly well. Not only America, however, because CNN and other major news outlets have become world brands, delivering news and information round the clock to audiences around the globe. This sharing of information and vicarious experience, through TV in particular, has created the global village predicted by McLuhan. But even the professor would likely be amazed at the depth of change created by this universal information sharing, which we now refer to as "globalism" – quite possibly the most important change of our generation.

The news business as it stands today is considerably different from the news business of the past. While that is stating the obvious, what is not so obvious is the continual change that occurs in how people charged with delivering public information do their job. As consumers of their product, we take things pretty much as they come, and go about our lives and work without giving too much thought to the ongoing struggle to attract us as an audience. While we take it as a given that automobile manufacturers and computer manufacturers are continually designing new products and innovations to sell us in order to gain a competitive edge, we don't usually view the news business as competing in similar ways.

A fundamental factor driving change is competition. This will continue as the driving force as long as the news media are free from government support and control – a long, long time we hope. Understanding this competition will help newsmakers in the instant news world respond more effectively to the demands of both traditional media and news consumers.

News executives have a clear-cut task: assemble an audience that advertisers will be willing to pay good money to reach with their commercial messages. The audience must have qualities that the advertisers desire, (money to spend above all) and must be in sufficient quantity to make buying advertising reaching that audience a reasonable investment for the advertisers. Accomplish this task, and the news executive will have the resources available to continue to build the audience. Fail at it, or succeed less well than competitors, and the resources to gather the news, effectively package and distribute it via printing presses and transmitters, will be very limited.

There are a great many options available to news executives to try to squeeze out a few more viewers or readers for their products. A few years ago, one regional TV station clearly was in some ratings difficulties and decided they needed to make some changes to recapture lost viewers. They must have conducted a brainstorming session to do some "out of the box" thinking, for when the changes were presented to the local audience the advertising proclaimed: "On March 10 (name of station) comes out of the box." The "out of the box" message was hyped to well beyond curiosity, almost to the point of nausea. When the great day arrived, we all discovered that they had taken away the desk from their news anchors who were now "free" to roam the set and stand and deliver the news. Audiences in no time found all the random movement distracting and uncomfortable and clearly the anchors were more comfortable sitting behind a desk where they could rest their papers and focus on delivering the news rather than figure out where they were going next. The "box" came back and the TV station went on to competing for local viewers on the same basis as they always have.

Competition for news audiences within each audience segment is focused on four key attributes: speed, depth, credibility and entertainment values. While this has not likely changed since the days when two different people in the same town put out a regular town newspaper, the emphasis changes considerably. As you will see, entertainment values are at a premium in this day of intense audience competition.

Speed

There are some old hands in the public relations business who continue to hold on to the belief (or is it vain hope?) that the media operate around "news cycles." For younger readers, I feel compelled to explain what a news cycle is. News cycles operate around deadlines when publications or broadcast news shows operate on a regular schedule. If a newspaper comes out a 5 a.m., a reporter's normal deadline may be 8 p.m. that evening. Unless it is a huge story, anything coming in after the deadline is going into the next news cycle. In broadcast, where news cycles really drove timing of releases, to make it on the 6 p.m. news, reporters needed to have the information a couple of hours in advance.

News professionals and communication professionals reading this will say that the couple of hours aren't reality any more. Exactly. Competition, cable TV, satellite broadcasting and the Internet have combined to make news an instantaneous business. Virtually every local TV news program features live feeds with satellite trucks and news helicopters flitting about the territory, setting up in just minutes, interviewing just about anyone they can get their hands on and running a "breaking news" story. And virtually every newspaper, local TV and local radio station have their own news Web site where the latest news is uploaded, regardless of the schedule, for printing or broadcasting.

The national news competition in the past used to exist between the three major networks at the 6 p.m. news hour. That audience has shifted, to a considerable degree, to the all- news-all-the-time channels on cable TV. Where CNN pioneered the concept and came of age in the 1990-1991 Gulf War, 10 years later the competition is fierce between the 24-hour cable news channels which now include two CNN channels, MSNBC, FOX News Channel and CNBC.

The primary focus of this competition is speed. There is a sense of urgency and immediacy surrounding all the coverage. The quality of the image doesn't matter nearly as much as the image being live or as close to live as possible and as close to the scene of the action as possible. In the ultimate picture of this new style of "immediacy," reporters will sometimes put just about anyone on camera that they can who may have even a remote connection to the event, until they finally resort to interviewing each other while waiting for real news to show up on the scene. In another somewhat silly attempt to convey immediacy, television stations will show a reporter amidst lots of equipment in their "satellite center" to show they are providing the news even as it comes off the satellite. Last night I watched a local reporter turn back to one of the monitors in the "satellite center" to view what was just then coming off the satellite feed. What makes this silly is any of the information coming in to the news channel can just as well be fed to the anchor desk, but putting a live reporter in the "satellite center" replicates some of the immediacy of being on location. The vital information is coming in over the satellite right now. Of course, it also provides an alternate set to add to the entertainment value.

Broadcast's strength has always been speed and immediacy. Print journalism suffered in the comparison. Occasionally there are ludicrous examples of how even daily print publications attempt to compete on a speed basis such as the example of our local daily hawking an "extra edition" on the streets following the Sept. 11 attack. Most newspapers understand that it is most likely that readers will have already heard or seen the basics via radio or TV by the time they pick up the morning or evening paper. When they pick up the paper, they usually have a few minutes or even longer to relax, enjoy the process of reading, and get information the broadcasters can't fit into their 30-second sound bite reporting style. Print publications almost always compete on the basis of depth rather than speed.

Depth

Years ago I went into the publishing business. I bought a monthly business publication that covered our local area with a population of about 150,000. The only daily in town showed a strong distaste for competition of any size. I knew they would come after me with everything they had. How to compete for the precious minutes the people in the business community spent reading? If I couldn't deliver an audience, I wouldn't be able to attract and keep advertisers. I knew I couldn't compete on real news stories – the newspaper would get me there every time. I couldn't compete on in-depth business trends, helpful advice, economic news or anything like that because the other national and regional business publications had far more editorial resources than I ever would. I concluded the only thing I could compete on was depth. Depth of information about what was going on with local companies, depth of analysis about local business trends and conditions, and mostly, depth of information about the community. Based on my training in college as a drama major, I was, and still am, convinced that we are mostly interested in people; first of all, ourselves. Secondly, people we know. Third, people like us, or people we can relate to. I made the business publication mostly about the people involved in the local business community and dedicated the magazine to building a real community of business people. Even though the local daily soon launched their own "business magazine," they couldn't match mine for depth and focus on people and soon gave it up.

The New York Times' famous slogan shows perfectly the commitment to depth: "All the News That's Fit to Print." *The Wall Street Journal* likewise competes on depth of business-specific coverage. National news magazines compete against other print publications, such as daily newspapers, by going one step farther in depth. Each week *Time, US News* or *Newsweek* digs deeper than the newspapers into the major stories of the day.

Here's the rub with the Internet: it has the capability of providing information at speeds considerably greater than the most efficient cable news organization and in unlimited depth. The cost of publishing a few extra pages of *The New York Times* is considerable. The cost of adding 200 extra pages to CNN.com is virtually nothing once the story is written. News organizations are demonstrating they clearly understand this by using their traditional media print pages and broadcast minutes to direct readers and viewers to more in-depth information contained on their Web sites.

Credibility

"Don't cry wolf!" ought to be the number one lesson in journalism and public relations schools. The ancient wisdom of Aesop very much applies to those who would provide public information in our day as much as Aesop's. As the little shepherd boy discovered, an audience will quickly turn a deaf ear to the purveyor of information who proves to be less than credible. As another saying goes, "Fool me once, shame on you; fool me twice, shame on me."

To that degree, all media compete on the basis of credibility. As newsmakers evolve into news packagers and distributors in the post-media world, credibility will be a primary concern. A corporation or organization that proves less than respectful of the truth will quickly cede its right and ability directly to the public to others who have no interest in protecting its reputation. The role of credibility in communication was clearly understood almost 2,500 years ago and articulated by Aristotle with clarity that has never been improved. He said there were essentially three modes of persuasion: *logos*, or appeal to logic; *pathos*, or appeal to emotion; and *ethos*, or appeal to the credibility of the speaker. Of these three, there was no question in his mind as to which was the most effective. The perception the audience has of the credibility of the speaker can and will outweigh every argument of logic or emotion. That credibility can never be compromised.

But credibility is much more than being trustworthy with the truth. You don't see news businesses competing with each other by saying, "You can believe us, not like the other guys," or "We tell the truth, they don't." They do, however, compete for credibility in other ways. One of those is by the particular slant that they may take. Because credibility, after all, is subjective. Senator Ted Kennedy would not be the most credible speaker to a Rush Limbaugh audience and vice versa. Credibility, therefore, has a lot to do with the particular biases of the audience.

Most major news organizations do their best to be credible to the widest possible audience. They do this in various ways. One is to be cautious about taking positions and trying to be completely objective, even while they understand that complete objectivity is impossible. Another is to intentionally balance the biases of their audience by including competing voices. On TV today, you see frequent examples of a conservative and liberal co-hosting a commentary program, or a radio station featuring a conservative talk show host one hour and a liberal host at another hour. Other news outlets simply state the philosophical basis they operate from and do not try to maintain credibility with all groups. Publications put out by radical environmental groups would not have much credibility with development or resource-oriented business readers, and neither would *Oil Exploration Today* have a lot of credibility with paid-up members of Greenpeace.

Another important aspect of competition based on credibility is accuracy. As was mentioned before, accuracy and credibility, while kissing cousins, are not exactly the same thing. Certainly, no one providing public information will be believed if they consistently provide inaccurate information. The Russians certainly found that out in the Kursk incident. However, there is a head-on battle between speed and accuracy, and today's audiences put a premium on speed. Many communication professionals who have been in this business for a long while have not noticed this very significant change. Getting it right is always more important. I am well aware that I am breaking every existing rule by suggesting that speed comes before accuracy. It does, with this condition: to maintain credibility when accuracy fails, a news provider must show that every possible effort was made to get the correct information and to be willing to face up and admit that inaccurate information was provided.

News viewers expressed serious anger during the 2000 Bush-Gore election when the major news organizations first called the Florida vote for Bush, then Gore and then determined it was undecided. Undecided indeed – for weeks. This was relevant information at nearly the highest level when it comes to national stories, and essentially every major news organization blew it. Calling an election before all the votes are in is a response to the demand for news speed. The only way the news organizations recovered any credibility is by explaining, in some detail and with a significant amount of repetition, that all news organizations contracted with the same organization to provide exit polls and these exit polls proved to be somewhat inaccurate. While not entirely satisfactory, it explained some things that were otherwise incomprehensible, placed the blame to some degree somewhere else and showed the news organizations were doing their best to provide accurate information. I use this relatively extreme example to make a point. Would any news organization today, given this situation, refuse to report what they know until they are absolutely sure of the accuracy of the information, while all their competitors go forward? I doubt it. Speed comes first. To abuse another saying, "It is better to ask forgiveness for being wrong than ask permission to be late."

Even though the problems in news coverage accuracy were so severe that congressional hearings were held on the subject, the Sept. 11 attack showed that those same news organizations remained committed to speed versus accuracy. Early reports were consistently wrong, and in some cases, seriously wrong. This can be easily understood given the confusion of the events. But they demonstrated that they will go on the air with what they have, clearly explaining that it is incomplete, unverified and potentially wrong, rather than risk being perceived as too late with the news.

One of the most painful illustrations of the consequences of ignoring the importance of speed occurred in January 2006. In the Sago Mine near Tallmansville, West Virginia, 13 miners were trapped deep underground. A Command Post was set up near the mine and a rescue team entered the mine equipped with breathing apparatus. The families of the miners waited anxiously for hours. Reporters from around the nation and world were doing live broadcasts awaiting word on the fate of the miners. At 11:49 p.m., word came through the crowd that 12 of the 13 had been found alive. The families gathered in the local Baptist church were jubilant, even more so when further word came that the miners were actually well enough to come and meet their families at the church.

The problem was it wasn't true. Apparently, someone in the Command Post had heard a garbled message on a speaker phone from the rescue team deep in the mine and, breaking Incident Command protocols, used a cell phone to convey the far too optimistic information to families outside. Reporters and editors, using "confirmations" from official sources, such as the governor and a US representative on scene, spread the good news to the world. In the morning, headlines proclaimed the miracle in West Virginia.

By approximately 11:30 p.m., the CEO of the mining company and other leaders in the Command Post had received the correct information from deep within the mine. Twelve had been found dead with one survivor in critical condition. Then, apparently, they agonized. How to tell the families celebrating in the church? How to go back to the crowds and the world with such devastating news? They waited for nearly three hours before ending the joy. Their reason? They wanted to make sure *this time* the information they provided was completely accurate.

Unfortunately for them, their concern about accuracy was understood as callousness, even cruelty. No one expressed an opinion that they did the right thing. There is a simple lesson here: when conveying vital information, speed counts. And if it is bad news, it counts even more.

This is a critical point, and a difficult one, for many of today's communication practitioners who have long operated under the entirely reasonable assumption that accuracy is the heart of credibility and, therefore, accuracy always takes precedence over speed. The message in plain terms to organizational executives and leaders is this: if your public information officer is pressing you to get the information out NOW, in spite of the fact that not everything is buttoned up the way you want it to be, consider the consequences. "Between a rock and a hard place" hardly describes this dilemma. But at least now you know how the professional news businesses are dealing with this same dilemma.

Infotainment

In 1984, communications professor and critic Neil Postman wrote a book called Amusing Ourselves to Death. Subtitled "Public Discourse in the Age of Show Business" it railed against the intrusion of entertainment values into how we deal with important issues. No doubt, Postman would be amazed at how the news business has been overwhelmed by the entertainment business 20 years later. Where there were once relatively clear lines between information and entertainment, now no lines can be drawn. This is the most important and influential trend in public information and of even greater consequence to the potential newsmaker/packager/distributor than the accelerating speed caused by the Internet and the unremitting demand for credibility.

There are a number of trends that have converged to create the current situation. Some of these are driven by culture, and others by the competitive nature of the news businesses. Activism, politics of attack, and growing negativity toward big business and globalization are important contributors. Add these important cultural factors into the reality of media and news competition, and it is not surprising that what has emerged is a blending of information and entertainment that I will refer to as "infotainment." Infotainment in its various forms is by far the dominant mode of public communication today, and as a result, must be clearly understood by executives and communications professionals who must deal with the contemporary journalists as well as directly with today's news audiences.

The End of the News Executive

The news executive has always been in a tight spot. He or she has two masters to serve: the news audience, which is the "customer" for the news product, and the advertiser, who is the customer for the audience the news product delivers. Serving two masters, as ancient wisdom tells us, is impossible. But the old-style news executive who had either complete control of the business, or at least a great deal of influence, made compromises based on a firm commitment to the value of legitimate journalism.

In major network and cable broadcasting, true news executives no longer have that position. Ownership and control, for the most part, has transitioned to executives who control corporations with many different business elements and who live by the quarterly report dictum of today's stockholders. General Electric now owns NBC, AOL Time Warner owns CNN, Viacom owns CBS, Disney owns ABC, and News Corp. owns FOX. Frank Biondi, former chief executive of Viacom, was quoted in a January 2002, article in *Esquire* magazine as saying, "I don't think there's anybody left who's got a news legacy running these networks."

Kim Masters, author of the *Esquire* article, states, "The news divisions are now little pieces of big machines and the people who run those big machines are hardly news junkies." Larry Grossman, a former president of NBC news, tangled with Jack Welch, the famed chairman of NBC owner GE, complaining, "All these companies have fallen into the hands of guys who couldn't care less about [news] and are dealing with it because it's a hangover from things past." Jack Welch, who fired Grossman, countered: "He operated under the theory that networks should lose money while covering news in the name of journalistic integrity."

This battle is at the heart of the infotainment trend that drives much of the news business today. From a corporate performance standpoint, executives can hardly be faulted for presenting programming that delivers the best audiences for advertisers. But what happens to serious journalism in the process? The question was played out on the national news when in February and March 2002, a public battle ensued between CBS and NBC over replacing the highly respected "Nightline," hosted by Ted Koppel, with the late night comedy program "Late Show with David Letterman." In fighting to keep his job and his program, Koppel resorted to the unusual step of requesting and receiving guest editorial positions in major newspapers. The op-ed piece was titled "'Nightline' makes profit for ABC, but Letterman could make more." Koppel spent a good deal of his limited space explaining how profitable the show has been for ABC, but conceding that "The Late Show" would generate more profits. He states, "…it is perfectly understandable that Disney would jump at the opportunity to increase earnings by replacing 'Nightline' with the more profitable David Letterman show." What clearly got under Koppel's skin was the comment by one of the corporate executives that his news program was no longer "relevant." Koppel writes, "…When, in short, the regular and thoughtful analysis of national and foreign policy is more essential than ever – it is simply wrong to describe what my colleagues and I are doing as lacking relevance."

Relevance wasn't really the appropriate word. What the executive probably meant to say was that "Nightline" was not entertaining enough; at least, not enough to compete financially with "Letterman." As it turned out, the negotiations failed, and Koppel continued with his "irrelevant" program until retiring in 2005.

The Prime Time News Magazine

We have seen, in the past few years, that news can compete very effectively with other forms of TV entertainment. But to do so, it has adopted many of the methods and techniques of entertainment, creating what I am referring to as "infotainment."

Primetime TV is now dominated by news programming. CBS's "60 Minutes" created the news magazine format, and a host of imitators followed. This new programming format, called a "news magazine," proved to be very successful for CBS and one of the most successful and longest running TV programs in history. ABC's "20/20" and "Primetime Live," NBC's "Dateline," and a number of cable TV imitators noted the success and came up with their own versions. In the process, there was a convergence of news and entertainment: primetime news programs merged with entertainment to create the news magazine formula and sitcoms merged with real-time stories to create a new genre (imported from Europe) in the form of so-called "reality shows." CBS's "Survivor" and "Big Brother" led to extreme and outrageous "reality" programming on FOX, such as "COPS" and "Temptation Island." Viewers are hard pressed to tell what is real and what is not real and, for the most part, don't care. They do care, however, that they are entertained.

Another form of infotainment emerged in radio broadcasting. Clearly, it emerged from the competitive realities of radio broadcasting, for this trend, "talk radio," virtually saved an entire broadcast band. Since the late 60s and early 70s, AM radio had been on the decline, giving way to the higher quality audio and stereo capabilities of the FM band. Since music emerged as the dominant means of gathering a radio audience, and FM could outperform AM in delivering music quality, it seemed only a matter of time before AM would go the way of the vinyl 45 rpm record and the eight-track tape cassette. But Rush Limbaugh, with his "Excellence in Broadcasting" network and his ability to create a rabidly loyal, if distinctly niche audience, almost single-handedly saved AM radio. Howard Stern fans would likely argue that the "shock jock" also did a lot to create the talk show format and save AM radio.

Sound quality didn't matter as much for talk. Broadcasters discovered that people liked to talk back to the radio. Now talk shows of all kinds, with every stripe of expert and every color across the political spectrum, are well represented. AM radio has new life, and the instant news world another segment of frequently loud and boisterous voices clamoring to be heard. The phenomenon of talk radio both accelerated the distribution of instant news and encouraged the now ubiquitous engagement of the audience with their information medium through instant interaction. Audience involvement, as any stage producer knows, has very strong entertainment appeal.

Print media is not at all immune from the infotainment trend. When, now retired, Gannett chief Al Neuharth, decided to launch *USA Today*, he was accused of creating a McDonald's version of a newspaper, where all news products would have the same dulling presentation and where the news was all happiness and fluff, all marketing and hype, all entertainment values and no real substance. Neuharth was on the money since his venture has developed into the second most circulated daily in the US. He was right in assuming that the American reader wanted a publication that was exceptionally readable, highly scannable, full of color and splash and light on details or in-depth heady coverage. As it turns out, there is an audience for both *The New York Times* and *USA Today*.

Infotainment is the natural consequence of aggressive competition for news audiences. The simple reality is that news producers need to give audiences what they want. We have already discussed that they want speed, depth and credibility. But news audiences also want to be entertained. They look in their news coverage for the same elements that grab and hold them in the movies, or in TV programming, or in the books and magazines that they choose to read in their limited spare-time. We are not entertained today as we have been in the past, with social interaction, with lengthy discussions over coffee and beer, and with hours of shared family activities. Social activities frequently involve going to the movies or watching a game on the big screen. We need color, action, high impact visuals and most of all, a good story.

The fact that infotainment has come to dominate specific publications and programming, as described above, is fairly clear cut and obvious. Where it becomes more insidious and, therefore dangerous to both viewers and newsmakers alike, is when those same infotainment values dominate the "hard news," – those traditional news programs or vehicles where the lines were more clearly drawn. There can be no doubt that those lines have been crossed. The evidence for this is not so much in the color, splash and insistence on compelling visuals that characterize much of news, but in the entertainment formula that is used to present the news. I call this the melodrama formula.

The Black Hats and White Hats

The melodrama has been a popular form of entertainment for perhaps as long as humans have entertained each other. The conventions of the melodrama formula can be seen in early forms of drama such as the commedia del 'arte of the early middle ages. The word "melodrama" in our culture brings to mind images of bewhiskered villains in large dark hats tying white skinned and flowing-clothed virgins onto railroad tracks while the roaring train can be seen approaching in the distance. A battle ensues between the dark villain and the white-hatted cowboy who rides onto the scene in a hurry to defeat evil and release the petrified maiden at the last possible instant.

The intriguing thing about melodrama is that, in spite of the fact that it is strictly formulaic and entirely predictable, it almost never fails to please. It is a handy and convenient device for the writer because he or she simply needs to follow the formula with only minor modifications to sustain interest and audience satisfaction. It is pleasing to the audience because the audience is spared too much discomfort of the unknown, while offering instead of uncertainty, the satisfaction of knowing that right, truth and justice will always win in the end.

The most pervasive entertainment value that has emerged in the last 15 years in our contemporary news media is the melodrama formula, and this is seen in our daily newspapers as much, if not more than, in our prime time TV news programming. The reason that it has become popular is that it responds directly to our need for story, for compelling narrative, for a suspenseful tale of good versus evil.

In a melodrama, there are only a few basic requirements, but they are essential. There is the need for the good character, the bad character and something or someone to fight over. The bad almost always looks like they are winning, but then the good comes in to rescue the "maiden" from evil. Today, this formula can be seen most clearly in those news programs which compete head-on for primetime entertainment, the TV news magazines. But the same formula can also be seen at work in local TV "investigative" reporting and in a great many print reports. The "maiden" is always the "public good" as seen by the reporter or news media. It may be public health, safety, protection of the environment, and in some cases, financial well being or quality of life issues. There is always a "black hat" and a "white hat." What makes it particularly formulaic is that seldom are shades of gray revealed. The white hat is mostly purely white and the black hat mostly purely black. The black hat is placed securely on the head of a person or group who is putting the public good at risk by what they are doing, usually by selfish pursuit of corporate profits or else through pure evil. The distinction between those two seems increasingly lost on a great many of today's news viewers.

With the melodrama formula in mind, the pattern becomes more obvious in many news stories. A company stands accused. Investigative reporters, activists, disgruntled former employees or even competitors have raised the issue to the media or the media has uncovered the accusation. The company has been marketing defective equipment, spilling chemicals, hiring dangerous workers, selling untested products, etc., etc. A cover-up is usually detected. In these situations, the accused has the black hat – automatically. The accuser has the white hat, regardless of credibility or motive. The maiden – the well being of the reader, and sometimes, of all society – is at risk.

One might think that journalistic responsibility and integrity would require some verification of the accusations before putting a hard-earned reputation at risk. But, when I have pointed out to reporters that the person making an accusation against a client was not credible, and was not speaking the truth, the answer I have received is, in effect, "That is not our concern. Our job is to report accurately what they say."

In some of the egregious cases of journalistic irresponsibility, the reporters and producers or editors themselves, cross the line of dishonesty, which is frequently the strategy of accusers. The situations in TV news magazines involving a news crew sabotaging a Volvo so that the roof would collapse on cue, and rigging a gas tank with an explosive to demonstrate how tanks can explode in a collision, are outrageous examples of a common trend. The primary difference between "investigative" reporting and straight news reporting is that the reporter plays the role of accuser instead of having an activist or opponent playing this role. Now it is the media not only standing by and being the storyteller, as in the author of the melodrama, but the author steps in to be the white-hatted cowboy.

While some of the more notable cases of reportorial excess have been in TV news, print reporters are far from immune. In some of the situations described in later chapters, print reporters have obstinately stuck to the "white hat/black hat" formula, even when the private or organizational agendas of those carrying the white hats was clearly demonstrated to them, and the lack of honesty in the information they provided clearly revealed. It is difficult to abandon the direction of a story when it plays well, fits the formula and provides the reader-interest the publishers and editors want.

Clearly, investigative reporting has greatly benefited our society. As has quality news reporting that brings to light failings in companies, government agencies, celebrities and other newsmakers. But there are two fundamental problems with the melodrama formula absorbing our news coverage. One is that it is fundamentally false at its premise and the other is it is so easily abused.

The reason that melodrama is not considered among the more elevated forms of art is that the very formula that makes it popular also makes if fundamentally false. Life, as we know, is not as clear-cut as having "good guys" and "bad guys". The maiden is usually not as pure, beautiful and helpless as is pictured in the standard melodrama. The good guys sometimes do bad things and the bad guys may turn out to have redeeming qualities. In other words, life is not black and white, but is filled with shades of gray. Great storytelling art avoids the melodrama charge by reflecting at least some of this complexity of life. Great journalism also reflects that the accuser is not always purely good, nor the corporate executive always purely evil – despite the fact that he may have been surprised getting into his car, and the only thing he knew to do in the face of those lights and cameras was to cover his face with the briefcase he was carrying.

Alaska Airlines' well deserved reputation for safety and quality was undermined in the aftermath of the Flight 261 disaster by relentless news reports calling into question its safety record and performance. Much of this came from a single disgruntled former employee who laid some very strong accusations against the company's maintenance policies. When companies are engaged in activities involving regulatory inspections, it is highly unusual to not have at least some reports that can be construed as damaging. Maintenance records involving Alaska were brought forth in the lengthy series of articles in the Seattle papers that supported the clear conclusion of the editors that the company was irresponsible. A once stellar reputation was very much damaged; but fortunately, it was not entirely destroyed, despite the apparent intentions of a disgruntled employee and complicit reporters. More responsible and less formulaic reporting would have included some perspective or context about Alaska's safety performance in relation to the entire industry, and would probably also have more closely evaluated the credibility and potential motives of the one person making the accusations.

This pattern is very much part of the formula. Once an event has occurred that has captured public interest, news media have an interest in stretching the story into days and weeks to capture and sustain the continuing interest. When an industrial facility had a dramatic explosion and fire killing some workers, it was, of course, of high interest to the community. For at least two years after the event, every time this particular facility was mentioned in any regional TV newscast, still or video, images of the fire were broadcast, regardless of any relationship of those events to the story being presented. What was imprinted into the public consciousness was the image of this facility and burning equipment. The attorney representing the families, who was always more than eager to talk to the media about his case, clearly wore the white hat and willingly aided the TV stations in their desire to stretch this story to the very limits.

So, one problem with the melodrama formula, when applied to news, is that it is false on its premise because it over-simplifies the truth. The other problem is that reporters with agendas who operate in a melodrama formula are too easily tempted to abuse the truth.

A newspaper in our region has taken a strong editorial position against a proposed energy facility on environmental grounds. There is no pretense of objectivity in the editorial stance, and surprisingly in this day, when the idea of fair reporting is still subscribed to by most readers, neither is there much of a pretense of objectivity in the news pages. As a relatively small paper, there was not the degree of separation between the editorial page and the news pages. In all but the largest papers, editorial page writers depend primarily on the reporters working on the story that leads to situations where the bias of the reporter is then magnified by the bias of the editorial writer. One of the reporters contacted a member of a government environmental agency repeatedly asking a whole series of questions. The calls came over a period of weeks and it was clear that the reporter was looking for this regulator to say something negative about another facility operated by the company proposing the new facility. Finally, the regulator said something that could be vaguely construed as negative. The next issue of the newspaper saw glaring headlines claiming that the agency was critical of the company. The outraged regulator, who saw how she had been manipulated, wrote a detailed complaint to the publisher. The reporter was temporarily taken off the story, but no retraction or correction was offered, even though the regulator clearly communicated that, in her frequent interviews with the reporter, she had communicated clearly the opposite of what had been reported. In a final irony, this reporter won several environmental journalism awards for these stories, which were entertaining, but fundamentally untruthful. Apparently, to win such awards, you have to be aggressive in pursuit of environmental protection, but not aggressive in pursuit of the truth.

Another extreme example, which I personally experienced, was with an Argentine newspaper at the tip of South America. My client was proposing a forestry operation in the area and environmental activists were strongly opposed and gave the small local news paper "information" about the project. This "information" included company plans to clear-cut the forest, (absolutely false) chip the wood (absolutely false) and send the chips to Japan for fax paper (absolutely false). The newspaper dutifully reported the accusations to the point that when representatives from the company arrived in town to make a presentation at a town council meeting, they felt physically threatened by the anger of the townspeople. We needed to get our story out, so we approached the newspaper about purchasing some advertising. "Certainly," they said, once a budget figure was agreed on, "Would you like that in form of advertising or a news story?" I immediately accepted the offer of a news story, which we wrote and was printed as "news."

Since the previous example of the power plant involved a Canadian newspaper, it may be comfortable for American readers to assume such abuses of journalistic integrity are limited to foreign news businesses. Anyone in media and public communication in this country would most likely be able to come up with his or her own "war stories." Another involved a US daily. Engaged in a pitched battle involving medical waste, my client had come under unrelenting attack from a local legislator. The newspaper delighted in the story because the legislator, in the tradition of Joe McCarthy, provided colorful accusations and good copy. It fit the formula perfectly: "Heroic public servant accuses big company of putting the entire community's health at risk for the sake of big profits." The reporter and editor clearly liked the story. So, when information emerged that made the situation gray instead of black and white, it was fiercely resisted. Accusations made by the accuser about the company's regulatory record and health and safety record of its own employees were presented in a way that did outright violence to the truth. When an attempt was made to correct the misinformation, the guest editorial was rejected because the editorial page editor couldn't "verify it as being true." When it was pointed out that never had any attempt been made to verify the truth of the accusations, and should that attempt be made they would be found to be false, the conversation ended.

When the formula must be followed, the truth is too easily sacrificed. That is the real risk of the melodrama mode of public information.

"Infotainment" represents a very significant challenge for newsmakers in the instant news world. It is the cultural and media environment that communication professionals and executives must live and work in. It is not a matter of choice, but of reality. To continue to pretend, as so many do, that news reporting is anything other than a business of gaining and maintaining audiences, is self-deception. The key to those audiences is speed, depth, credibility and infotainment. As newsmakers enter this world – willingly or unwillingly – they must learn what the audiences expect and what their competitors can be counted on to do. From that, they must formulate the policies and strategies to compete effectively in this increasingly strange world of public communication.

5.
When Opponents Grab the Microphone

At the time of the first edition of this book, about half of Americans were using the Internet. As I write this second edition in early 2006, four years later, between two-thirds and three-fourths of all Americans use the Internet.

But there is another even more significant change. Most casual users of the Internet use it to gain information, to read and view materials presented by others. That too is changing. More and more Internet users are actively publishing their views, engaging in community discussions, uploading information. Internet use has broadened, but it has also become far more active and interactive.

A few of those active Internet users might not like you or your organization. In fact, if you present a sizeable target, they may make it their hobby, or even their career, to make life as miserable for you as possible. Their reasons might be pure, in that they may think they are performing a public service, or they may be less than pure, seeing the opportunity to damage or destroy your reputation as a means of building their own. Having opponents may not be anything new, since opponents have been around for a long time. The difference is they now own the most powerful transmitters and printing presses the world has ever created.

Suppose along the way in your business career you did some damage to the career of a co-worker who since then went on to bigger and better things. The anger seethes. It happens. But now, she is suddenly hired as the executive producer for CNN. She is the kind of person incapable of forgiving or forgetting and she doesn't mind stretching the truth to get even. Make you nervous? All of your opponents who have computers and Internet connections have in their hands the power to create an audience and communicate their idea or version of the truth. It's no longer a situation where they need to buy out a broadcast channel or purchase a newspaper to get the public attention and ear. They can do so for essentially no cost while working in their bedroom in their underwear.

In late 2001, the energy trading giant Enron crashed. In a matter of weeks, the company's stock went from a high of $90 to as low as 28 cents per share. Shortly after this, stories emerged in national newspapers reporting that, while employees and ordinary investors were losing their life savings and retirement accounts, Enron executives were handing out multi-million dollar bonuses to each other. A story as large as this, enhanced by the Andersen shredding scandal, stays on the front page and on the TV newscast schedule for some time. Most stories erupt very quickly and then almost as quickly go away, replaced by a new breaking news story. What doesn't go away so easily is the anger and despair of those who feel they were burned by executive incompetence, deception or worse. Shortly after the Enron news broke, a number of new Web sites were launched by the victims of the disaster, dedicated to continuing the story, communicating in excruciating detail all the information they could find and publish. One of those sites offered assistance to ex-employees interested in telling their stories to the media by helping them contact reporters who had expressed interest in talking to unhappy former employees.

Five public information trends have emerged, which, when combined, pose an unprecedented risk to the reputations of high profile people, companies and organizations. These five trends are:

- The growing cynicism and negativity in our public discourse
- The movement of the media away from traditional news reporting to "infotainment"
- The emergence of the powerful activist/opponent
- The ability of these powerful opponents to create and effectively use their own means of information distribution.
- The eager involvement of politicians

While we can identify them as independent elements, as you will see, these trends weave together in a complex tapestry of dependence so that the impact of all five together becomes much more significant than if each were to develop and operate independently.

A Time of Cynicism

Few will contest the idea that we live in a deeply cynical time. The real life tragedy of Sept. 11 probably did more to relieve us of some of this cynicism and return to a more realistic view of life than anything else could have. Nevertheless, as has been pointed out by numerous commentators, Americans have become increasingly cynical of the political process and of the economic forces that deeply affect them, but over which they have apparently little control. This can be seen in voter turnouts, in the frequent "throw the bastards out" votes, in the continually degraded political discourse, such as the highly negative and effective "attack ads," and in the growing anti-globalism backlash as seen in the World Trade Organization protests in Seattle and other host cities.

There is a "chicken and the egg" question here in regard to whether the media created this trend or contributed to it. Most communication historians will point to Watergate as a critical point in our history where, in conjunction with the Vietnam debacle, the American people lost trust and hope in politicians and the political process. At the same time that our elected leaders and their associates shamed themselves and us, the investigative reporters emerged as heroes. It was a role they accepted with a little less humility than might be appropriate. A turning point in the respect shown by the media toward those in elected office might be the interchange between President Nixon and ABC's aggressive reporter, Sam Donaldson. When Donaldson was asking questions of the President, Nixon asked, "Sam, are you running for office?" Donaldson quickly retorted, "No sir, are you?" The fact that this likely does not seem disrespectful today demonstrates the degree of change in the relationship between the media and those involved in the political process.

Similarly, the decline in respect for business institutions, businesses and individual business leaders is also due in significant part to the incredibly poor behavior and low moral standards of so many in the business community. Don't misunderstand me, the numerous stories of scandal, corruption, moral failures and greed that demonstrate this problem in the business community are matched by the same kind of character and value disappointments in every walk of life. Business leaders have no monopoly on greed, lust, dishonesty or corruption. The same behavior can be found in the professions, church leadership, education, organized labor, agriculture and every other occupation. Many prominent news stories of early 2002 demonstrate this, ranging from child-molesting priests to highly respected historians who plagiarize. That's what makes the current situation somewhat unique and interesting. Moral and character failure in the business and political realms is not unique – it just has become the focus of reporting as well as popular entertainment. A clear evidence for this decline is the study conducted by Media Research Center in 1997.

This study examined nearly 900 TV entertainment shows. It showed that businessmen commit more crimes on TV than anyone; in fact, they commit three times more crimes on television than career criminals! Most murders on TV are committed by businessmen, again by a factor of three. Businessmen are more likely to cheat than contribute positively to society (28.7 percent versus 25 percent). Let me emphasize – this isn't reality; this is TV's picture of reality. However, as is frequently said in advertising and public relations, perception IS reality.

Because the public in general holds the view that most in business are corrupt and evil, it plays extremely well when the media present them in this light. In fact, portraying characters that go against the grain of public opinion is a risk that most media managers are not willing to take – particularly when the melodrama formula is working out quite well. As one network executive stated, as quoted by Eric Dezenhall in his book titled Nail 'Em, "We need villains. And if we portray businessmen as not caring about society or their employees, would we be all wrong?"

Public discourse is where we have most dramatically seen the slide into negativity and cynicism. In 1978, when I became involved in managing a state legislative campaign, I attended a campaign school in Olympia taught by a grizzled veteran of the political wars. Since I was a 20-something political newcomer, he seemed old and grizzled to me. During the course of his seminar he stated that voters do not vote for candidates. By a strong margin, they usually vote against candidates. While not explicitly stated at this time, because it was 1978 and not 1998, the meaning was clear: your campaign should be about why the voters should not vote for the other candidate more than about why they should vote for your candidate. That view may surprise many in the public today, especially when they are now used to hearing candidates at the beginning of a campaign talking about how they want to run a clean campaign and simply talk about their record or their plans. However, most who have been on the inside of a campaign instinctively know that this is what most campaigns, particularly hotly contested ones, have been about for some time.

This negativity was amply demonstrated in the campaigns involving both Presidents Bill Clinton and George W. Bush. Clinton was simultaneously one of the most vigorously and perhaps viciously attacked candidates ever, and at the same time he and his political teams virtually perfected the only response that has proven effective against vigorous and vicious attacks: to attack. His remarkable saga as "the comeback kid," well chronicled in campaign advisor George Stephanopoulos' book <u>All Too Human</u>, demonstrated the truth of the adage, "the best defense is a good offense." The story of Clinton and his personal failures is sad, primarily because he had to go to that way so often against others. Ultimately, his greatest challenge, of protecting his presidency from collapse, was won by his remarkably effective attack on Special Prosecutor Ken Starr and the "right-wing conspiracy" behind the investigation. All he needed to do, like a great defense attorney, was create sufficient doubt in the minds of Americans of the fairness of his accusers and the political battle was essentially won.

The Carville-Stephanopoulos "war room" strategy developed in the first campaign has proven remarkably effective and has been repeated by most campaigns since then. It consisted of two basic principles: stay on message regardless of attack ("It's the economy, stupid!") and attack the attacker. The sooner the better. The Dole campaign, while not a stellar example of effectiveness, nevertheless adopted a similar approach in trying to beat any criticism from gaining momentum by countering it before the attack had an opportunity to really develop in the media.

The election of 2004 was marked by extreme vitriol as well as the pervasive and innovative use of the Internet as a campaign tool, particularly in the primary campaign of Howard Dean.

Media Infotainment

Speaking of presidents, the media have had much to work with in the past few years. There are the tales that include a sitting president caught in serious criminal activity and paying to keep it quiet, of a front-running political candidate with a mistress on his lap while cruising on a luxury yacht, and then there's the one about another sitting-president groping White House staffers and taking sexual advantage of young interns. All these played very well into the hands of media business executives charged with the responsibility of filling more and more air time with "news" that would lure TV audiences away from competing network's sitcoms. It raises the question again: did the media create infotainment to compete, or did it fall into it by simply reporting the unfortunately all too entertaining shenanigans of our nation's leaders? When it ran out of politicians misbehaving, was it simply forced to turn to other powerful people and expose their frequent frailties and failings? A hint to the answer is found in the personal life of President Kennedy. The numerous indiscretions well known to the media of the time, but unreported, indicate that the times have changed and changed greatly.

The question, while perhaps interesting, is hardly the point here. What is the point, as was discussed in the previous chapter, is that infotainment is the style of news du jour. As a result, it is what newsmakers in the instant news world must contend with. It is pointless and counter-productive to pretend that we still live in an era of "just the facts" reporting – let alone "respect those in high office" reporting. In those days, the concerns about bias and objectivity related more to getting the quotes straight, rather than forcing every story in a tight, predictable melodramatic formula of white hats and black hats.

The interweaving of these two trends now becomes clear. The public holds a perception of misbehavior on the part of our political and business leaders and is quite interested in stories that demonstrate this perspective. News business executives need to deliver the audiences that would normally turn to evening drama or sitcoms, or the readers who would pick up Danielle Steele, Dean Koontz or Tom Clancy. Some of the greatest moments of success for the media, if you leave aside great drama of good versus evil such as the Gulf War, came during the Watergate and Lewinsky scandals. The public's temporarily insatiable desire for all the tidbits, historic or not, have fed the development of the all news channels initiated by Ted Turner with CNN and Headline News. These cable "all news, all talk" media are now joined by the Internet/cable teams of CNBC, MSNBC and FOX News. Such good versus evil stories have also fed the development of other important trends in public information, including talk radio and the almost endless pundit shows such as "The Capital Gang," "Hannity and Colmes," "Hardball with Chris Mathews," and so on and so on.

Now we need to add one more important element to this tapestry: the accuser. For without the accuser, the media is left to be the prosecution as well as judge and jury. Even though the investigative styles evidenced today show little concern about the impression left by this mishmash, most "hard news" outlets prefer to have a person or group other than an investigative reporter make the accusations against the black hats. Particularly because the accuser need not respect the same level of honesty and integrity or adherence to the truth that most investigative reporters need in order to preserve credibility.

Activists and Other Opponents

Grassroots political activism has a rich and storied history in the American democratic experiment. Some of our most revered national heroes were activists of the first order going back to the American revolution. Activists are frequently colorful characters who have had profound impact on the course of history. Cary Nation, of the temperance movement, Susan B. Anthony, of the women's right to vote, Harriet Beecher Stowe, in the anti-slavery effort, are a few of the remarkable women activists who contributed to our American story and traditions. Martin Luther King, Jr. is deservedly a national hero on the level of our most respected leaders and presidents. Certainly there are a number of others who also had profound impact, but who live more in infamy than in fame. Senator McCarthy and John Brown come to mind, as does the activism of Eldridge Cleaver, Tom Hayden and others from the cultural revolution of the 1960s.

While activists have always been an important part of our democratic process, it is quite certain that at no other time in history have so many made a career out of it. Nor have activists been so instantly successful at gaining fame, or been so ingrained as an accepted, every day part of our lives and culture. We have become, in some respects, a democracy that depends on activists and our news media have become information/entertainment vehicles that depend on activism.

The career of one activist, of which I am perhaps too painfully aware, is instructive of some of the trends. This person, whom I will call Jean, began her activist career more than 20 years ago. One of her children became ill with a serious disease and she became convinced that the cause was an industrial facility located within a few miles of her home. She took her accusation of disease-causing emissions to anyone who would listen, including to the state capitol. In meetings with local representatives, she demanded that this company be put out of business to prevent other children from dying, weeping hysterically during her tirades. When her demands did not result in the action she desired, she literally camped on the lawn in front of the state capitol building. There she made a great discovery, which would serve her well during the next 20 years of her efforts at bringing this company down: the media loved it. Her accusations were widely reported without regard to the possibility of whether there could be any truth to them. Photos of her attempting to get the ears of the governor and state legislators were printed in local and regional newspapers. One result is that she gained instant fame in her local community. This celebrity status was elevated when she received a national award for activists. Another result was the state launched an epidemiological study to test her theory at a cost of tens of thousands of taxpayer dollars. The ironic thing is that the officials knew her claim was medically impossible because the particular disease her child suffered from was not transmitted via airborne contaminants. Nevertheless, the study went forward and resulted in a very predictable report showing that not only was there not an increased incidence of this disease as she claimed, but that it was medically impossible to contract the disease through the method studied. The newspapers ran an inside page story on the study but it never stopped her from repeating the now discredited accusation. Twenty years later she still boldly states the accusation as if it is truth and as if the state study has verified her claim.

If that were the end of the story, it would not be so instructive. Since state or local health department action would not shut this company down, she would find other means. She ran for the office of County Council member and won.

By this time, she had a well-established relationship with the local newspaper. It was a mutually beneficial relationship. She provided exceptionally colorful copy and was bold and relentless in her accusations against this locally owned company. Oh, she also tried a few other targets to attack, but only against this company could she create the vitriol needed to gain attention, supporters and media attention – at least on a sustained basis.

The battleground shifted from the emissions to the very existence of the business. She worked closely with a competitor, leveraging her position as an elected official to help them gain legal standing that otherwise would not have been possible, and then helped them sue the County to change laws that affected the operation of the company. Despite the fact that a community-wide survey showed that more than 80 percent of the populace supported the environmentally-positive activity of the company, the 200 angry citizens who believed her accusations of the death-dealing activities of this company persuaded the other council members to support her efforts. The result: the company's primary business activity was halted and, only by astute business moves, was it able to salvage its business and sell out most of its operations to a larger company.

It is important to understand that her method of doing business was by intimidation, temper tantrums, wild accusations against anyone who stood in her way and the perfection of the "90 percent lie." This device is where you take 10 percent of the truth and distort and exaggerate it so that the net result is information that is completely untrue. But, when pinned down, the accuser can always go back to the 10 percent and blame the listener for going beyond that kernel of truth. It is a specialty of a great many of today's activists and can make even the most harmless records look vile. The tenor of public debate with this person on the County Council became so negative and intimidating that by a 6-1 vote (she voted against it, obviously) every other member of the Council voted to censure her for her behavior on the Council. Astoundingly, the local paper criticized all the other council members and commended her for her bold protection of public interest. They were not about to have such a convenient marriage of accuser and reporter put at risk by the facts of horrible public behavior and serious disruption of the democratic process.

There was yet another part of this company that was still operational, so it became the next subject of attack. She had attempted to put this portion of the operation out of business a few years earlier by successfully passing a citizen's initiative that would ban the import of materials used by the company knowing that most came across the border from Canada. The initiative was a clear violation of the Interstate Commerce clause of the US Constitution and, since this was before she was elected to office, the County refused to pay to defend it in court. She formed a citizen's committee to defend it, but the initiative was summarily dismissed as illegal. Undaunted after her success in destroying the company's main business, she attacked with another initiative after failing to get the necessary Council votes to put the company under. The company foolishly refused to fight the ordinance publicly and it passed overwhelmingly. When it became clear that this too was illegal, for a number of reasons, including constitutional reasons and that the County would not defend it, she put the initiative in the form of an ordinance and, based on the supposed overwhelming public support, secured a unanimous Council vote.

The battle waged over several years with many court appearances. While the company's legal position was solid, its name was so tainted in the community that it was virtually impossible to gain any support for any efforts it might make that would involve getting permits – even to change processes that may be positive for the public. The company no longer exists.

The question, of course, is "why?" Why did the company allow it to get to this, since there has never been one shred of evidence presented that the business activity the company was engaged in was the least bit harmful to any member of the public? Why did this person dedicate 20 years of her life to a cause that she must know is based on personal motivation and not any realities of public risk? Perhaps, most importantly, why did the newspaper continue to keep from the public the outrageous and newsworthy excesses of this public figure while continuing to treat her information as credible – even when it is clearly demonstrated that it was not?

If this were an isolated instance, it would not be worthy of consideration. The reality is that it happens all the time, in almost every community, in one form or another. This was an ongoing story on a very local level. This same story is playing out right now at the national and international level and in virtually every town, community, city and state. If your company or organization has some significant profile, there's a very good chance that you are currently contending with activists in situations fundamentally similar to what has been described.

The Alar scare, in which unfounded accusations were made against a substance to improve the market appearance of apples, is one of the most notorious examples of activist excesses. The actress Meryl Streep lent star quality and high credibility to claims that proved to be totally unfounded. But, by the time the media got around to reporting the psuedo-science behind the claims, the damage to the apple industry was immense and the public had lost interest in the story. The limited amount of backtrack reporting by the media went largely unnoticed and did little to restore public confidence in an important food and industry. Virtually every industry that manufactures products for public use or consumption can point to national and regional "Alar situations," in which bogus science put forward by activists has been accepted without scrutiny by the media and has caused very significant damage to safe products or industries.

The most instructive and common situations involving activists involve environmental issues. Environmentalism has become one of the most significant forces in our individual conscience and our economy in the last 20 years, and for very good reason. Human existence has a profound impact on our world, and in general, we have not been good stewards of the resources we use. As I write these words, I find myself in the Mexican city of Mazatlan, where clearly visible from the harbor is an oil-fired power plant that apparently has little to no environmental controls. All day long it has spewed an endless cloud of dirty smoke into the otherwise clear, sun-filled sky. It added dusky, rose-gray color to the morning and evening skies, and hung like a shroud over the entire city and mountain region throughout the day. Seeing that ominous cloud reminded me of the benefits we enjoy in our prosperous America where we have been able to afford the revolution in pollution control. I have yet to meet a person who did not consider him or herself an environmentalist. All of us with a stake on this earth and a concern for future generations cannot avoid favoring any effort made to protect and preserve resources and, most particularly, those resources such as air, water and food on which we all depend.

While I am profoundly grateful for the many accomplishments of the environmental movement, and respect the daring leadership that many in this movement have provided, I am also too painfully aware of the excesses and the damage that the marriage of convenience of activists and media can cause. Today's corporate leaders and communication professionals need to be very aware of the risk of activism, particularly if the business or organization has global reach. This is due to the fact that a result of the globalization of communication is that activists and opponents now operate in a global community, as the next example will illustrate.

My client was a smallish company with huge ambitions, and it launched the largest private forestry operation in South America. They acquired vast tracts of forestland on the southern tip of South America, mostly on the island of Tierra del Fuego. The forest there consisted largely of a hardwood tree that provided excellent furniture grade lumber. They set about the project with high hopes and a lofty aspiration of setting a new global standard for environmentally sound forestry. There would be no clear-cutting; scientific studies of an eco-system that was poorly documented to date would be provided. They would set aside huge areas as permanent forest preserves; they would establish local lumber processing to support a much diminished local economy, etc. They appointed as "land steward" one of the most respected experts in environmental forestry, and gave the land steward unprecedented control over their plans. The land they purchased included permits that would allow them to begin harvest virtually immediately. But in their efforts to do things right, and gain adherents in the environmental community, they opted not to make use of those existing permits, choosing instead to go through an exceptionally lengthy and expensive planning process.

The effort proved to be disastrous. More than 10 years later, the company has withdrawn from the project and is trying hard to stave off bankruptcy precipitated by its ill-fated foreign venture. While they did succeed in gaining the support of many in the environmental community, those who understood what they were trying to do wanted to keep their support quiet so as to not confuse and undermine their more extreme supporters. The primary story is told in the methods of a very few – less than five – extreme environmentalists with as much persistence in keeping the company from cutting trees as the company was persistent in carrying out its effort to gain approvals.

In earlier days, the company had been the target of some members of Earth First, an eco-terrorism organization that threatened the company owner's children and vandalized company offices. While there were two people involved in criticizing the company's activities, their protests were covered extensively in the local newspapers creating a "track record" of environmental ire. Years later, this negative press record came back to bite them, when the Northwest island which was the focus of these protests became almost a household word in the national newspapers of Argentina and Chile. This, in itself, is a significant lesson for companies who face opponent accusations. A permanent record is created that, if not balanced by complete reporting and a significant number of other positive stories, represents a long-term risk when put in the hands of those who wish to damage reputations.

How did the company's relatively minor problems in the Pacific Northwest become international news? Because the activists in the Northwest quickly made common cause with the activists in the southern tip of South America. A few of the more vocal activists from the Northwest traveled to South America, were paraded in front of rallies and held meetings with government officials. The leading activist in South America traveled to the Northwest and became the star attraction at the protest rallies held in the company's hometown. It was almost a situation of one-plus-one equals millions, at least that was the perception that was created. The story that emerged wasn't one of a small company attempting to set a new standard for environmental forestry; it was a demon corporate giant who, having ravaged the forests of the Northwest out of existence, was now turning to do the same in South America. That story was far more compelling to the newspapers covering the story than that of a company dedicated to responsible forestry and reviving the economies of all remote towns – and to making a profit.

In talking with one of the executives about lessons learned from this disappointing effort, one was that the original permit should have been implemented immediately. Their efforts to "do it right" would likely have been easier if they had proceeded on the original basis, and negotiated changes in those plans in exchange for the opportunity to expand their operation. Another lesson is that the mainstream environmental community, fearful of alienating the more extreme elements, is virtually powerless to support companies or individuals who attempt to conduct industrial activity in a positive manner. While they received tacit support, that could not be translated into a moderate environmental consensus, for obvious economic reasons. The environmental groups did not want to put their fundraising efforts at risk to support something they believed in because of their concern of alienating their more extreme supporters. Finally, a key lesson was the power of a very few people to undermine the best intentions and tens of millions of dollars of persistent effort. That power is based in part on their persistence and dedication to a cause they deeply believe in, but mostly by their willingness to do anything and say anything, regardless of the truth. This willingness, combined with the eagerness of the media to promote controversy and strong accusations – to put white hats and black hats on the usual suspects – means that gaining political support for even an unusually enlightened project is tenuous at best.

The power of the few was clearly demonstrated in the battle over a natural gas-fired power plant planned for development just on the US side of the Canadian border. The local paper carried the headline: "Ten Opponents Successful in Stopping Power Plant." This headline enraged those "ten" because they claimed support of more than 80,000 citizens opposing the project. The truth is fewer than 10 – two or three, really – combined with the power of the media on both sides of the border intent on sticking to their infotainment melodrama script were able to stop the cleanest power plant in the region from being built. This potent combination resulted in the first-ever state permit denial of a power plant in the midst of the worst power shortage in the region's history.

The assumption might be that the proposed plant did indeed represent environmental risk. The truth is the opposite: at that time, there was no cleaner gas-fired plant planned, permitted or operating. It was denied not because it violated any environmental regulation on either side of the border, but simply because a few people were very successful in creating the perception of public concern. I say the perception of public concern, because in the county where the plant was to be located, polling showed anywhere from 60 percent to 75 percent of the people supported the project.

If the plant was exceptionally clean, if there was strong local support and if the state panel was established to permit such facilities without being unduly influenced by "nimbyism," – the "not in my backyard" phenomenon – how could such a thing happen? The simple and true answer lies in the combination of activist/politician and media infotainment. In this case, the two key opponents were both elected officials. One, a County Council member in the US county where the plant was to be located, and another in a similar position in the small British Columbia city across the border in Canada. Both were bright, articulate women with pleasant demeanors that masked the anger and bitterness that characterized their efforts.

Eric Dezenhall pointed out some of the consistencies in these kinds of activists, although in his experience, most were not elected officials. He said: "I don't like attackers, but my job has taught me they are not all evil. They can be the people next door who complain about chemicals in food and fat in popcorn and muffins. Once I strip away the rage, I find a desperate person looking for credit, recognition or celebrity. I find an exile from an exciting world that has passed him by."

The combination activist/politician is not a new phenomenon, but it may be far more widespread than in the days of Joe McCarthy. Their success, despite their frequently narrow focus, can be attributed in part to the remarkable treatment they often receive from the media. As mentioned before, the activist/politician and the media enjoy a marriage of convenience when one provides the colorful copy, frequently outrageous accusations, and bitter controversy that the other happily transforms into the melodrama formula. This was certainly true in the situation mentioned earlier of an activist/politician dedicated to destroying an industrial facility, and also was the case of the two who fought the power plant.

The convenience in this marriage is about money. As Dezenhall pointed out in discussing the Alar situation, all parties involved in the accusation stood to gain financially, while the defendant, the apple industry, had much to lose: "The NRDC (National Resources Defense Council – the accuser) is an agenda-driven entity that relies on fundraising and a high profile to prosper. Fenton Communications

(NRDC's PR agency) is a for-profit PR group, and "60 Minutes" is the most profitable franchise in the multi-billion-dollar CBS empire. They all benefited from the controversy. NRDC raised its profile, Fenton pleased its client, and "60 Minutes" got high ratings. If they were motivated exclusively by public welfare, they might have waited for evidence before making accusations. As it was, they shut down an industry – the definitive conclusion required of all witch hunts."

A common characteristic of the successful attacker is their unabashed use of the dramatic statement or hyperbole. Providing attention-getting quotes is another reason why the entertainment-oriented press goes to great lengths to report on, and defend, these activists. Someone who provides the kind of copy and headlines needed to sell papers, attract an audience and get people talking around the water cooler is of significant economic value to news publishers.

One of the most stunning claims offered by the elected official involved in the power plant siting controversy was that the company was intentionally setting out to kill people. This outrageous accusation was based on the fact that emissions are an unavoidable result of burning fossil fuels and scientific evidence that shows air quality has an impact on mortality. The logic was that if you add to emissions in the air, you are no better than a person caught in attempted murder. Of course, the same logic could be applied to the person who gets in his car in the morning knowing that the exhaust emissions are adding to an already burdened environment. Such hyperbole and emotionally-charged accusations are characteristic of virtually every melodrama where there is strong public interest.

A visual example of this kind of statement is the coffee table book published in the mid-1980s, during the outcries about loss of forestland, which contained nothing but pictures of clear cuts. Now, it is true that there are enough clear-cuts in the US to create a sizeable coffee table book, but the impression left is that there are few if any trees left standing – an impression contradicted by the fact that since the 1950s, the US has been gaining more forestland than it is losing.

In the industrial facility melodrama discussed earlier, the elected official/activist in public hearings made dramatic claims about trucks involved in the operation, including doors falling off and dripping horrible contents onto public roads. She also repeatedly claimed, in the press and in public hearings, that a worker at the industrial facility contracted a life threatening disease. She did this knowing full well that the state agency had repeatedly denied his claim on the basis of his not being in the company's employ long enough for it to be medically possible for him to have contracted the disease there. Activists frequently don't see the need to bother themselves with the truth. The point is what can be most effectively used to generate news stories and discredit your hated target.

True Believers

While truly effective attackers and activists make full use of the media's strong interest in headline-grabbing accusations, the characteristic of most activists that I find most company executives and communication professionals are least prepared to deal with is what I call the "true believer" mentality. Modern democratic society has developed a deep fear of fundamentalists of all stripes. Extreme fundamentalists of all types have demonstrated their willingness to commit outrageous acts of terrorism or murder, feeling fully justified by the righteousness of their cause. This is as true of Al-Qaeda coming from the Islamic religion as it is of white supremacists coming from the Christian religion. Extremist anti-abortionists have demonstrated that in their understanding of God and morality they are fully justified in bombing clinics and killing doctors in cold blood. What characterizes these "true believers" is their view that the end justifies the means. This belief is what makes the anti-abortionists so dangerous, the Islamic terrorists so hard to comprehend and the radical white supremacist an object of fear. We know that these people do not conform to what most of us believe about right or wrong. They believe that the justice of their cause qualifies them to do anything and everything to those who oppose them.

This true believer mentality is not reserved for the most extreme religious or political fundamentalists. In a much more moderate form, it is a characteristic of a great many activists and it is why combating their attacks is a difficult game. They simply don't play by the same rules. While most would never sink to illegal or violent activities, many of the "true believer" variety of activists do believe that the justice of their cause gives them great latitude in the tactics they employ and with the way they deal with the truth.

The ironic thing about this is that the activist comes to the public eye through the media and invariably has the white hat on. The company dragged into the spotlight starts with two strikes against it. First, since the accusation has been made, it already has the black hat on. Second, even before the accusation was made, it is presumed that its leaders are bad people chasing profits at the expense of the public good, and whenever company officials speak in their defense or tout their record, from the jaded news media's standpoint, they are just "spinning."

Activists come into the public perception battle with several advantages. One we have already discussed, and that is the pre-disposition of the media to award them the white hat without investigating their credibility or motives. Another is they see such battles as largely emotional and effectively appeal to the fears and anger of the audience. Another is the simplicity with which they approach what are often complex issues; this simplicity plays well with how the media is able to treat the news. Finally, they seem to understand better than their corporate opponents that the real battle is over credibility.

This seems to be particularly true when the activist or opponent is of the "true believer" mentality. As a result, there tends to be a very disjointed debate as both sides spar. The company or organization under attack focuses on the "facts," such as the extent and nature of emissions, and to carry on this discussion in a fairly formal, somewhat friendly but very professional tone. The activist, on the other hand, tends to focus on whether or not the company can be believed or trusted. The nature of the discourse is frequently much more personal, informal, passionate and unambiguous. While companies clearly want to be careful in what they are saying for legal as well as accuracy reasons, and they want to be dignified and professional, opponents are not equally hampered by these niceties. They clearly understand that ultimately the battle will be won or lost on the public perception of credibility or who is to be believed.

The reason this is such a powerful advantage is that credibility is the most powerful of all means of persuasion. As pointed out earlier, the Greeks clearly understood that credibility (ethos) – the believability of the speaker – was a more important factor in persuasion than the best logical arguments or the most powerful emotional appeals.

This all-important issue of credibility will be discussed later, but it is important to note the strategic advantage most activist opponents enjoy in this. The contemporary rules of the public debate are that they can wholeheartedly, and without too much regard to the truth, attack the credibility of their targets, while the company responding needs to maintain "the high road" and focus only on the merits of the logical argument.

The two elected officials who have served as our models of activist/opponents have both perfected the techniques of undermining the credibility of the companies they oppose. In the power plant issue, the early debate focused on greatly exaggerated claims about environmental risk and damage. When those claims had largely been discredited, the focus shifted much more to attempting to undermine the record of the company and the methods used to gain approval. For example, in a public hearing, the opponents focused an inordinate amount of time on the "discovery" they made shortly before the hearing began that, according to them, the company had paid to have their supporters show up at the hearing. It was one of the first times that the number of supporters had nearly equaled the number of opponents, and that fact was of clear concern to the opponents. The accusation of the company paying its supporters to attend was a shock and a surprise to those of us who had worked hard to get community members supportive of the proposed facility to attend. The truth, as we discovered later, was that one local union strongly supportive of the project had offered to pay a small amount to cover the cost of fuel to its members who attended the meeting. The union members there were a minority of the supporters, and those who accepted the small payment were even fewer. The critical point was that the company knew nothing about those arrangements and would not have supported them had they been asked. But the truth, as usual, is irrelevant. The opponents who made much of this in the public hearing accomplished their goal. The news media, and perhaps the state panel listening to those speaking in favor of the facility, were now skeptical of the authenticity of the support.

The County Council member opposing the plant pulled a similar stunt that almost proved physically dangerous. A public rally held by opponents on the steps of the county courthouse had attracted a crowd of a couple hundred opponents. At the last minute, to create a bit of balance, we had recruited a few supporters to hold up signs in support of the project. These few received strong abuse from the opponents, to the point where one decided he had had enough and left in disgust. One of our staff members grabbed his sign and was holding it when the County Council member took the microphone. She focused the crowd's attention on the three plant supporters holding signs and announced that they were paid representatives of the company. She got the reaction she wanted. The crowd of opponents was incited and became physically threatening. Rather than risk injury or further incite an ugly crowd, we took the signs down and left the rally.

Companies engaged in these sorts of public issue battles may wish to keep the debate focused on the merits of their proposals or on the facts of the incidence causing concern. However, they need to be prepared for the very strong likelihood that the activists will shift the debate to whether or not their company is evil and whether they, as leaders, are evil. The starting point for those arguments will be that the company is big and that it has earning profits as its single purpose. But that is the starting point. Next will come an exposé of the company's regulatory compliance record. Then, any negative news reports about the company or its leaders that can be accessed through today's Internet research tools will be rehashed, but with the most negative spin imaginable. Company leaders should also expect that if they or their company have ever been sued, the accusations of the legal opponents will be quoted at length and treated as if the accusations are the final judgment and truth. Finally, if the personal or professional ethics or behavior of the company leadership, any employees or even friends and associates is less than squeaky clean, these failings may be trotted out as if they were core to the issue at hand. In a very real sense they are, no matter how unrelated to the subject, because the opponents understand that this is about whom is to be believed. They trust that you will stick to the facts and issues of the controversy and not counter with raising questions about their credibility.

Now They Have the Mike

Understanding opponents and their tactics ought to give organizational leaders and communications professionals pause. They have some cultural advantages, some rules of engagement advantages and, in many cases, they have the passion and freedom of true believers. Now add to that the ability to communicate freely, quickly and powerfully with a rapidly growing Internet community around the globe.

As a general rule, activists, opponents and their organizations have been far more eager, skillful and willing to employ the communication potential of the Internet than the companies and organizations they attack. It's not because the companies don't have a lot at stake – they have millions or billions of dollars of brand equity at stake. It's not because they don't have the resources. Of course, most have far more communication resources including Internet access and tools than their opponents. The reality is that it is precisely because of the strength of the company that makes the activist's use of these tools so effective. It might be called the judo effect, where the very strength and advantages of a company are used against it.

Look what the Internet offers someone with the dedication and commitment to attack you. A Web site containing all the accusations and evidence or psuedo-evidence supporting the attackers claims can be launched in minutes at essentially no cost. The billions of pages of information on the Internet provide a rich source of information for those looking to do damage to your reputation. Communication between others who share concerns is accomplished at no cost and at the speed of light. Coalitions can be built – not in months or weeks, but in hours. An audience can be attracted with relatively little time or effort – particularly when attackers make use of the rapidly growing databases of like-minded people and organizations around the world. Momentum is created easily by mass emailing every bit of progress in the battle against the company to the growing audience around the world. By the time the savvy attacker brings the media into the picture by simply directing them to their Web site, a compelling case for widely supported public outrage has been built. The reporter's job is now much, much easier. No need to dig for angry people to interview, or to dig for the "facts" of the situation – it is all conveniently provided in instantaneous form. In fact, reporters who choose to do so can simply go to the Web site to find names and contact information for people who would love to be quoted or go on camera. Then, when the report comes out in the media and the Web site address is proclaimed, the attackers' efforts immediately become magnified.

Organizational leaders, and communication managers to some extent, treat these Internet attacks with much less significance than, say, an attack article in a major newspaper. But they are deceived, because the Internet provides many more advantages to leverage the story and multiply its effects than a single hit in the traditional media. One very large international company came to the realization a little late after having ignored the Internet attacks too long. It was only until they noticed that the momentum buildup on blogs, forums, and discussion groups had reached such a fever pitch that it was significantly undermining their growth plans. Only then did they initiate a plan to counter the Internet chatter.

Yesterday, at the office, we received an angry note via our client's Web site from a young person opposed to the power plant project we represent. She was angry because she did a search online to gather information for a school report about why this plant is so awful. Instead of finding the opponents' Web site, she found the proponents – ours. She didn't like the information she found there at all. It explained why this plant was environmentally clean and responsible. What was most interesting was the tone that suggested we had somehow tricked her by having a Web site that was in favor of the project when she clearly only expected a site opposed to it. Might this attitude also be somewhat common in the general public? Certainly, they expect a manufacturer or even an industrial facility to have a Web site extolling the virtues of their product. But do they expect them to have one that counters arguments against them, or defends their environmental record, or touts the positive things they provide for their communities?

The two main uses of the Internet in public issues are to communicate information (or the organization's version of relevant information), and to build and activate a common interest group. Before looking at this second activity, we'll review how activists are making use of the Internet to communicate their version of a public issue or incident.

A Platform for Attacking Credibility

The tactics used by many activists identified earlier are clearly evident in a review of activist Web sites. We identified the "90 percent lie," in which a miniscule amount of truth is used to leave an impression that is fundamentally untrue. We talked about the activists' typical strategy of attacking the credibility of the company or its leaders, particularly when their factual or logical argument for opposition has been weakened. We also talked about the powerful, informal and emotional style of discourse and their use of overstatement and hyperbole.

An opponent's Web site about a proposed power plant in California is instructive. In this situation (in which I had no involvement), the opponents had strong support from the city's mayor and unanimous support from the city council in opposing the plant. Then the energy crisis happened and despite the strong local opposition to the facility, the California Energy Commission approved the plant. A review of the opponent's Web site subsequent to this approval clearly demonstrates that their primary objective was, and is, to damage the reputation of the company involved. There was no discussion of their perceived problems with the plant. Instead, it was all about the company's falling fortunes, in this case Calpine's, in the aftermath of the Enron debacle. Every negative article about stockholder concerns and slumping stock prices was rehashed on the opponent's Web site, along with the opponent's own take on the bad news the company is facing. While this has virtually nothing to do with the proposed power plant of the organization (their

Web site identifies two area women as the founders of this organization), it does contribute to their effort to undermine company confidence and credibility.

A more blatant effort to undermine credibility is the next section of their site that purports to expose the companies lying about the proposed plant's steam plume. The Web site states,

> "It takes the District Attorney to get Calpine to tell the truth. Throughout the two-year approval process Calpine maintained, despite plenty of evidence to the contrary, that the Metcalf Energy Center would not emit a visible plume. Recently a concerned neighbor contacted the District Attorney's office to see anything could be done to get Calpine to tell the truth. Unfortunately there are no laws against lying in such a manner but the District Attorney did meet with Calpine to discuss this issue. Here is the before and after of Calpine's Web site:"
>
> [Before]
>
> *Will there be a steam plume?*
>
> No. The Metcalf Energy Center will include "plume abatement" technologies in the project design. This means that the water vapor that is released from the facility will not be visible, even on cold days. Calpine and Bechtel are investing several million dollars in this design feature in order to meet the high visual standards proposed for North Coyote Valley.
>
> [After]
>
> *Will there be a steam plume?*
>
> In modern power plant construction, the water vapor normally rising above the cooling towers or stacks is called a "plume". The Metcalf Energy Center will include "plume abatement" technology in the project design in order to meet the high visual standards proposed for North Coyote Valley. The system is designed to prevent prominent plumes during normal weather conditions year-round when equipment is in normal operation.

A careful reading of the two statements shows the nature of the "lie" that Calpine is accused of. The second statement states that the plume abatement technology employed "is designed to prevent prominent plumes during normal weather conditions year round when equipment is in normal operation." Apparently, there is the possibility of abnormal weather conditions and abnormal operating conditions that could result in plumes that the abatement technology cannot effectively manage. And, therefore, the straightforward "no" offered by the company originally is seen as a lie.

The conclusion to this clarification offered by the company in response to the

District Attorney's inquiry is, according to the opponents, "One more reason why Calpine should not be trusted."

If this is the primary basis for undermining the company's credibility, it shows how far the opponents need to stretch. But what it most clearly demonstrates is that the issue is not really about plume or no plume, it is about whom is to be believed. Because opponents and companies are, in effect, forced to operate by different sets of rules, the opponents have a strong advantage in the credibility "claim/blame" game.

Building Audiences

When Apple released its iPod Nano mp3 player in 2005, it created another product launch sensation. But not long after it got into consumer's hands, some noticed the front on their Nano's was very easily scratched. Internet conversations and blogs started to discuss this disconcerting problem. Apple wasted no time. Having been burned in the previous year by ignoring the blogs and Internet chatter relating to its replacement policy on iPod batteries until activists had built up a solid head of steam, Apple was not about to let it happen again. Apple straightforwardly acknowledged a problem with some iPod Nano screens due to one of their suppliers. It offered to replace defective Nanos, and apologized for the problem. Yes, as a recent Nano owner, I was interested. I heard about this in the mainstream media and my first hearing of it was Apple's apology. Would it have been better for them to let this stay in the Internet world and hope that it went away, rather than raising it to the mainstream media? Absolutely not. They killed the chatter before it had a chance to build a head of steam and put their credibility at risk.

The use of Web sites by activists to present their version of the controversy is important; however, the far more significant use of the Internet in these battles is the ability to create audiences and to efficiently communicate to large groups of people. This is what brings this kind of battle into the post-media world because previously, anyone wishing to communicate quickly and to large groups of people was forced to use the media. Paid advertising, large-scale direct mail or news stories favorably presenting your point of view were the communication options. Not today. The Internet, much more than a means of publicly presenting information that audiences can "pull," has the ability to pro-actively "push" information, and in the process, build audiences or communities around shared interests. It is this ability that activist groups have used to great effect and which represents the true power of the microphone in their hands.

The fact that activists and others using the Internet as a communication tool can relatively quickly build audiences is demonstrated by the "blogger" phenomenon discussed earlier. Andrew Sullivan, one of the most successful of this new breed of

Internet publishers, started Internet publishing in fall of 2000 and now routinely has 30,000 or more readers per day. Writing in the April 2002 issue of *Fast Company*, John Ellis states, "What amazes the mainstream media community about the bloggers is how quickly they've established themselves. Sullivan is, without question, the most influential print journalist in Washington today." That was in 2002. By early 2006 when this update is written, blogging has taken on a life and power that would have been hard to predict four years ago. It increasingly drives corporate behavior (as in Apple and Dell), it scares many a corporate and organizational CEO into sleeplessness, it was responsible for the rapid demise of one of the gods of traditional journalism, Dan Rather, and it has engaged literally millions of ordinary citizens in the act of journalism.

Using the Net to Network

One key to the success of Internet publishers is the way in which they link to existing groups, communities or networks to quickly build audiences. In the pipeline accident discussed in the first chapter, a small group of local activists took up the cause of pipeline safety immediately following the accident. Thanks to the Internet, it probably took them all of 10 minutes to link up with small, but powerful, groups of activists in other parts of the country already dedicated to the cause. The power plant opposition Web site contains numerous web links – including links to organizations fighting causes completely unrelated to the concerns of this group. A "we'll scratch your back if you scratch our back" strategy is in place that enables one group to tap into the resources of another and create a much greater impression of political clout.

A quick review of activist Web sites demonstrates that one of the most commonly used words is network and networking. This ability to forge alliances and to tap into resources of other groups is one of the reasons why activists, who usually represent an extreme political position, have been effective far beyond their numbers to secure legislative and opinion change. It is current Internet technology that gives this basic and wise strategy wings. All the many advantages of the Internet from research, individual and mass email, shared information resources, compelling presentation, no-cost instant publishing – all these make the task of an activist easier and less expensive.

The Web site for the Video Activist Network, www.videoactivist.org, is instructive and gives a hint into the future of activism. This organization promotes the use of video technology in the hands of amateurs to enhance the effectiveness of their causes. A particularly popular application of this strategy targets police brutality. Certainly, the disgusting images of police officers in the WTO riots in Seattle did much to turn public opinion against the Seattle Police, with one result being the political defeat of the one-term mayor in office during the riots. The video activist

Web site provides a variety of services including the opportunity to present your activist video on their site in either downloadable or streaming video formats. The section providing advice on how to get maximum impact out of the video catching the bad guys in action illustrates the point being made here. The first two suggestions are to use email and a Web site. Advice is given about asking for web links so that "viral marketing" techniques can be used to facilitate distribution and exposure of the video.

The emphasis on the Internet as a means of inexpensively reaching audiences is clear. Those savvy enough to build audiences, capture email lists and contact data, network with ever more powerful cohort group – those have the power of the media in the laptop in their back bedroom.

When the Politicians Get Involved

It has become a virtual certainty that, when an accident or issue hits the public consciousness with enough force, political activity will ensue. We have become so accustomed to this that we may have to look back in our history as a nation to realize that not every industrial accident or large-scale business failure in the past resulted in congressional hearings and sweeping new laws. Today, however, it is assumed that outraged citizens will call for, and get, the attention of elected officials to the problem covered in the news today. Politicians react instinctively to the opportunity to address a pressing and current problem, while getting much needed publicity. I have yet to hear a politician respond to a problem without suggesting that there is some legislative cure for which they will take personal responsibility for making happen. New laws and regulations are the inevitable result.

The Oil Pollution Act of 1990 stands out as a primary example. This sweeping act, which monitors and controls the environmental behavior of the nation's oil companies, was created out of the Exxon Valdez disaster. One affect of this and similar laws has been subjecting people engaged in activities that result in damage to the environment to severe criminal penalties. I heard a state environmental official tell a group of oil industry managers that any oil spill will involve criminal investigation. This, no doubt, was an overstatement. But within the oil industry, for one, there is a new type of job. They are called "go-to-jail-jobs," which simply means that the role includes supervising processes in which there is a risk of going to jail should something bad happen. Clearly, in this world, there are no more "accidents." Behind every unfortunate event, the immediate assumption is of negligence, evil intent or profit-driven apathy – but never an accident.

The issue is not whether this is good or bad, or whether the legislation and regulations that result from these high profile situations is positive or negative. From a public issue management standpoint, it is vital that today's leaders and communication professionals understand that when the politicians get involved, the incident takes on a whole new dimension.

In the pipeline accident mentioned earlier, the activists, strongly supported by the grieving family members, immediately attacked the regulatory body responsible for pipeline safety. They effectively pitted one federal agency against another, and put the head of the pipeline regulatory agency in a very difficult spot. Her natural and reasonable reaction was to play it as tough as possible against the company involved.

Imagine for a moment that you have an outstanding regulatory record. In dozens of years of operation you have had no major citations and you have one of the best safety, health and environmental track records in the industry. But something bad happens. It is to be expected that the activists will attack whatever they can find in your record in order to make you look bad. It is also to be expected that the news media will report those accusations and consider that your efforts to put them in context are "spin" and "defensiveness." But now, the very people in high places that you had worked hard to develop positive relationships with based on your excellent performance, turn on you. Just when you need them to state the truth, that you are a careful and responsible operator, they treat you as if you are a pariah. Not that they have a choice. It is you or they – your business or their career. If it appears you are too cozy, or they are not being sufficiently harsh, the pressure mounts. Now, not just from the press and the activists, but from state representatives or senators and members of Congress. Once the black hat has been firmly settled onto your head, even your closest friends in high places will appear strangely distant.

But things can get worse when the momentum is built for real political action. All that is necessary for momentum to build is for one or two elected officials to determine that the situation in which you are involved is the political horse they are going to ride. At that point, it doesn't really matter if they are tilting at windmills, and real, toothy legislation will never result. From a reputation management standpoint, the incident has suddenly turned from a sprint into a marathon. Now you have more than one player whose interest it is to keep the story front and center. The political opportunity dies when the public focuses on another subject – and then the horse dies. So now, the news media have one more source intent on keeping the story hot. We can no longer talk about the marriage of convenience between media and activist. When politicians join the fray, a mutually beneficial relationship grows between all three parties, with the result that the black hat becomes even more firmly fixed and the battle is guaranteed to last a long time.

The pipeline incident in my hometown resulted in over three years of legislative activity at the state and national level. The legislators who sponsored and drove the legislation used their successful efforts as primary elements of their election campaigns five and six years later. That means that the news story continues. The company's bad name continues to be reported because of these political activities years later. Reporters doing their job need to assume that readers need background. If your company is involved in such an event, as long as the legislative process drags on, your name will continue to appear in the background of these stories. It is very difficult in these circumstances to be very effective in public efforts at rebuilding confidence when there are continual reminders of the events in question and your role in them.

Here, then, are the problems: Activists with the power of the media. Politicians eager to jump on emotionally charged, public outrage bandwagons. News reporters needing to tell a gripping story to compete effectively against other entertainment opportunities. A public audience tired of all this – jaded, cynical and angry. It is no wonder that few corporate leaders feel adequately prepared to deal with reputation crises of large magnitude. The instant news era of the Internet does indeed magnify the risks. But it also magnifies the opportunities of dealing with those risks.

It's time to turn from the problems posed by this instant news world to the solutions and opportunities it also represents.

6.
How the Rules Have Changed

Today, a significant number of companies conduct incident drills. Some of these companies, particularly in the oil industry, do so in part to meet federal requirements. While the primary purpose of these is to exercise the operational response, or the work done to contain the incident and clean up the mess, practicing the public communication function is also an important part of these drills. In one drill I observed, as a provider of the communication technology used, the issue of old rules vs. new rules became very clear. The person who assumed the role of PIO or public information officer was of the "old school." While others on the communication team, younger and less experienced, were working hard to get out an initial press release, the veteran advised them, "There's no reason to get this out before 2 p.m. because we'll have plenty of time for the evening news cycle."

Someone forgot to tell him in the era of instant global news, of multiple 24-hour news channels, of satellite trucks and the hunger for "breaking news," of intense competition and, mostly, of the widespread use of the Internet to gain public information, every minute is a news cycle. Scheduling releases made sense when everyone would wait. Now the news is distributed all the time any time. It's just one example of how understanding some of the fundamental changes occurring in the preparation and distribution of public information forces a reassessment of the normal way of doing things.

We have identified three streams of change in public information: the coming of the Internet with its demands for speed and directness, the development of infotainment as a popular style of news reporting and presentation, and the enhanced power of the activist whose ability to influence opinions is based in part on the other two streams. These converge to create a new public information environment.

When the environment changes, the old ways of doing things don't produce the same results. Someone has described insanity as doing the same thing over and over but expecting a different result. It may also be insanity to do the same things in a radically changed environment and expect the results to be the same. If the environment has changed, if the rules have changed, if the way the game is played has changed, doing the same thing over and over again will indeed produce a different result. If the temperature drops, wearing the same coat you wore yesterday will no longer keep you warm. Conducting the business of corporate communications, crisis management or issue management in the same old way when the public information environment has changed will not produce the expected results.

While there is no possibility of fundamental agreement on rules for such a complex subject as public communication, these "old" and "new" rules are suggested as a means of stimulating thinking about how things change in response to changing conditions.

Rule 1:

Old Rule: Meet demands of the media.

New Rule: Meet demands of a wide variety of stakeholders who expect immediate and direct information.

There are a couple of good reasons why the old rule was written and continues to be practiced today. First, because in the media dominated world, the way to quickly get the news out to all stakeholders was through the media. That was how they were going to get the information anyway, so the best strategy was to concentrate your efforts on telling your story the way you wanted it told. Secondly, public relations were a neat corporate division that defined boundaries of activities. Advertising people dealt with the public in selling the product or service, human resource people dealt with employee communication, the finance department handled financial communication to stockholders, and the public relations people dealt with the media. While this has been changing and more companies and organizations have communications executives that manage external communication with all audiences, the vast majority of public relations professionals that I have dealt with continue to view their primary task as managing media relations.

To illustrate the new complexity of today's instant news world, answer this question: Who are the media? Are they only reporters, publishers and editors from traditional media? Or do they include bloggers, citizen journalists and Uncle Randy who is extremely unhappy about his company and establishes a Web site and an email list dedicated to undermining the company's credibility? The White House press corps was stymied by this question when a blogger received press credentials and became the center of the news because he wrote pro-administration blogs. The fact that we can't easily identify who are the media, who should be considered legitimate journalists and who should not, illustrates that we cannot as easily segment the world as we used to.

In the instant news world environment, the neat divisions between media and audiences lose their relevance. Key customers need to know what is happening and the impact on the company when they read about their supplier in the news and it is wearing the black hat. The most pressing financial news information suddenly isn't about the upcoming quarterly report; it is about efforts underway to rebound after the terrorist attack that hit the headquarters. Fence-line neighbors need – for their very health and safety – to find out what is happening in the facility, and if they should evacuate. Agencies responding to a major incident need to be informed continually of the unfolding response, even though they may be in another part of the state or country. If the event is in the news, elected officials will have a great many people asking them what they know about it and what they are doing about it and, as a result, they will be pressing hard to be "on the inside" of the response. One huge lesson that came out of Sept. 11 was the critical need for multiple communication methods for employees and their families. There is no higher urgency of information when the lives and livelihoods of friends and family are at stake.

In this new information environment, leaders and communicators need to think through various scenarios with the questions: who will have high relevance and high demand for information? Given today's instant news expectations, how will they expect to get the information from us and when will they expect it?

Rule 2:

Old Rule: Follow news cycles.

New Rule: New cycle every minute.

We discussed this rule briefly at the beginning of the chapter. When talking with public relations professionals, this is usually my first clue that suggests whether someone is operating in the instant news world. It tells me whether or not they actually realize how profoundly the news environment has changed.

News deadlines are becoming extinct. Certainly there are media outlets that have regular deadlines, particularly print media. But those deadlines now apply more to the "in depth" follow up stories, not the major announcements that inform the public of what is going on. The news magazine coverage is extremely important. But it provides the context, background and details after the public has gained interest in the story that they got via broadcast, off the street or from their electronic news service on their desk. Even this important service is threatened by the virtually unlimited detail and background that can be inexpensively published on the Web and which is provided to audiences on their terms.

In several drills I have observed or participated in recently, the public information expectation was that the first release of information would be somewhere between one and eight hours after the incident began. When asked about what his expectation was regarding the initial release of information, Scott Miller, the respected environmental reporter for KING5, the NBC affiliate in Seattle, replied, "Immediately. It may not be realistic but that's what we have to deal with." The expectations have clearly changed. As we will discuss later, the consequence of not meeting expectations is the very real risk of being viewed as unresponsive and therefore, irresponsible.

Rule 3:

Old Rule: Bad news usually goes away quickly.

New Rule: Bad news can be controlled by opponents and politicians and frequently has a long life.

There's good news and bad news about today's news environment. The fast pace and priority on the instant news channels of broadcast and Internet tends to make stories come and go quicker than ever. Breaking news, after all, can only last so long. The depth of coverage is limited, as is the time it stays on the top of the news editor's priority list. The bad news is, the story can hang around a lot longer than it used to because the story is no longer controlled by the media alone.

Two factors can result in stories hanging around that would otherwise disappear into the ether of old news. One is that opponents have the tools to keep a story alive; the other is that many stories result in political interest, and this interest inevitably results in stories becoming protracted.

If the situation you find yourself in results in activist or opponent activity, you can count on the story being around a lot longer than you would like. When a person or group has a vested interest in keeping the story in the headlines, it will normally have a much longer shelf life. Any new information, any problem with previous statements, any new developments, such as legal actions, are fair game for the activists to reactivate the story with the media. It is not the reporter who won't let go that is the concern here; it is the activist who, for various reasons, has a personal stake in making certain the story doesn't die. Not only does he or she have the opportunity to keep it in the media's radarscopes, he or she has the broadcast tools to keep delivering information or misinformation. The audience may be smaller, but it can be troublesome and demand ongoing company resources for a surprisingly long time.

The widespread use of search engines makes this problem much worse. If your company is highly visible, and has attracted attention of an activist or a group of activists who are establishing a lot of chatter on the Internet, you may be surprised to find out what a search engine request shows. Internet visitors may have to wade through a list of anti-company Web sites before they even get to your company. And many of those sites may be made to look like they are actually providing helpful information about your company. It's as if your most hated and feared opponents established a building right in front of your main entrance and forced all visitors coming it to be exposed to their lies, misinformation and personal attacks before they can even enter your place of business.

Similarly, when elected officials get involved in the story, their involvement inevitably creates an entirely new dimension. Now it is not just the story about the controversy or the event. The story evolves into what the people or the government are going to do to make certain such behavior doesn't occur again or go unpunished. From the media standpoint, each new development on the political front requires at least a brief rehash of the event or controversy that led to the action, with the result that your company or organization will be once more featured, and not in a way you would choose.

The old rule, very much in place in most organizations, is to muddle through the story while it is in the headlines, then get back to business as quickly as possible. That strategy must change because in many situations, the story will last months and potentially years. Ongoing damage to reputation must be anticipated. A recovery strategy must include the possibility or likelihood that the company or organization will not take just the main hit of the breaking news or headlines, but the pain of a thousand cuts. Strategic considerations include how strongly to communicate directly with the public and key stakeholders, for how long, and what resources are needed to focus on this issue even long after the public furor has receded.

Rule 4:

Old Rule: Accuracy above all.

New Rule: Speed above all.

The old rule is a very good one, and many communication professionals are going to roll their eyes when I suggest that this rule has changed. After all, there is nothing more damaging to the effort to build confidence in the public than providing false information. Indeed, credibility is everything. This vital topic will be explored in much greater depth later. The problem in the world of instant news is that credibility means more than just being accurate with the information. Credibility is based also on providing that information very quickly. In fact, speed may be more important than accuracy when it comes to credibility.

When the competition for fickle news audiences depends to a great extent on who is first with the information, the media frenzy can be overwhelming. In this environment, it matters less to the reporters, editors and producers what the information is and who it comes from, than that they have real information to convey. At the scene of an accident, it will usually be considerably more valuable to get an on-camera interview with an eyewitness who says he thinks he saw four people taken away by ambulance, than to wait and get official word from someone in a position to more accurately determine the number of those injured. After all, the reporter could be faulted for providing inaccurate information if he or she speculated, but reporting on someone else's speculation is just reporting.

I do not mean to suggest for a moment that responsible reporters have little care for the truth. Certainly they do, because they also know that their future as a reporter is dependent on their credibility and the credibility of the stories they present. But I am saying that no self-respecting reporter will wait patiently while the right company official checks and re-checks the facts when those "facts," or presumed facts, are available from other sources. Any doubt about this behavior can be erased after the mining tragedy in West Virginia in early 2006. After a garbled message from the rescue crew was misunderstood and communicated to families through unofficial channels, the press picked up the story of the "miraculous" rescue of 12 miners. The story carried for hours around the world. The media later admitted they did not have official confirmation, but they accepted no responsibility and in the public's eye took no blame. They simply were reporting the "truth" as it was then understood on the ground.

The question for the leaders responsible for protecting the reputation of the company or the organization comes down to whether or not they wish to be the source of information about the issue or incident; if not, they must be willing to allow others to provide the facts and the perspective for them. It is well-established public relations doctrine that to have any real influence on the course of story, the company involved must be the source for as much information as possible. What many have not realized, is that the pace of reporting has so increased that if they are not able to respond very quickly, they have given away this important opportunity to impact the story.

The accuracy vs. speed dilemma is at the heart of needed changes in communications planning for most organizations. Crisis communication plans normally identify, in some detail, the organization structure appropriate for various types of crises and who is to approve what information when. These very reasonable measures are put in place to make certain that the organization speaks with a single voice and that the leadership has the opportunity to maintain control of the message at very critical times. These plans now need to be re-evaluated. If the approval process in place cannot deliver the information with the speed required in the "now is too late" world of instant news, those plans must change.

There are three basic reasons why most companies and organizations today will fail to meet the speed and accuracy demands of the instant news world: people, policies and technology. To respond effectively, the communication team – which includes the communication professionals, the executive leadership, lawyers, consultants, response managers, etc. – needs to clearly understand the speed and accuracy demands and needs to have a well-honed command/control/communication system in place to meet those demands. The crisis response policies need to place a very high priority in the response on the public information function, providing the highest level access of responders and executives and provide specific speed/accuracy response guidelines. Finally, the technology needs to be in place that will allow these frequently far-flung team members to implement the policies and work efficiently together to meet this difficult demand.

It must always be remembered that credibility is what is at stake, and credibility depends on speed and accuracy but is not equated with either. Miller, the environmental reporter quoted earlier, pointed the way out of this dilemma, "Tell us what you know, when you know it." In other words, if you have clearly established facts, don't wait to accumulate a complete story to provide them. Give them to the press now. If you don't have all the information, give them what you have and tell them what you don't have and when you may be able to provide it. Never, ever speculate and never provide information that you are not certain is accurate. But, don't hold back with what you do know. Communicate now.

Rule 5:

Old Rule: Legal review optional.

New Rule: Legal review required.

Every situation is different, and certainly there are going to be public issues and news events in which the role of attorneys is minimal or nonexistent. But it has become clear that attorneys are increasingly involved in situations involving public interest, the news and the reputation of the company. This is true for a couple of reasons. One is that the overwhelming majority of crises that affect companies have a direct legal component. Most corporate crises involve legal action or are caused by legal action. The company or individual executives are being sued, or are suing or are being investigated for regulatory or criminal violations. The second reason is that there is a much higher risk of legal action coming from an accident, environmental event, or product or service issue. Finally, and perhaps most significantly, there has been a strong trend to criminalizing corporate behavior. That used to be said primarily in relation to environmental damage or safety failings. Now, with a number of high profile executives in prison for very long terms due to accounting violations, the criminal potential of C-level activities continues to be expanded.

What this means is that communications professionals, either working as consultants or operating in communication departments within companies or organizations, need to consider that attorneys are going to be part of the response team in most situations of high public interest. Let's be very straight up – the working relationship between the professionals dealing in the court of law and the professionals dealing in the court of public opinion is often uncomfortable. This difficult topic will be addressed in more detail in a later chapter. What is important here is to understand that at the very time there is a premium on speed of response, there is a significant addition to the communication team – a group of attorneys –

who usually march to the beat of an entirely different drummer. If court cases were handled like news stories, the evidence would be collected and presented in an hour or two, and the cases would seldom extend past a couple of days. The court of public opinion has no patience.

Since speed of response is as critical as getting legal approval on statements, there is no way out of this dilemma other than to get everyone who will be part of the communication response on the same page as it relates to the public information requirements. There is no question that only executives with strong leadership and who are aware of the new instant news demands can truly make this happen. In both preparing for and responding to a news event, few public information professionals have the power to overrule attorneys (nor should they). Executives have the responsibility to look out for the best interests of the company, and therefore need to weigh the frequently competing requirements of the court of law and the court of public opinion. It is only the executives who can pull these two forces together to make certain that the public information demands are understood and the preparation is in place to enable a speedy and accurate response.

Rule 6:

Old Rule: Provide minimum needed.

New Rule: Provide what the most detail hungry audience requires.

The media are no longer the only audience of today's communicator. Reporters are just one of many groups of stakeholders who expect and demand information from you. Meeting the very different information needs of the very different audiences represents a new challenge for most in corporate communications.

Although I continue to be surprised by it, it is clear that many seasoned public relations professionals subscribe to the "less is better" theory of providing information to the media. There is some justification for the idea that the company should provide only the minimum information needed. Don't tell more than what they ask for, never volunteer anything and if you know something bad might come out, wait until it is out before providing any information on the subject.

That is a matter of communication strategy, and while in general I don't subscribe to the thinking behind it, in the instant news world, it is largely a moot point. It is moot because communicators are not dealing with just the news media anymore.

Leaving the media aside for a moment, the person or persons responsible for providing public information about the company need to take into consideration a variety of stakeholders. They start with employees. Employees whose livelihoods depend on the success of the company and whose social life may well revolve around many other people employed in the company have a high relevance/demand quotient. Their view of management will depend to some degree on how vital information about important public events is conveyed to them. Employees, even more than some other stakeholder groups, are both audience and media. The messages they communicate carry high levels of credibility and if they are well positioned to communicate with other audiences that are important to the organization, they play a key role in providing information.

Large customers, stockholders, government officials, bankers, neighbors and community leaders, are some of the other groups who may very well have a high relevance/demand quotient. In this instant news world, they simply cannot be brushed off. They demand and expect information, and if they are important to the future of the company, it is obvious that their demands need to be met.

In terms of quantity of information, the media's demands vary greatly. Reporters for national news outlets can only deal with the minimum of information, while local and regional reporters, and those representing specific interest groups such as trade publications, have a much higher demand for detail. Reporters for major news organizations have exceptionally high relevance/demand in the very early going of a major story. After all, their reputations, and the reputations of the news organizations they represent, are at stake in getting information to their audiences as quickly as possible. But for most stories, this relevance/demand dissipates relatively quickly. The relevance of California Congressman Gary Condit, for months the subject of numerous news reports about a missing intern, disappeared in the dust of the World Trade Center disaster. But while news media relevance can disappear quickly, the relevance to other key stakeholders is not likely to disappear. Voters in Condit's congressional district continued to have a strong interest in the congressman's actions, even after the Sept. 11 attacks.

To meet the demands of these other groups, today's communicator needs to be prepared to provide in-depth, ongoing information about the issue or event, and needs to be prepared to do that for a considerable time. Because that is the situation, they also need to be prepared to continue to provide it to the news media during the entire time, because the public information provided to stakeholders is, after all, public information. It would take a very small company to be able to provide relevant details to its employees without fear of those details finding their way to the media. Similarly with stockholders, neighbors, etc. While the news media may have lost interest, the continuing flow of information may result in renewed interest, or at the very least, a continuing source of information indirectly provided to the media. If it is going to find its way indirectly to the media, and your interest is in protecting your credibility with the media, it makes sense to provide them the complete details directly.

Rule 7:

Old Rule: Assume some level of news balance.

New Rule: Someone is going to be wearing the "black hat."

It is very difficult to devise an effective response strategy if there are fundamental differences in understanding of the news business. I would be so bold as to say that most executives still believe that, within today's news business, there still exists the underlying philosophy of fairness, objectivity and telling the whole story as carefully and truthfully as possible. At the risk of being cynical, that is not my observation. I am not saying in the least that today's reporters are bad people, or that they have evil intent. It's just not how they see the game being played. They know their bosses have their eyes continually on the ratings meter, Web stats, and newsstand sales. Ratings are determined largely by how the news story they are covering, or how they are covering it, grips the audience. Compelling visuals, heart wrenching human reactions, clear-cut good vs. evil, ironic twists and surprise endings – these are the elements they look for in telling the every day stories that may involve your company or organization. In other words, the ability to entertain is critical to the successful news organization.

Anger and frustration were clearly written on the face of the executive responsible for a large industrial facility. Another news story had come out about an ongoing and serious legal issue. There had been no attempt to understand the underlying meaning of the legal action the company had taken. There had not even been any call or conversation. The facts were gathered from the court record, and the headline in the local paper made the company look rotten. There was nothing untrue about what they had written, it was the interpretation, the subtle nuances of writing, the "spin" the reporter had put on the story that was troublesome to the executive.

This was a very mild mannered executive, so the depth of anger was surprising, and it was clear he expected me to do something about it. I couldn't explain it at the time, but there was little to do. No retraction could be requested – the facts were there. The headline is almost always written by someone other than the reporter and is usually taken from the first paragraph or two of the story, and in this case (as in so many others) the headline writer caught the reporter's spin and spun it another round or two. The later parts of the story provided more balance, but the headline writer clearly didn't get that far, or didn't care, given his or her orientation to the story.

Mostly what I needed to explain to the executive was that in this particular situation, in the greater controversy of which the legal action was a small part, the media had placed the black hats on our heads. Given that context, the story wasn't overtly bad. What we needed to do, rather than react to a particular story, was get the black hat off our head. That was a bigger challenge and a more important one than reacting to one day's reporting.

Communication strategy is greatly affected by the anticipation of how the news media will perceive and present a story. That's why gaining a gut level understanding of the new media environment and the instant news world is fundamental. It's vital not just to communication professionals who need to develop the strategic recommendations and implement them, but also for the organizational leaders who need to approve and participate in them.

Fortunately, because the news media often adopt the same approach to attracting and keeping audiences, and their attention as the entertainment industry, the new rules are quite predictable. Does the subject in question have anything to do with the health, safety or well being of the public or of individuals in the community? Is there a hint of crime, corruption, conspiracy or scandal involved? Is there any heart-wrenching human impact that can be visually recorded or powerfully presented? Are there antagonists involved who are willing to make bold, outlandish statements or accusations? Are there powerful people in trouble? If the answer to any of these questions is yes, the media will decide that the story has some compelling interest and will drive the story in a way that takes advantage of that compelling interest. The urgent question that communicators need to consider in that early response time is "who is going to be wearing the black hat and who will be wearing the white hat?"

Rule 8:

Old Rule: Wait for them to call.

New Rule: Credibility depends on getting to them first.

I remember the conversation well, and especially the patronizing smile on the face of the senior public relations manager in this situation. Yes, important new facts had come out in an accident investigation; facts that the reporters would gather soon. No, we would not contact the reporters and proactively give them the information. Hell, they hadn't been treating us all that nicely, why should we do them any favors? Besides, it's better if they ask us the questions and we can respond. Who knows, maybe they don't even have the information yet, or maybe something else will come along and it won't be such a big deal. Why try to make it something bigger than it is?

I pushed. After all, this was in my community and I had worked hard to gain the respect and trust of these reporters. I wanted them to know that if I had information of importance to them that I could release, they would get it. Trust, respect and credibility are the most important tools of the trade.

In a different situation, a client had a small-scale incident. Given extensive coverage of equally small incidents, it was likely that even a minor situation would get coverage. In this case, it was my call to make and I had the trust of the facility management. I released the information as soon as I had it. One of the managers at a lower level went semi-ballistic. How stupid of us to draw the attention of the media to something that they might not even find out about. Certainly, emergency agency notifications had been made and all the local media were tapped into those notifications, but it didn't mean we had to bring it to their attention too. The senior manager was now in a spot of having to settle the argument. What was at stake is how we would handle proactive release of information for future events. I explained that I was brought into their overall situation because of extensive negative media coverage. My primary concern in working with the media was for them to trust the company and me. Not that I would tell the media everything they wanted me to or give them "inside" information. But the reporters should trust that if I was able to give them information that they needed, they could count on me to provide it. And they could also count on me to help get management to understand what information they needed and when. I wanted their trust and respect and I wanted the company to have the trust and respect of the local reporters and editors. I explained to the manager that to gain that, we needed to be forthcoming. He agreed. There was no coverage of the minor incident.

One of the changing circumstances of the instant news world makes this situation easier to resolve. As we will see in the next rule, proactive and direct communication is becoming the required strategy. If you are going to proactively tell your story to employees, stakeholders and members of the public, you might as well tell the media directly. In this open, instant information world, telling one is telling all. Even bad news goes down much better if it comes directly from the source.

Rule 9:

Old Rule: Let the media tell your story.

New Rule: Tell it yourself.

A recent discussion with an executive responsible for crisis management for one of the world's largest companies illustrates the philosophical divide between the media and the post-media world. We were discussing use of the Internet in a major crisis. While he and I were proponents of the idea of "push," the consensus of the management team was "pull." The managers decided that if the company experienced a major crisis, they would supply information on their corporate Web site but would not proactively distribute that information to those interested. If somebody wanted information, they could come to them and ask them for it. This included the decision not to prepare server infrastructure that could withstand the potentially millions of hits their servers would take should a number of people decide they wanted to "pull" the information from their sites. They decided their best strategy was to be information reactive, and not worry about whether or not they could actually react.

An instant news world strategy requires the capability of instantly "pushing" information to pre-determined audiences as well as the ability to accumulate audiences on the fly. It means thinking in advance about whose opinion of you is vitally important, and making certain they have the story correct and straight from the horse's mouth. It means being instantly responsive to those who are interested enough to inquire, and making certain that they are proactively fed information as updates become available. Fundamentally, it means building credibility by meeting or exceeding their information expectations.

What the managers of this large company apparently do not yet understand is that information expectations have changed and are continuing to rapidly change. As more people have access to the instant information technology of the Internet, and as they gain an understanding of the potential this represents for a company to communicate directly and personally with them, they will not be satisfied with "pull." If my daughter is in an accident and my best friend knows how she is doing and is aware that I don't know, but doesn't pick up the phone to call me, will that friendship be damaged or destroyed? Absolutely. Friends don't let friends remain ignorant. Especially about something that is vitally important to them.

What those managers are indeed saying is, those people who invested their pensions and life savings in our stock don't deserve to be informed of events that may deeply affect their futures. Those employees who have dedicated their lives to making this company successful don't deserve to hear from us how a crisis may change their lives. Those neighbors and community members whose health, safety and sense of security may be threatened by our actions can just check our Web site or read in the newspaper what we are doing to protect them. They don't deserve or need to hear from us directly.

All's well and good if the stakeholders have no expectation of communication. But today, if they have no expectation of direct, personal, instantaneous communication, it is either because they are in the ever decreasing minority who do not understand the potential of current communication technology, or because they have already lost faith and trust in the corporation. If they have the communication expectation, and they are treated as these managers plan to treat them, it is a virtual certainty that they will lose whatever faith and trust they may currently have in the company.

Several months after I had the conversation with that executive, the company had an incident that was covered in the national news. In news stories taken from the Associated Press and written in *The Wall Street Journal*, it was noted that no company spokesperson was available for comment and all the information about the event came from the government agencies responding to the incident. The "pull" theory was clearly not working to the advantage of the company's reputation. Since that time, however, the company had several large-scale incidences that brought to the attention of senior management the need to improve communication. It has since adopted strategies and technologies that are making it one of the best in the business at communicating with its key audiences.

What most surprises me about the "no need to be proactive attitude" is that frequently it is these same people who complain about how poorly they are treated in the press. It is these same communicators and executives who authorize the spending of millions of dollars in paid advertising to get their message out. This can only be attributed to the fact that they do not understand that they too have become broadcasters. They have the power of the media in their own hands. They can tell their own story. But, they choose to continue to allow others to tell their story for them, even while expressing complete distrust in those whose hands they have placed their brand value and their very future.

The rules of public communication are being re-written almost daily. As our legal system is struggling to keep up with changes brought about by new technologies, such as in the protection of artistic and intellectual property, so today's business leaders are struggling to keep up with the changing rules of public information. That challenge is not likely to go away any time soon.

7. Communication Strategies for the Instant News World

How has communication changed as a result of the advent of the "instant news" world? What do you communicate and to whom in a world where "now" is almost always too late? That is the overriding question for communicators responsible for reputation and brand value management in the early years of the twenty first century. Or another way of putting it: How do I get the right information to the right people, right now?

Nearly every day in the national and international news, we can observe companies large and small struggling to maintain hard-earned reputations. Once high flyers are brought low – often by their own misdeeds –but other times because of unfair, unwarranted attacks. Names like Enron, Arthur Andersen, Martha Stewart, Firestone, Odwalla, Worldcom, Exxon, are just a few of the most prominent ones to either be destroyed or significantly damaged by reputation crises. There are many others such as Ford, Shell Oil, Merck, Marsh McLennan, AIG and many others like them who have been damaged and who move forward, carrying with them the scars of reputation battles.

No effective communication strategy can cover for people and their organizations who foolishly squander the public trust. When real and serious problems become known, those problems need to be addressed and addressed quickly. An alert management will root those problems out and solve them before they become an organization-destroying public embarrassment. Each and every day, executives of companies and organizations are discovering and responding to problems within the organization that could result in serious public perception problems: sexual harassment, safety lapses, environmental issues, illegal activities, questionable ethical behavior, accounting discrepancies. When alert and responsible managers take positive actions, there is usually no news to report. It is when these things go on without being noticed, or continue on uncorrected after being discovered, that a reputation crisis becomes possible. Worst of all is when there is evidence of a cover-up.

A quick review of recent reputation crises makes it clear that there are two very different starting points in dealing with a crisis. If the accusations are false, the response is to address the negative perceptions caused by the false accusations. However, if the accusations are true, or even partly true, the communication response is wholly dependent on the organization recognizing the wrong, and very quickly communicating the recognition and the changes made. This is one of the most important elements of reputation management, and it bears repeating: if you have done something wrong, you must admit it, accept responsibility and explain how you are going to fix it. If you have not done anything wrong, you must aggressively address the accusations and the false perceptions raised by the accusations.

Unfortunately, too many perceive public relations as fundamentally dishonest because too often corporate or organizational communication has been disingenuous. But lying or hiding the truth doesn't work. The truth will come out. That's why the communication team can only do its work if the company is indeed innocent of the charges it faces, or has publicly acknowledged the problem and moved quickly to rectify the problem that has been identified.

It has become painfully clear in the past few years that companies and organizations depend on the good opinion of a great many people in order to operate. In some respects, this is not new. The village cobbler would probably see his business suffer if his customers and fellow villagers believed him to be a lout and a crook. But now, we live in a global village with many people who have the motivation and capability of accusing huge companies with valuable brands of being louts, crooks and environment destroyers. The role of public opinion in the ability of the company or organization to operate and grow might be called the public franchise, or a community license to operate. It is an unspoken agreement, an unofficial consensus of various groups. It is granted virtually automatically; in other words, when a company or organization comes to the attention of these groups that make up the "public," there is a certain level of presumption of innocence (I say "certain" level because business people in general are seen in a negative light in the public). But this presumption is fragile and easily lost. When companies lose their public franchise or license to operate, they cannot effectively operate. ValuJet lost it and became a new company. Amway lost it and its transition to Quixtar demonstrated that it cannot easily escape the negatives attached to its brand. Enron lost it, Firestone lost it, Martha Stewart lost most of it and valiantly fought to restore it. The industrial facility referred to earlier in the discussion on politician/activists lost its public franchise and ultimately found itself so boxed in and restricted that it had essentially no room to maneuver. The company no longer exists. And neither does Arthur Andersen. Andersen's legal problems were serious, but not enough to destroy the company. What destroyed the company was their clients' unwillingness to stick with the firm when it showed little interest in fighting for its reputation and its public franchise.

While communicators cannot prevent the mistakes, misbehavior and carelessness that often causes this loss of public esteem and subsequent loss of brand value, communicators and executives are tasked with protecting that value whether the organization deserves the scorn and disrespect or not. One very sad reality of this instant news and infotainment dominated world, is that far too often the accusations are not justified, or the consequences paid far outstrip the faults that caused the controversy in the first place. In these situations, it is most certainly a communication issue.

How does one go about devising a communication strategy that will protect that public franchise and brand value? Are there differences in that strategy required by the instant news environment?

Strategic thinking starts with a clear picture of what a happy result will look like. To quote Mr. Covey: Start with the end in mind. Or, another way of putting it: what is your picture of winning? It is very difficult to play a game if the members of the team do not understand or agree on the definition of winning. Far too many executives have a negative view of public relations expenditures, and it is almost always because the communication professionals have suggested solutions without clearly defining the desired end result of those tactics.

The goal, or definition, of winning may very well be different if the organization is in a pre-crisis mode, or in the middle or recovering from a reputation crisis. If your organization has any risk for a reputation crisis at all, you are currently in one of those three modes. Regardless of the specifics, once there is an understanding of the public franchise, and the fact that relationships with strategic individuals constitute the core of a businesses' value, the definition of winning will always resolve around creating maximum value in the minds of the right people. In other words, ultimately the goal of a communications effort is to create, strengthen or recover relationships. It is to help the right people place a high value on what the organization does for them.

It is not communications per se that create the value. Value is generally created by action. What does your organization do that creates high value for its critical stakeholders? Does it perform well to generate an acceptable or exceptional profit margin and share price? Does it demonstrate through its actions that it cares about the neighbors near it and the community in which it lives? Does it provide the benefits, work environment, opportunity for challenge and growth that employees desire? Does it fulfill customer needs in a way that is unique and highly valued by customers? These are the activities of companies that create value. The role of the communicator, then, is to understand where value is created in the mind of the stakeholders, and communicate the truth of those activities in ways the stakeholders can understand and appreciate. When communication efforts are effective not only at conveying the valued actions of the company, but also in conveying to the company the perceptions, concerns, and interests of the stakeholders, those efforts also create value in and of themselves. The fact is, we want to be listened to and we want those important to us to take the time to communicate what is going on.

It seems to me that gaining the confidence and loyalty of the right people is, or ought to be, the bottom line goal of virtually any organization, whether it is articulated that way or not. From a communication strategy standpoint, it is very helpful to think of the goal of the communication effort as building relationships. Relationships, after all, depend on communication. So the starting point of communication strategy is some form of the statement: We want the right people to place a high value on our existence. Now, how do we do that?

It starts with determining who those right people are. The specifics of any communication strategy are going to deal with the following questions listed below. Nothing in these questions is specific to the instant news world. However, the answers may vary somewhat from the more traditional views of public information and communication strategy.

The key communications strategy questions:

1. Audience: To whom do we need to talk?
2. Message: What message do we need to convey?
3. Listening: What do we need to hear from them?
4. Voice: Who needs to deliver the message?
5. Media: How should we communicate?

Audience: Whom do We Need to Talk to?

The media world response is clear: reporters. But in the instant news world, communicators need to look past the reporters to the recipients of the information. The key questions are, "who has a high degree of interest in the information about our company or this event and why?" "For which audiences is this information highly relevant and who has high demand for it?" Certainly reporters have high relevance/demand because their jobs and futures as reporters depend on delivering the information that delivers the ratings and readership.

The communication team needs to think like a CEO at this critical point. Companies and organizations exist only because certain people value their existence. If no one places a value on whether or not the organization is there, it will not be there for long. So who values the organization? If it is a government agency, the value is in the minds of the elected officials who authorize funding and their willingness to fund is directly related to the value they perceive their constituents see in the agency. A police agency, for example, will suffer severe consequences if the public it serves perceives it as ineffective, or worse, evil and corrupt. An environmental agency will lose prestige, funding and perhaps its existence if the elected officials believe their voters see nothing good coming from the agency's efforts. For companies, the question of value extends to a whole number of people. Do the employees value the company? Hopefully. But realistically, usually in relation to how easy it is to replace the company's contribution to their income, the fulfillment of meaning and purpose in their lives and the social networks they have built and enjoy. Do stockholders value the company? Directly in proportion to the company's performance in meeting return expectations. Do customers value it? In direct proportion to how easy it is to replace the products or services with alternatives. Do members of the community in which it is located value it? Only as it applies to their own hopes and aspirations for quality of life in their community. When the CEO and other top leadership have a clear understanding of the importance of meeting the expectations of these various audiences, the communicator's job is easier. If the entire focus is on operations, with little to no regard for identifying and building high value relationships, the communicator probably needs to start here, as challenging a task as that may be.

This problem becomes critical when the top executive is not the one with overall stakeholder and brand value responsibilities. A plant manager, for example, will be focused more on his or her traditional measures of performance, including plant reliability, profitability, throughput, etc. Then the communications manager needs to counsel the executive to help them see that the best opportunity for them to come out of this situation with their future prospects bright, is to think like the CEO of the company and extend their concern to all stakeholders of the company.

It becomes crystal clear when you look at the value question that everything centers around the old question central to marketing and sales: WIIFM, or What's In It For Me? That is what everyone wants to know. Thinking like a CEO at this point means thinking about who values the organization or on who the company depends for its existence, and then having clearly in mind why they value it, or what's in it for them. Analyzing potential audiences from that standpoint will quickly lead you to a list of groups with individual priorities, and that list is most certainly the first step in a communication strategy.

A simple chart may help identify audiences and priorities in communicating with them:

Group	Value	Priority
Executives	Opportunity to build their careers while being well compensated	
Employees & Families	Same	
Stockholders	Competitive or better return on investment	
Fence-line Neighbors	Minimal disturbance of their lives while contributing positively to the community	
Customers	Providing needed products or services in a way that is not easily replaced	
Lenders	Business performance that assures repayment	
Media	Source for speedy, reliable information that will facilitate fast, accurate reporting	
Suppliers	Reliable and secure source of revenue	
Contractors	Similar to suppliers or employees	
Analysts and Industry Consultants	A direct, trustworthy relationship that will contribute to their being "in the know"	
Elected Officials	Positive perception in the minds of voters	
Regulators	Compliance and respect. Confidence that their career will not be threatened by behavior of company executives.	
Community Leaders	Continuing contributions to their community in the form of taxes, resources, positive role of employees in community, etc. Do nothing to threaten the community's security and well being.	

In thinking about priority, the question needs to be: whose poor opinion of the organization most puts the enterprise at risk?

While a priority column is listed, prioritization varies from organization to organization, and even varies depending on the situation. What becomes clear when reviewing the list is that there are important people in nearly every category who need to have a positive opinion if the organization is to be successful in the long haul. That positive opinion needs to have some "stickiness," or some depth that will enable it to withstand any bumps and bruises along the way. When attacks come, you want those people whose opinion of you matters the most to give you some benefit of the doubt.

When your company or organization suddenly finds itself squarely in the public eye, all those various audiences will gain an impression about the organization. It is not really a question of whether or not to communicate, because should you choose to remain silent, a strong message will be sent. In fact, the only way you have any hope of managing the perceptions is by communicating. To choose not to, or to communicate too slowly for today's instant news requirements, means you are putting your message in the hands of others. Those others may well have agendas very much contrary to your own.

It's helpful to look at various reputation crises experienced by different organizations and see what messages were communicated and what public perceptions resulted. In the aftermath of the September 11 attacks, the Red Cross faced one of its most serious reputation crises when it was revealed that plans were being made to use excess funds raised for victims for other purposes. The early message provided by the executive director was that this policy was reasonable given the outpouring of donations, the need to prepare for other emergencies and the fact that they carefully worded their televised appeals to allow for this policy. It was the wrong message. Ultimately, after congressional hearings and much discussion on the cable TV pundit shows, the Red Cross admitted this was a mistake and would use the funds only for what most people understood they were donating them. By this time, the high-profile executive director had left, a board-executive rift was revealed, and the organization's reputation for compassion and integrity was significantly tarnished.

Can there be any doubt that Firestone sent the wrong messages in the weeks leading up to its massive tire recall? In a sense, it didn't really matter what the specifics of the messages were. After all, most news viewers didn't read their press releases. The most important day of their company life, the day of the product recall, their Web site crashed under the weight of the hits, meaning their voice to communicate directly was silenced by poor preparation. It didn't matter, because whatever Firestone said came off as too little, too late. This is one of the strongest reinforcements for a central premise that, in this post-media, instant news world, speed is perhaps the most important message. It is dreadfully easy to get behind the news and accusation curve, and extremely difficult to get in front of it. But the consequences of getting behind can be dire. Not only did Firestone inadvertently send the message of "too little, too late," they also sent the message, "it's not really our fault."

There are two huge message mistakes that are made repeatedly when companies come under fire. One is, "it's not our fault," and the second is, "we did something wrong but we tried to cover it up." The first one is a message that is frequently overtly conveyed and the second one is conveyed by others, based on the information or misinformation about company actions. Even the hint of a cover-up almost immediately changes the nature of the story and the reporting. A cover-up to the news media is the equivalent of blood in the water for sharks. If there was any question about who should wear the black hat in an emerging story, the question is immediately resolved if there is any real evidence of cover-up, or even a scent of a cover-up.

The executives of Arthur Andersen certainly experienced this. Until a partner in the Houston office led an effort to shred documents investigators needed to evaluate the propriety of Enron's financial dealings, there was only uncertainty about what role, if any, Andersen may have played in the Enron financial disaster. But, after the shredding, the press, Congressional investigators and the public clearly placed the black hat on the formerly highly regarded company. From that point on, almost anything said by the company in their defense was looked upon with a much higher degree of skepticism.

In the Olympic Pipeline accident, the company was notified that a criminal investigation had been launched almost immediately following the release and ignition of gasoline into Whatcom Creek. State law requires the company pay for, but not provide, an attorney for any employee accused of doing something criminal while in the normal exercise of his or her duties. So the company notified the individuals involved and they immediately hired their own attorneys with the company paying the bill. Government accident investigators, company attorneys, the US district attorney's office attorneys, and of course, the media all wanted to talk to these employees immediately. Their attorneys, having just been dragged into what was obviously a very serious situation, immediately gave them the advice: "Don't talk." They were told that no one could force them to discuss the situation because they could plead the Fifth Amendment. Now, the Fifth Amendment in the minds of the public is something that guilty people, particularly mobsters, use to avoid incriminating themselves. When the media heard from the federal investigators that the employees were not answering their questions about the accident, but pleading the Fifth, a cover-up was scented. At that point, no cover-up was intended at all; attorneys just thrown into a highly charged situation needed to take a little time to find out for themselves what their clients had done or not done. But because the company did not, and would not, clearly explain the situation involving employee's legal rights, it stood guilty as charged of directing their employees to not cooperate and hide the truth. Several years after the incident, if you ask a reporter or member of the community about the company, the first thing they will comment is the company's refusal to allow its employees to cooperate with investigators. This is a false perception, but it stands, and will stand forever, because no real effort was made to communicate the truth.

While it may be easy, with the benefit of hindsight, to see message mistakes made by others in the heat of a crisis, the question here is what the message ought to be. One thing should be clear from everything that has been presented to date: whatever it is, it had better be fast. A slow message is almost invariably a "too little, too late" message. Beyond speed, here are a few things to consider in developing your message:

What You Do is More Important Than What You Say

Actions have always spoken much louder than words. While it is easy for the communication team to get focused on wordsmithing and crafting messages, a good communicator must think like a CEO. If many of the key audiences place a value on the health of the enterprise, and the health of the enterprise is very dependent on the public trust, what specifically is being done in light of the circumstances to build public trust? The great temptation when the media lights go on and real problems have been revealed is to start thinking about the expensive legal battles to come. That's why communicators and the legal team so frequently tangle at this point. The lawyers are paid to think about protecting the company in court. But, if public trust is lost, there will be nothing of value to protect in court. Actions must be taken, even strong and painful actions, to protect the public trust and maintain the confidence of the key audiences.

Be Human, Show Compassion and Empathy

In any situation in which there are victims, the public sympathy will be with them. This is natural and good, but it is also how the infotainment game is played. Victims are critical to the story and effective communication of their pain and suffering is an essential element of telling a compelling story. From the company's perspective, that pain and suffering may be overstated or even completely false (unfortunately there are many people eager to claim victim status even when they have had nothing to do with the incident, as even September 11 demonstrated). However overstated or false it may be, the public sympathy is going to be with the victims, and a company shows callousness to the victims at great peril. A company or organization whose priorities are focused from beginning to end on those who have been genuinely hurt by what has happened, whether or not the company is to blame, is a company that gains and deserves the respect of the public.

Accept Responsibility

Here's the really sticky one. Who do you respect? Do you respect someone who does whatever they can to push responsibility on someone else and look for the slightest excuses or flimsiest reasons to say, "It's not my fault?" Or do you respect someone who says, "I am taking responsibility for this mess." The problem is simply that the public wants someone with the character to stand up and say, "I accept the consequences of my actions." The attorneys, meanwhile, fully aware that everything said in public will show up in court, want the company to completely avoid saying anything that may cause a problem in court. The two positions cannot be easily reconciled.

One reason why this is so difficult is that the word responsibility has multiple meanings. It can mean: "I'm accepting responsibility for cleaning this mess up while we find out who is at fault." It can also mean, "I am responsible, therefore I am stating that I am the sole cause of this disaster." The two are very different but easily confused. In the oil industry, the law requires that the "responsible party" – that is the actual term used in the law – assume responsibility for the cleanup, regardless of fault. The responsible party is the one who owns the product at the time of the release. A common question of reporters in a spill is "Who is responsible for this?" An appropriate response is, "While the cause of this incident is not yet known and is under investigation, we are accepting full responsibility for the response and the cleanup." This separates, at least to some degree, the issue of fault, blame and financial responsibility for the response.

There's a similar problem with saying, "I'm sorry." On more than one occasion I witnessed attorneys, executives and public relations professionals discuss at length with a horde of reporters waiting whether or not the executive should say, "I'm sorry" or "I'm very sorry." No kidding. "I'm sorry" could mean, "I understand and regret the pain and suffering those who have been affected by this situation have experienced." Or, it could mean, "I'm really sorry our negligence caused this suffering." The two are very different.

When difficult conflicts emerge relating to whether the court of public opinion takes precedence over the court of law, the answer must come from the executive level. It is the CEO, Chairman of the Board or Executive Director who is charged with the responsibility of looking after the best interests of the company. These people must understand that there is a strong possibility of conflict in crisis situations, and they must be prepared to use their best judgement. It is not exercising fiduciary duty to stockholders, employees and other key stakeholders to turn over executive decision making to attorneys (or communication professionals for that matter) and then hide behind the screen of doing what the professionals told them.

When thinking about that issue of priority of court of law versus the court of public opinion, CEO's now have some strong models to evaluate. Martha Stewart most likely would not have gone to prison and seen her stock value tumble by hundreds of millions of dollars if she had simply stated when first accused of insider trading that, "I have made a mistake, I should have known better, I am sorry I let you down. I have learned much from this and am willing to accept the consequences of my actions." It is very likely she would have been given a fine and perhaps probation, but the public would have respected her for admitting mistakes and accepting responsibility. Similarly, Arthur Andersen as a company did not need to die. Leaders could have dealt directly and openly with the partner in Houston responsible for shredding documents. They could have said, "We are dismayed by the actions of our partner, and accept responsibility that we have created a culture in which those kinds of decisions would even be considered. We are doing some soul searching to identify how we can make certain in the future that we always expect our partners and staff to perform in the highest ethical manner." I firmly believe Arthur Andersen would be with us today, and we'd all be better off with another strong player in the high-level accounting business.

The point is, and I want to make it as clearly as I can: Doing what protects you in the court of law may always seem the safe choice, but frequently it is not the right choice.

Be Straightforward About What You Know and Don't Know

Transparency, honesty and openness are the qualities we look for in a person. At no time are these more important than when someone is trying to fit you with the black hat. But the very natural reaction, particularly when the lawyers are giving strong advice to keep quiet, is to hunker down, say the minimum necessary and "spin."

In the very earliest stages of an incident or emerging issue it is critical to be open and direct with both the media and stakeholders. The problem is there is little information. Unfortunately, this provides no excuse to keep quiet. The information that is available needs to be carefully and completely disclosed, but perhaps even more important, there needs to be communication about what is being done to get the information that the audience wants and is not yet available.

Reporters and the public always want to know, as quickly as possible, the cause of an accident. An airliner goes down in good weather taking hundreds of lives. Of course, we want to know what caused it. But unless a crowd of people was standing around while someone shot an anti-aircraft missile at it, the cause will likely not be known for some time. The common rule when providing information about an accident or incident is to avoid speculation. This is sometimes easier said than done because reporters would love to get a direct quote or an on-camera statement from someone who leaves some strong indication that supports a favorite theory of the reporter. The best method of dealing with this line of questioning is to state, "We simply cannot speculate on the cause right now. Our concern is for those who have been affected by this and dealing with the cleanup. We have experts already in place looking at what has happened and why it happened, and we want to know for ourselves as well as providing that information to the public. But it will take some time to investigate this and understand fully what happened and why."

One of the very best examples of this being done correctly was how NASA handled the Columbia disaster in 2003. Just 16 minutes before completing its flight, the Columbia disintegrated in view of national news cameras. The very first questions were: What happened? Who is to blame?" NASA never ducked the issue, never attempted to be evasive, even when the questions became unreasonably accusatory and of the "black hat" nature. Instead, they said debris hitting the wing – the immediate focus of attention – was one definite possibility, and that a full, independent investigation would determine the cause – but that right now the agency was focused on the human tragedy. The fact that lives had been lost, lives of their co-workers and friends. They communicated the care and compassion that was appropriate, they never ducked the blame question, but they also refused to be sucked into an unreasonable blame game that the reporters seemed so insistent upon.

A major reason why companies and organizations do not appear to be forthcoming early on as a story breaks, is the speed vs. accuracy dilemma. The strong and reasonable desire to get it right causes a lot of closed door scurrying, discussions and delays. If the public could look behind the scenes, they would see well meaning people wanting to make certain that everything they say is correct and beyond question -- people concerned about keeping their integrity intact. But the public cannot see behind the closed doors, and therefore, what they observe is a company refusing to talk or so slow with their information and statements that the news of the minute or the hour has long left them in the dust.

If you ask reporters what they want and expect in this instant news world, they will say, "Tell us what you have right now. Tell us what you don't have. And tell us when you are going to get it." It's that simple. If you don't have confirmation on key facts, such as injuries, then the limited information you have cannot be presented as factual. The answer then is, "We do not currently have reliable information on any injuries, but we will get that to you as soon as possible."

The real difficulty emerges when it becomes known inside the organization that the company or organization has done something wrong. The smoking gun is found. Once the communication team gets over the shock of realizing that the black hat may indeed fit, the discussion turns to whether the media will find out, and when and by whom. The common practice in dealing with such a situation is to prepare a holding statement. This document contains the official company line to be used when asked any anticipated difficult questions. However, if we look at the basic principles we have already outlined, this difficult situation perhaps calls for a different response. We said that credibility is everything. You lose that and the game is over. We said that the public wants openness, honesty and transparency. We said that the best policy is to tell what you know when you know it. We said that the word "cover-up" almost immediately changes the story to something more sinister, entertaining and long lasting. These principles inevitably lead to the conclusion that the best policy is to be the source of the information. Do not let the investigators uncover it for you. Do not allow some unhappy employee the sweet opportunity to make the claim that he or she brought you down. However, before telling what you know, there is one more important principle to remember that is especially critical in this kind of situation: What you do is much more important than what you say. If problems have been identified, confidence and credibility depend on the public and stakeholders knowing that you understand the depth and significance of the problem, and are taking the appropriate measures to insure the problem is resolved and does not reoccur.

For a tragic example of failing at telling what you know and don't know quickly enough, we can look at the Sago mine disaster of late 2005. Thirteen miners were trapped for hours when the word came out that twelve were found alive. Families rejoiced in the nearby church and news headlines around the world proclaimed the miracle in West Virginia. It was no miracle. Someone misunderstood the garbled radio message from the rescuers, violated the communications protocol of the Incident Command operation running the rescue, and communicated the false good news to the families. Reporters didn't verify it before running with the story. Worst of all, the company executives struggled for three hours with how to stop the celebration and tell the families and the world the truth that all but one of the thirteen had been found dead. Anger about safety issues in the mine was quickly displaced by a passionate rage about this inhumane three-hour delay. In the instant news world, there is no patience when you have information with high relevance.

Message: What message do we need to convey?

It may appear that, in talking about providing information in the early going of a crisis event, there is no such thing as a "message." As events unfold, it is the facts and specific information surrounding the event and what the company is doing about it that is conveyed. However, there is a difference between information and message. Ultimately, the only thing that really matters in communication is the perception of the audience. That's why there is such truth to the statement "perception is reality." The message, in this sense, is what the recipients of the information are understanding about the situation and the players involved: it is their perception.

News viewers or readers may gather information about a financial scandal, or a massive legal battle, or an environmental disaster involving your company. But the question is, "what are they thinking about the people involved and the quality and character of the company involved?" The Chinese character for crisis has two meanings: danger and opportunity. In a previous book, Friendship Marketing, I stated that trust is normally built in a relationship when there is a problem between the two parties. Not that you want to create a problem to create trust, but how you handle a difficult situation with potentially conflicting interests says a lot about your character, and, therefore, whether you are to be trusted by the other party.

Understanding the distinction between information and message is helpful in understanding the role of presentation in the communication process. An effective response with all the right words can be greatly diminished or destroyed if presented by an officious looking spokesperson with his or head down reading a script. A smirky smile can create a damaging impression when the message is one of sorrow and regret.

One company's leaders decided to hand a written statement to the waiting television crew instead of having a spokesperson on camera to deliver the message personally. The handing over of the message by a low-level communication staff member was the visual presented on the television reports. The words were strong and effective, but the message was clear and contradicted the words. The message was: "We are afraid to be seen on camera."

One of the most difficult jobs of the communication manager is helping executives who need to represent the company in the public to convey the right message with the right information. If personal characteristics or lack of ability in this regard prevents the effective communication of the right message, alternatives need to be found.

It is very helpful to keep near the top of your mind, during the most difficult and dark days, the relationship goal you have in mind. You want those people who are important to the present and future of your organization to place a high value on your existence. You want them to want you to be here. Evaluate every action of the company, every communication with the public and stakeholders, everything visible in the response and recovery efforts with the question: "does this result in the people important to us wanting us to be here?"

If we go back and review the list of potential audiences, and their reasons for wanting us to be alive and healthy, the connections between what we do and say and their interest in us should start to become clear. The employees, for example, assuming they place a high value on their employment and the company's ability to continue to help them meet their needs, do not want to see the company trashed in the public eye. They do not want to be embarrassed when they meet someone new and tell them where they work. They want a company that is healthy and respected. Stockholders want a company with the leadership to get through difficult situations, who can right the ship, get it back on course with minimal financial and public franchise damage, and get back to the business of providing a healthy return on investment. What is critical to them at this stage is observing strong, dynamic leadership focused on rapid recovery, while demonstrating true compassion for those affected by the events.

While it is very important to evaluate the various audiences in thinking about a central or umbrella message, the result needs to be creating that single message.

To attempt to communicate too many divergent messages to too many audiences means that any and all messages will be lost. The brilliance of President Clinton's first campaign strategists was that they understood this clearly. There are so many things to talk about in a presidential campaign, and opponents will go after whatever relatively minor item is successful in undermining credibility. But campaign strategist James Carville and crew stuck to the basic message: "It's the economy, stupid." The basic message a company or organization must communicate during a crisis needs to have this kind of simplicity and strength. A single, overriding message will usually be communicated; the question is whether the organization will control it and whether the message is the one the organization wants the world to hear. Exxon sent a loud message throughout the early days, and even long weeks, following the Valdez disaster. It was communicated most loudly through the absence of the top leadership who said, in effect, "even though I have the capability of travelling the globe through my corporate jets and I can go anywhere I want, when I want, this situation is not significant enough for me to attend to it personally." The message needed to be that the company saw this as a disaster of the highest magnitude, and it was providing all its resources to contain it, clean it up and find out what happened so it could be prevented in the future. That message was never conveyed.

When thinking about message then, it is absolutely necessary to start with the audience. What do you want them to think of you? Do you want them to see you as caring? As taking appropriate and effective action? Do you want to be perceived as a company and as leaders with character, people who own up to mistakes, who are concerned about the impact on others, the community, the environment? Thinking about these things will help direct the words that need to be presented as well as directing the best methods and people to present the message.

Listening: What Do We Need to Hear From Them?

For communicators, there is a natural tendency to forget one of the most basic tenets of communication: communication is a two-way street. It involves interaction, give and take, listening as much as talking. At no time is this more true than in situations in which the media are telling the world about you in the way they want to. Effective listening helps you understand how perceptions are evolving and drives the most critical strategic decisions.

I am convinced that one reason this is not commonly practiced is that corporate executives have accepted the accounting view of life that says the worth of a company is measured in the bottom line. In the "relationship value" model, the value of a company is found in the value placed in the company's existence and well being by those people who benefit from it. The bottom line is merely a reflection of that relationship value and is frequently a lagging-indicator. The real value, then, is in the perception of those people on whom the company's future depends: customers, bankers, stockholders, key suppliers, employees, etc. Knowing what they think, how their perceptions are being altered by the events of the day is critical to the executive team and is, and ought to be, the purview of the communication team.

It is surprising that more communicators are not stronger champions of key stakeholder listening. Knowledge, after all is power, and the knowledge of the perceptions of people critical to the organization is very significant power. Being the one to suggest this and then deliver the vital information serves the executive leadership with information that is critical to their effective decision-making, and elevates the communicator in the minds of the key leaders. More than just about anything else, it can put the communicators on the executive team. Even if communicators are not motivated by the opportunity to become more strategic in their role in the company, they ought to consider that listening is part of their responsibility. The communicators need to be not just the mouth for the organization, but the ears as well. When the future health, or even existence, of the enterprise is at stake in a public crisis, it is more critical than ever that communicators exercise both sides of their responsibility.

Perhaps one of the main reasons why communicators, and executives for that matter, are somewhat reluctant to consider listening is because of the presumed trouble and expense. Listening is generally understood to mean large-scale scientific opinion surveys with high degrees of statistical accuracy, relatively long lead times, and the necessary process of reviewing endless charts and numbers. There is definitely a time and place for this kind of listening, but it is not the kind of listening we are talking about here. What is suggested here is much simpler and less costly.

The listening that should occur in the midst of a media event can be put into two groups: informal and formal. Informal listening is just a habit. Every opportunity to find out what people are thinking should be exploited. Reporters are not just people who are seeking information from you, they are potentially excellent sources of information about any and all aspects of the situation and because it is their job to get information from a variety of sources and may indeed know more about what is going on than you do. They also have opinions about how the public perceives the situation, and their opinion about public opinion is critical. Reporters do not write in a vacuum, and they usually believe that the approach they are taking is consistent with how the public understands the situation. If they think the public perceives you as wearing the black hat, they will be fairly reluctant to put the black hat on someone else. Their sample size is usually related to a few friends, co-workers or family members, but it nevertheless is sufficient for them to develop relatively firm opinions about public perception. It is one reason why when media coverage diverts significantly from public perception, as you may determine from your more formal listening, one of the most important things you can do to change the reporting is to show their understanding of the public's response may be in error.

Informal listening applies not just to reporters, but to every stakeholder and audience group. Members of the communication team who have the opportunity for direct interaction by phone or face to face conversation should be strongly encouraged to ask how the people they are talking to feel about the situation, how the company is doing, what could be done differently, and how they think this situation will resolve itself. This information, anecdotal as it is, needs to be relayed back to the communication managers and, if trends emerge, needs to be conveyed to the executive leadership.

Formal listening is similar to informal in that members of the team are tasked specifically to identify people to talk to and then interview them. There is no need for statistically valid sampling at this point. There is a need to avoid bias in the questions asked, but this is usually done by using common sense. Questionnaires that clearly appear to be used to gather numbers to be entered into a computer for processing should be avoided because, frankly, people don't care to give their time and opinions simply to become an anonymous number. People are very interested in sharing their opinions and recommendations if they perceive they are being listened to as unique individuals, that their opinions really matter and that what they say may make a difference. Those items should all be realities in the way interviews are conducted.

How many interviews should be conducted? Common sense suggests enough to set a clear, but not necessarily unmistakable, direction. If you ask twenty people the same question and you get the same or similar response from eighteen of those, you have some degree of assurance that you have your answer. But if you ask twenty people and you get fifteen different answers, it is probably a good idea to keep asking.

The point to be made here is that while there is a place for formal, scientific and expensive surveys, they are not the only way to get vital information. When it is perceived that there needs to be a $30,000 survey that will take two weeks to complete, the response is usually then we won't do anything. It's a shame because vital information needed for effective communication response can usually be gained in a few hours and at very little cost.

In one major incident referred to earlier, we did the informal and formal listening focusing on community influencers. We conducted fewer than thirty interviews and gained valuable information for the executive team on the perceptions within the community. A few weeks into the situation, a much larger public relations company with a worldwide practice joined us, and we shared the results of our snapshot community listening with them. Predictably, they told the client that a $20,000-plus statistically accurate survey was required and pooh-poohed our little effort. Three weeks later, the results of their survey were presented. It showed no substantial difference from what we had already learned. In the meantime, we kept on with our informal and very low key formal listening and found that in the two weeks between sampling and presentation, the issues were changing substantially, as were the perceptions. But since the experts from the big firm had convinced the client that our informal listening was of no value, the ongoing listening had little impact on strategic and communication decisions. This would not prove helpful to the client in the long term.

Fortunately, today's online communication methods encourage and enhance listening opportunities. In fact, the Internet is valued so much by consumers in part because it provides them a high level of control over what they participate in and how they do it. Today, communication centers facilitate listening by integrating inquiry management, as well as providing the opportunity to develop quick surveys that can be used to help measure public opinion. These are becoming standard, so that if a company or organization in crisis does not use them, their absence also sends a message. But the message says that the company doesn't care about the opinion of the audience – not a message most companies want to send.

The effectiveness of a communication effort needs to be measured. Managers are soon taught that you can't manage what you don't measure. Public relations professionals, in my mind, too often hide behind the general perception that public relations results can't be measured. The reality is public communication is highly measurable. Because the only thing that matters is the perception of the audience, and this is very measurable on both a large- and small-scale. The communication process is not the picture of a hose squirting information in a single direction, it is a waterwheel collecting information and distributing it. Critical information collected is "How are we doing?" This information is vital to keep the communication process rolling.

Voice: Who Needs to Deliver the Message?

One of the most profound insights of John Naisbitt's 1982 bestseller, Megatrends, was "high tech, high touch." This simply said that as technology becomes an ever more pervasive force in our lives, we have a compensating need for more personal interaction. This has been clearly demonstrated in the use of email, one of the most startling and significant communication innovations of all time. One might have assumed, like express package shipping or faxing which preceded it, emailing might have been primarily a business tool. It is indeed a powerful business tool, but it is much more a personal communication tool. Email and its close relatives, chat rooms, instant messaging, etc., are used primarily for interpersonal non-business communication. In a world in which work and careers are driving people out of small communities, new communities are being formed and personal ties are maintained by a high tech tool initially envisioned more as a business tool. The social networking aspect of technology is, at this writing, the most important development in Internet use, spawning a whole new range of thinking, products and innovations under the theme of Web 2.0.

A major focus of this book is the use of technology in communication. Technology has transformed the media and is threatening its monopoly status, and the only response of those facing reputation risk in this instant news world is to fully engage the technology available to provide speedy, direct communication. But, technology requires a counter balance, and that is the personal touch.

The CEO of Exxon defended his decision to stay at his headquarters on the basis that communication technology allowed him to effectively manage the response from his office. He was right, but it didn't wash. While President Putin didn't claim that his dacha was properly wired in order for him to manage the Kursk business, the effect of both their decisions was the same. The media reported their absence and the public interpreted it as personal disengagement. Vice President Cheney was roundly and appropriately criticized after his unfortunate hunting accident in early 2006. The criticism was not that he shot and wounded his 78 year old friend, but that it took four days for him to come before the national news cameras and say that yes, he was the trigger man and that he was very sorry.

The people at the top need to be highly visible and very involved in the situation. Anything less looks either like hiding or obliviousness. An outstanding example of executive involvement was the role played by Alaska Airlines CEO John Kelly following the crash of flight 261 in January of 2000. And what communication specialists will undoubtedly study, in years to come, as the ultimate example of executive leadership in an overwhelming crisis, is Mayor Rudolph Giuliani of New York. His presence and very human but straightforward communication style during those horrifying days resulted in his being named *Time* magazine's person of the year, in a year dominated by other people at the center of historic events.

One thing that must be considered in this new world of direct communication is that the chief executive can only go so far. Mayor Giuliani and others who have done well in the public eye have done so in part because they made themselves highly accessible to the media. But doing this diminishes the time and availability for other key people, such as customers, stockholders, employees, etc. The burden of personal and direct communication must be shared. The entire executive leadership team must take a role in personal and direct communication at the time of the incident. This is, of course, not to say that their entire responsibility should be communication, as they have their job to do as well. But part of that job needs to be communication.

Media: How Should we Communicate?

Of all the questions dealt with in this chapter, this is the one that reflects the greatest change as a result of the instant news world. We identified the audiences to be communicated with earlier. But this isn't new. All those audiences were there before. It's just that the understanding for most of them was that the only option for fast communication of information was through the traditional news media. Since reporters were the ones beating down your door looking for information, it was natural to focus on meeting their needs and to presume, by doing so, you were meeting the information needs of everyone else.

The Internet has changed that because it creates the possibility of direct communication. Those deeply affected by what was going on always had a strong desire for relevant information, but they had no expectation because there was not really a practical way to communicate directly. It was natural in the media world for them to expect to receive the relevant information from the media only. Now there is a growing realization of the potential for direct, personal and fast messages to those people who have a reason for wanting that information. As that realization grows, companies or organizations that ignore that expectation will do so at their own peril. That is the real opportunity and risk of the coming post-media world.

Those people living next to an industrial facility that experienced a large fire, and who sent an email to the company asking if they should evacuate, had some expectation that they would get a response. In fact, they probably had an expectation that they shouldn't have had to send an email, but should have been told directly. Instead of being proactively informed before inquiring, these people did not even get a response for over two weeks. Do they really think it is because the company doesn't have the computer or Internet resources, or the people resources to answer their life and death question? Clearly not. Their only thought can be that the company doesn't care enough about their well-being to even get back to them. The company communication manager's response: our job was communicating with the media. It was this same company who was severely criticized by the media because the information they needed for their stories was only available from the fire departments and agencies responding.

The best and most effective way to communicate has always been direct and face-to-face. Romances by love letters have their attractions, no doubt, but the lovers usually write about the day when they can communicate face to face. Rarely when the lovers are face to face do they pine about how eager they are to get back to writing letters from a distance. We made the point earlier that the executive team must be actively involved in the public communication. Ideally, the CEO would meet personally with every person affected by the events. That isn't possible, so a sort of information triage is always the order of the day. If we can't have what we really want, which is direct, personal, face-to-face communication between those who matter and those who can do something about it, what is our next best option? We mentioned earlier that getting other executives involved was very important in extending this personal outreach. But even that will only take you so far.

If the basic principle of effective communication is make it as personal and direct as possible, we can establish a hierarchy of communication methods:

Face to face

Telephone

Personal letter, fax, email

Special section on Web site

General Web site

Media

As you go down the list, each one becomes less personal and less direct. It is immediately obvious that the use of the media to communicate to those whose opinions matter deeply to the organization is not ideal. It has been commonplace in a breaking news event simply because there were no options because speed was always primary. A front-page news story would outpace a letter any day of the week. The six o'clock news would certainly outpace most of the methods of getting information out quickly – even within organizations, such as to employees.

But the Internet changed that. Now direct, personal and immediate communication is possible. If it is possible, it will become expected, and it already is in many respects. A company can send an email out to its employees within minutes. Every company of any size also has the opportunity, should it decide to make use of it, to use the Internet to communicate proactively with all the key stakeholders whose perception holds the key to its future. Even though they have the capacity because the technology is very much available, very few companies have the will or the current capability. This can only be explained by a failure to understand the current media environment.

The audience wants what it has always wanted. If the information is relevant, if it bears directly on their present or future hopes or plans, then there is a pressing urgency for the information. When they know it is possible the urgency changes into a demand, and not meeting that demand can be catastrophic.

There can be little question that the use of the Internet is already, and will be increasingly, more critical for a company to protect its reputation and maintain a too fragile public franchise. The Internet offers the opportunity to provide immediate, direct and personalized information: one-to-one communication on a mass scale. Done right, it blends the high tech and high touch in a way that Naisbitt could not have imagined. Sir John Browne, CEO of oil giant BP, could not communicate with everyone affected by the Texas City refinery disaster of 2005. But his team did post on the crisis Web site that was launched for the incident a fifteen-minute video of him at the press conference. His compassion, concern and determination to do better spoke loudly and directly.

As compelling as the video of the CEO was, it could not fully replace personal communication. Communication strategy in this instant news world that does not focus on the requirement for direct, personal and immediate information to critical people is doomed to failure. Strategies that blend personal and direct communication with the best, fastest and most direct use of communication technology are the winning strategies.

8.
Preparing the Organization and Team

Executives are an insecure lot. As a result of watching the very public destruction of countless corporate reputations, executives are very well aware of the risks they face every day in a world dominated by instant news, infotainment and the Internet. They have seen the steady decline of CEO tenure, and have observed that in a great many cases, the public embarrassment of the company has been the primary reason for premature CEO departure. Several studies since Sept. 11 have shown that over 80 percent of executives feel their organizations are unprepared to deal with a significant crisis. They are smart enough to know that if their organization is unprepared to deal effectively with a news-making event, as the leader, they are extremely vulnerable. What makes this strange is that while there is a powerful need, there is little being done to prepare for the new realities of public communication.

Having dealt with dozens of companies at various levels over the past few years on this issue, it is clear that the primary obstacle to effective preparation is the organization. Within most organizations, there are enough obstacles to adequate preparation that only those leaders and concerned employees with great commitment and stamina are able to overcome them. Ultimately, organizational problems are problems of leadership. In plain truth, the fact that so few companies and organizations are prepared to manage a reputation crisis is a failure of both communication leadership and top executive leadership. Only strong commitment from individual leaders is sufficient to overcome the inherent opposition that exists to effective preparation.

One top manager of a large industrial facility clearly understood the need for adequate preparation. The person in his organization who would be responsible for the public communication in a major event was unconcerned. His computer keyboard was stored on the top of his computer and has likely never been touched by him. He was within a year of retirement and learning something new was simply not a high priority in his life. He had long-standing working relationships in the community and believed that should disaster strike, his job will be to answer the questions from the media, and then go on with his normal routine. He's a nice guy, well-liked, with a long history of loyal service to the organization. Aside from replacing him, working completely around him or forcing him to change, the manager decided he had little choice other than to wait out the time remaining before his communication manager retired.

One large multi-national company convened a global teleconference to discuss their preparations, including the ability of their technology infrastructure to handle a major news event. While there were some on the call very aware of the new media environment and the importance of adequate preparation, the prevailing viewpoint was that it was sufficient in a time of crisis to simply post some information to the company Web site. If the demand for information exceeded the few thousand hits per day that the company servers could handle, it would be OK if the site went down while they worked to put together a more robust solution during the crisis. It is one of the more extreme examples of the head in sand response, but, as I was told, "We are not interested in paying for insurance." In other words, there was no leadership inclination to invest in the ability to publicly communicate effectively in the event of a crisis. This story would not be so illustrative if the company in question were not a leader in an industry that was seriously damaged in the public eye because of one company's failure to communicate adequately.

Happily, in the time since this was first written, leaders throughout that company have completely changed direction. No doubt they were influenced by significant crisis events that took a serious toll on their reputation. Now, they have become a global leader in crisis preparedness and "instant news world" communication strategies and technologies. It is too bad that it took organization-shattering crises to accelerate the change.

One of the most consistent obstacles to preparation is the disconnect between various areas and departments in a larger organization and the fact that they do not share common agendas. The Internet is a technical issue, and therefore Internet infrastructure, access, use policies, applications, etc., typically fall under the purview of the Information Technology department. In a public communication crisis, the communication team and executive leadership need to have full and unimpeded access to the communication power of the Internet. But this kind of access normally conflicts with the natural desire of some IT managers to maintain their position of masters of the technology. The very natural fear is that providing non-technical people with the tools they need to make full use of the technology will diminish their role and value in the organization. There is inordinate fear of the curtain being pulled back to expose the wizardry they perform. They are exceptionally cautious about any effort that may result in this kind of exposure. They also seem to be afraid that if a new idea or new technology is brought to the attention of top management and it didn't originate from them, it will weaken their position. The "not invented here" syndrome is very much alive. In all fairness, some of this "turf war" is related to the responsibility that IT managers have to maintain the integrity of their systems. The Internet, being an open, uncontrolled and largely uncontrollable sort of technology, represents huge risks to IT managers whose job is it to insure the safety and security of the organization's technology resources and business data.

Leaders who understand the importance of preparation and planning are not stymied by the obstacles, no matter how many there are and how entrenched they may be. They subscribe to the old saying, "Don't tell me how rough the water is, just get the ship in." Getting the ship in, in this case, means addressing the four key elements of preparation:

Policies

Plan

People

Platform

Policies

Communication policies exist on two levels: a broad statement of intention that indicates the commitment of the organization to communicate effectively with those people who need information from the company, and a limited level of detail about how policies are going to be implemented. In other words, a short list of "dos and don'ts."

To communicate or not to communicate? How quickly and with whom? These are the core questions that must be answered at the very highest levels of the organization, and the difficult nature of these questions is one of the main reasons why far too many top executives would rather shove the public communication question in the corner. Establishing policies means making decisions and, in the case of public communication in this new era, it means making some difficult decisions with the entire enterprise at stake. Very few executives come to the task with a professional background in communication. Most come via financial, legal, managerial or technical training and experience. This is not to say they are not interested in or ineffective in communication; it is highly unusual to rise to top positions without considerable communication skills. But it does mean that communication is frequently seen as not central to the business, and therefore best delegated to those whose responsibilities are also, therefore, limited.

While communication policy at the highest levels can be seen as a board level decision, certainly no one can establish policy as critical as this for the future of the organization, other than the CEO. However, frequently a communication manager, or even communication team member, concerned about these issues, can instigate the discussion and facilitate the process of developing an appropriate policy. These are some of the key questions in developing such a policy:

1. How vital is the role of communication to the existence and mission of the organization?

2. What does a successful communication response look like and how will it be measured?
3. Does the organization consider it important to communicate information of high public interest?
4. Recognizing the dramatically changed nature of news and public information, what is the organization's goal as it relates to speed and accuracy of information?
5. What groups or audiences will receive priority in communication?
6. Will the organization be reactive or proactive in the distribution or publishing of information?
7. What role will the organization's leaders play in the communication process?
8. How will it be determined whether a crisis exists, and what level of response is required?
9. To what length is the organization willing to go to protect its credibility?

While each organization must answer these questions independently and with integrity, a primary purpose of this book has been to provide the background about changes in the public information environment that requires new thinking and a new approach to some of these questions. Some guidelines that may apply to your organization are offered as a means of starting the discussion.

1) How Vital is the Role of Communication to the Existence and Mission of the Organization?

In the previous chapter we discussed the concept of the public franchise. This is simply the idea that a company or organization cannot effectively operate without at least the tacit support of the public. From a marketing standpoint, we can look at this as brand value. If the brand has become tarnished and confidence is lost, the company is severely damaged, and may even need to go to the extreme measure of abandoning the brand entirely. ValuJet took this measure, as did Firestone and Amway. Arthur Andersen stands as a stark example of extinction caused by loss of brand value. The public, in effect, has veto power over the goals and aspirations of the company. What makes this so frightening is that the franchise can be lost not only by misdeeds on the part of the company, but by the actions of activists, by online reputation terrorists, by misinformation, or by an overly aggressive reporter, intent on telling a good story for ratings purposes. The only real protection is the ability and willingness to respond very quickly to reputation threats.

We also discussed how the value of an organization was linked to a great extent to the value placed on it by key people: stockholders, customers, employees, community leaders, etc. When it is understood that there is actual economic value attached to these perceptions, the shepherding and protection of these perceptions takes on a very high priority. It is these issues that should help determine the organization's response to this important policy question.

2) What Does a Successful Communication Response Look Like?

A communication policy, like a public relations plan, should include a clear statement of goals. The goal of most communication is relationship building. The goal of a communication effort for a company or organization ought to be to create, enhance or protect the relationships with the people who are important to the enterprise's present and future. A crisis represents a considerable threat to established and future relationships, but as mentioned earlier, it can also represent an opportunity. Handled properly, an effective crisis response and its communication can build an organization's respect, credibility and brand value. An appropriate communication policy statement should say in some form that it is the intention of the organization to manage the response and the communication of that response in such a way that the credibility of the organization and the respect with which it is held are enhanced. In other words, based on the way the crisis is handled, the goal is to have the people who matter to the company place an even higher value on the company's existence.

3) Does the Organization Consider it Important to Communicate Information of High Public Interest?

The basic question here is whether the organization leaders wish to speak to the public and interested audiences themselves, or be content to allow others to speak for them. Others include the media, activists, opponents, competitors, employees, industry pundits, government officials, etc. It ought to be obvious, but in viewing the actions of many companies caught in the headlights, it appears that their communication policy states they wish everyone else to speak for them. This appearance, in the age of instant media, is likely caused by the speed issue. In other words, by the time the organization is prepared to speak, others have already spoken for them, and the media and the public have gone on to the next breaking story. The affect on the public is the same: the company has not spoken.

That means in this new era, the decision to communicate is equally a decision to communicate very quickly. It is virtually instant communication or no communication at all. Which leads to the next question.

4) Recognizing the Dramatically Changed Nature of News and Public Information, What is the Organization's Goal as it Relates to Speed and Accuracy of Information?

The evidence of instant news is all about us. Each day and night on TV we see it clearly, and each day as we use our Internet devices to gain instant information the point is made. Yet, when I recently asked some industry communication people their expectation about getting an initial press release out in a drill scenario, they indicated that if it got out the first day they would be doing well. *The first day?* The reporter referred to earlier made it clear that if they don't have a statement from the company when the news breaks, they will go with what they have. It is now or it is too late. A communication policy and plan should clearly identify when statements from the company about fast breaking events should be issued. This compelling reality brings the instant news world problem home. If the organization cannot find a way to communicate effectively and properly in that "golden hour," the first hour after the event, it is flat out not prepared for today's instant media world.

It is obvious that it is not sufficient to simply state: "We will respond with a public statement within one hour of the initiation of the incident." Because the critical question is: "How?" No doubt a very fast response is required. Our government may state it is the policy to land a person on Mars next year. But without a realistic commitment of resources and the technological capability of doing it, creating such a policy is an exercise in silliness. Much of the further discussion about the plan, people and technologies will be focused on how to make a fast, accurate public information response feasible.

5) What Groups or Audiences Will Receive Priority in Communication?

This question has been a non-issue in public relations since the days of Edward Bernays, recognized by many as the first spinmeister or public relations professional. To many involved in public relations today, the question still does not make sense because public relations has long been equated with media relations. But, as we have pointed out, the media have simple served as a necessary intermediary to communicate with the audiences that really matter. In this post-media world, their role and significance is undergoing fundamental change, which does not mean that reporters should now receive a lower priority. It simply means that today, every one of the audiences is a priority audience. Their demand and expectation for immediate and direct communication is the fundamental change that defines the post-media world.

If you have to choose between communicating to the Governor or taking care of the County Executive of the county where the facility exists, to whom do you respond? How about the Governor, the County Executive, the publisher of the local paper, *The Wall Street Journal* bureau chief, your stockholder and the eldest son of a worker who was killed in the accident everyone is interested in? What is your priority?

These are the very difficult and very real situations that executives and communication managers need to deal with. It may be more comfortable to let things sort themselves out in a real situation, but undoubtedly a price will have to be paid. A crisis can almost be defined as a situation in which circumstances and demands overwhelm the capability to deal with them. That will most certainly be true of communication demands. In communication planning, the keys to this dilemma are technology and delegation. The technology available today allows for instant and direct communication with the key people – provided there is the proper preparation. Delegation makes it possible to prepare the team in advance to cover all the bases. It may very well be advisable that, while the CEO is given the responsibility of dealing with the families of those involved, another senior level executive or the director of communications may be the one to coordinate the Governor's visit.

6) Will the Organization be Reactive or Proactive in the Distribution or Publishing of Information?

The basic question here is what will you do when there is bad news to tell? Will you wait until asked? Will you want important audiences to hear it from you first, or do you want to communicate with them after the media have told the story in their way, with whatever bits and pieces they can quickly pull together?

No doubt it is my bias that makes me marvel at the companies and organizations at the beginning of the twenty-first century who consciously pursue a communication policy of having others tell their story for them. It is well established that public speaking is the number one phobia. But does this phobia extend to the highest levels in a corporation and to the degree that they wish reporters whose job it is deliver as large an audience as possible, and activists whose future depends on creating a sense of public outrage, to speak on their behalf? This is exactly the policy defended by communication professionals in some of the world's largest and most successful companies.

While some explicitly state that the media will speak for them, a far greater number have a policy that states they will provide and disseminate information but they are clearly unprepared to do so. Being unprepared to do it in a way that meets today's media and audience demands means they have a de facto "no communication" policy. It does no good to say you will be open, direct and straightforward in your communication when no preparation has been done to make that possible. If it is your intention to proactively provide bad news (or good news for that matter), then responding positively to this policy question requires having the capability of performing.

7) What Role Will the Organization's Leaders Play in the Communication Process?

This simple question contains one of the most important communication policy decisions to be made. In a reputation crisis, the organization's leaders must be visible, engaged and, if appropriate, on the scene. In a large-scale event, the communication task is overwhelming enough that perhaps several on the executive level will need to be very actively and visibly involved.

There are certainly circumstances in which the CEO, undoubtedly talented in many areas, simply does not come across well through public media. In that case, the situation must be confronted directly (easy for me to say, hiding behind this computer screen), and other company or organization leaders designated to be the face on the company. It should be understood that reporters have a strong preference for getting their information from executives or managers, rather than spokespeople who are professional communicators. Perhaps they believe that, despite extensive media training, executives are more likely to slip up and give information or juicy quotes than trained professionals. More likely they believe that better, purer, less laundered information will be provided by those responsible for making decisions within the company. As a general rule, reporters respond best when they see they are given access to the decision-makers and this often results in better reporting.

There is no doubt a lot of misunderstanding about the role of spokespersons, and not only on the part of reporters. The executive from one company I talked to, who had little inclination toward open and direct communication, said the company had designated a low level administrative assistant as their spokesperson for the primary reason that this person wouldn't be in a position to really know what was going on, and therefore wouldn't be tempted to give out information the executives felt was inappropriate.

In addition to determining the role that executives will play in putting a public face on the company during a reputation crisis, another important policy decision relates to the information approval process. Who will decide what information goes out under which circumstances? Who has the right to approve public information? What role will attorneys play in these decisions? What about other outside consultants, such as crisis experts or experts on specific response topics? How will the editing, vetting and approval process work in actuality? In a media world where now is too late, the answers to the question of approvals may very well make all the difference between an effective and botched response.

There is probably no more important role the organization's leader must play than refereeing the almost inevitable battle between the legal team and the public communication team. It has become increasingly common for company attorneys to take a very prominent role in decision-making about what the company says (and does) in a crisis. It has even become common that it is the attorneys who speak on the company's behalf. There are very good reasons for this, primarily because a crisis seems to inevitably involve legal action, either immediately or down the road. Many attorneys are in fact very effective in the role of public spokesperson, which is not difficult to understand given their usual gifts with language, persuasive ability and knowledge of the law. But executives who decide to use attorneys in this role, or who base their public communication decisions on legal advice, need to be very aware of the considerable dilemma involved. Because in my experience, the most serious reputation damage occurred unnecessarily as a direct result of attorney involvement, and that experience has been confirmed by conversations with numerous other communication professionals.

An attorney's single charge is to protect the enterprise in the court of law. The charge of the public relations manager or communication manager is to protect the enterprise in the court of public opinion. It is far more common than not in a news-making crisis that the best course to protect the organization in one court puts it at considerable risk in the other court. That's why I say the conflict between attorneys and communicators is almost inevitable.

Most attorneys' natural reaction to an event that will likely lead to legal action is for the company to say little or nothing. That is understandable given the highly fluid nature of the events, and the fact that anything that is said publicly can and will be used against the company in court. Accepting responsibility, expressing sorrow, expressing a strong desire to prevent such actions or accidents again, expressing a past record of preventive activities – all these represent very genuine risks in the court of law. But not speaking, or speaking in legalese, or couching everything that is said in terms and styles clearly intended to protect the company in court is counterproductive to the main goal of the communicator, which is to protect and enhance credibility in the minds of the people who really matter to the future of the enterprise.

What is the solution? The solution should first rest with the attorneys and communicators. It is disgustingly easy to get into a power game at this delicate stage of a crisis. The issue quickly becomes not what is in the best interest of the company, but who can establish dominance or control of the situation. I have observed both attorneys and very experienced communication professionals allow their arguments to go to ridiculous extremes, making it clear it wasn't about protecting the organization, it was about protecting their ability to influence the direction taken.

An increasing number of attorneys are very aware of the inherent conflict between these two courts, and will give their advice with that understanding. They may say, "If I look at it purely from a legal perspective, here is what you should do or say. However, I understand what that would mean for the company's credibility and, therefore, you should consider if the long term consequences to the company are more significant with loss of credibility than the legal risk." Communicators, on the other hand, need to take the time to listen to the attorneys and find out what the legal risks really are. In many situations, if there is some discussion and the power-tripping is ended, a solution can be found that minimizes the legal risk, while still allowing the company to speak in a way that protects its credibility. Not always, unfortunately.

That means that the CEO or organization leader has a critical role to play here. The CEO's job is to protect the present and future of the organization. The dilemma between the two courts is very real, so tough decisions need to be made. A legal cost must sometimes be paid to protect the public franchise and the viability of the company in the future. And sometimes a decision must be made that harms the organization's credibility in order to protect the company's legal position. In those cases, I much prefer to make an honest statement about why the company cannot speak, or why it is taking the position that it has because of the potential consequences in court, but taking such a position often leads to a new round of warfare with the attorneys.

I am making a strong point of this because it is a crucial issue, and because too often I have seen CEOs take the position that protecting the organization means turning decision making over to the attorneys when a large legal action is involved. Clearly they believe that protecting the company's legal stance is the best way to protect their positions. My only reminder to CEOs who have this philosophy is to assure them that most CEOs today experience a short tenure not because of adverse legal action, but because the customers and/or the public has lost confidence in them. Do not be too quick to assume the best way to protect the investment of the owners or shareholders is by allowing the attorneys to take control.

8) How Will We Determine Whether a Crisis Exists and What Level of Response is Required?

There are many excellent resources on defining crises and appropriate responses. We won't cover well-trod ground here. The point to be made is that the communication and crisis response managers need to have clearly in their minds the circumstances that require various levels of response. In the aftermath of Sept. 11, the National Guard and other agencies such as the Coast Guard have developed various alert levels with fairly clear definitions of what threat conditions require which level of response. Some agencies have four levels, others use three. A company or organization that plans properly for reputation threats will likewise have various levels of response with a corresponding response plan for each level. The greater the threat, the more of the leadership team and response team is pulled into the response, with clearly defined roles and expectations for each member.

It is not always easy to see in the early stages of an unfolding story how it will play out and how much of a crisis it may become. This is one good reason to have an experienced crisis communication professional available to provide threat assessments and to provide guidance in evaluating the direction a story may take. I have been involved in many situations which had the appearance of becoming major reputation-threatening crises, but which never developed. To over-react in the early stage could have caused damage, and could actually have precipitated unnecessary media coverage and stakeholder concern. On the other hand, situations such as Arthur Andersen, Firestone/Ford make it clear that the crisis momentum can get rolling quickly and, if the company underestimates the impact, it is forever behind the curve, with little possibility of catching up.

When a client was faced with what promised to be highly publicized legal action, we prepared a response and a press release to convey that response. The question became, "do we release it or not?" To release it without a large-scale effort on the part of the plaintiff's attorney would likely create a story that otherwise wouldn't exist. To delay or not release would mean that our side would likely not get told. When the plaintiff's story appeared on the AP wire, I could see that the story was released and in a very early stage. We emailed the release to all reporters we thought might be interested. When very little media coverage appeared, we concluded that one possibility was that with our response, reporters could more easily see that the plaintiff's attorney's release was a publicity-seeking story, and decided it didn't have strong news merit.

9) To What Length is the Organization Willing to Go to Protect its Credibility?

This is the fundamental preparation question. It starts with an assessment of brand value and the potential risk to the enterprise's future should its public franchise be damaged or destroyed. From there it goes to the establishment of a clear link between credibility and reputation. When raising my three teenagers, I appropriated the great NAACP college ad slogan, "A mind is a terrible thing to waste" to repeat to them more frequently than they wanted to hear: "Trust is a terrible thing to waste." I will appropriate it once more. For a respected company or organization, credibility is a terrible thing to waste. The loss of credibility is the loss of public confidence and the potential loss of the public franchise.

Credibility is a character issue and character values are ascribed to organizations as well as people. Firestone's trust was lost once it was believed, fairly or not, that information about tire manufacturing problems was ignored or hidden by management. Large tobacco companies are spending millions and millions of dollars attempting to restore credibility by talking about their good work in war torn areas and communities, but the reality is for years executives hid the truth about what they knew about the risks of smoking. Their bald-faced lying will perhaps never be forgiven, and the willingness of the public to respond with draconian measures that put civil liberties at risk is an example of the cost of loss of credibility.

The real problem with this issue arises with an honest discussion about what credibility means in the instant news world. This will be discussed at length in a later chapter dealing with the future and the need for "truth filters," but as companies and organizations more frequently find themselves taking on the role of the media in public communication, credibility expands in importance beyond anything we have yet seen. People reading information from a Web site, or from an email message coming from the company, need to know that the information is reliable, that it does not represent the company spin, that it is completely honest and truthful.

Credibility is fundamental honesty. It is not just a matter of how carefully you choose your words. It is much more a matter of speaking the truth clearly in a way that is understood and that contains the whole truth. The most difficult challenge to credibility in communication emerges when it becomes known that people within the company did indeed make mistakes, were negligent or even operated illegally or unethically. If this information is not public, should the company communicate it, or wait for it to be revealed by other sources? This is the real meaning of the question to what length will a company go to protect its credibility? If credibility is important or critical, the answer to that question is obvious. If protecting the company financially in a court of law is the ultimate value of the company's leaders, then credibility will almost invariably be lost. There is very little no-man's-land in this highly dangerous battlefield.

The public longs for the character and credibility of a John Procter who, in "The Crucible," went to the gallows rather than sign an untruthful public confession, crying out as he did, "Because it is my name, it is my name." We long for people and organizations who risk their own lives for personal honesty, knowing that in this time of public ownership and stockholder pressure, how short that supply of personal honesty and character truly is.

A quick perusal of news stories in this age of instant news and infotainment will show that cover-up is a most consistent theme. A company that knows something and does not tell it straight out is almost always accused of cover-up. The lead accountant on the Enron account for Arthur Andersen destroyed key documents relating to the Enron situation. He protested that he was following the advice of the company's attorney who responded that she only said to follow document destruction procedures. The legalities are a moot point. What is absolutely crystal clear is that the credibility of Arthur Andersen was at stake and already damaged by the decision of one of its partners. He may have followed legal advice and company policy, but the result was the appearance of a cover-up, and that is toxic to a reputation. While the company responded by firing the partner involved, and he consequently pleaded guilty to federal obstruction of justice charges, these actions did not substantially help the company. By that time, their waffling on matters of character and policy, their stated intention to fight the criminal charges, their inconsistency between what the company officials were saying and their lawyers were saying resulted in a profound loss of public confidence and a flood of account losses. A March 30, 2002, *New York Times* headline summed up the problem: "Leaderless at Arthur Andersen When Direction is Needed."

There are no simple answers to this difficult question, but a communication policy needs to address it because it lies at the heart of the entire response. Hypocrisy will be exceptionally visible when a policy says one thing, and company leaders do something else. What is essential is that communication leaders, executives and the attorneys they will rely on sit down together to specifically discuss and hammer out a policy and plan to answer the question of how far the organization will go to protect its credibility.

Plan

After the fundamental questions have been answered in a document that represents the organization's communication policy, that policy must be implemented through a well-prepared plan. Here are a few questions to consider in developing that detailed communication plan:

Plan Questions:

1. How will the communication team be organized?
2. How will the communication organization evolve based on the scope of the issue or incident?
3. What are the key roles in managing a communication effort and who will be assigned to those roles?
4. What equipment and resources will be required to communicate effectively?
5. What key organization messages need to be communicated during a public event?
6. What approval process will be used to ensure messages and information

released are accurate, appropriate and reflect the values and priorities of the organization?

7. How will outside participants such as lawyers, consultants, communication contractors, etc., be integrated effectively into the effort?
8. How will the many questions from the various audience groups be managed and answered?
9. How will we coordinate and manage participation from the various units in the organization?

Like most corporate documents, the best plans are short and sweet and to the point. While your written plan may have a lot of background information and text, it should also have a "cookbook" section. The longer text can be read at leisure as part of the preparation and training activities. But during an event, a good plan needs to operate like a step-by-step set of instructions. The cookbook plans are the ones that will be most useful in the time of an actual event and can serve as an invaluable guide for the team that has been assembled to respond.

People

When my children were young in the early 80s, like almost all their friends, they got into video games big time. Like most parents, we questioned this use of time and what it might mean for their futures. Aside from the frustration of not being able to make Mario perform with anything near the degree of skill they demonstrated, it was my view that they were indeed preparing for the world of the future. "This is the way the next war will be fought," I opined to my wife. Not only that, but because an entire generation was being raised on fast-paced action on the computer or TV screen, and the intense movements on a handheld controller, I was convinced that employers of the future were going to have to replicate this kind of action into their work, or have a generation of workers terminally bored.

This has become reality in ways I could not have dreamed. Most automobiles are now manufactured using mouse and joystick controls handled by a few highly trained and very bright computer engineers operating billions of dollars of technology. We bomb the caves of Afghanistan and the strategic targets of Baghdad from 50,000 feet guiding smart bombs and "daisy cutters" into the smallest spaces with computer aided devices, using controllers not unlike what my kids were using with Nintendo. And today, we communicate with millions around the world with game-like digital production interfaces.

The post-media world – the world of instant news, instant media and infotainment – demands a new kind of communicator. The "slap you on the back, everybody's his best friend" style of public relations professional that dominated the capital/media world is as out of place in this new world as the Kalishnikovs proudly owned by the horse-riding mujahideen are in the new world of pilot-less aircraft.

There is no doubt in my mind that the primary obstacle to change and to adequate communication preparation is the fact that the very people who have risen to the top of their profession are too often living in the comfortable media world of the past. To tell them that their new world will live on an Internet platform, and that they must be conversant with advanced database management, broadband communications, and digital image production is to tell them that much of what they have built their careers on is now irrelevant. No wonder there is resistance.

The solution is not to throw that valuable experience away. Nor am I suggesting that no one born prior to 1975 can succeed in the instant news world. But, I am suggesting that change is necessary, inevitable and must be demanded. Age is not the issue. My father, who has been interested in technology since he hid a radio from German occupiers in his native Holland during WWII, is an avid computer enthusiast and spends countless hours learning the latest digital video and image manipulation technologies. My mother, also in her mid 70s, has recently discovered what a marvelous tool the Internet is for keeping her children and their spouses, grandchildren and great grandchildren connected.

Those involved in public communication today must clearly understand that technology is a primary driver in their lives. The ones who will succeed and grow in the new news era will embrace this fact and anticipate the changes rather than resist and dread them.

Communication leaders today must also step up to a new level of responsibility within their organizations. We have seen the elevation of the corporate communication manager in the decision-making hierarchy in recent years, but in many organizations, this function is still relegated to lower level junior managers, or a sub-function of human resource managers. Communication managers need to take a strong role in the company strategy and decision making because so much of the present and future of the organization rides on the effectiveness of public and stakeholder communication. Lines between marketing and public relations simply do not make as much sense in the era of instant, direct communication. If the purpose of the organization is to develop and maintain high value relationships with the right people, it ought to be obvious that effective communication with those right people is a fundamental element of what the business or organization is all about.

At a recent gathering of public relations professionals, one of the most popular sessions had to do with "gaining a seat at the table." The speaker offered suggestions on how public relations contractors or corporate communications staff people could become more "strategic." While the topic was timely and the presentation well received, many suggestions were less than meaningful. Being strategic means making contributions that are important to helping fulfill the mission of the organization. Yet, there was essentially no discussion about the critical role of communication in the function and operation of the business, or about learning to think like a CEO. A communication professional of real benefit to the executive team is one who deeply understands, and is committed to, the mission of the organization. He or she understands the role of internal and external communication in fulfilling that mission and has the ability to develop, build support for and implement communication solutions that are effective in advancing the organization's mission.

One task today's communication leader must assume is preparing a team to manage the communication process in the event of a reputation crisis. If the organization does not have a communication leader with the qualities described above, the CEO or other senior executives need to assume this role, or bring in the outside expertise needed to prepare an effective communication team.

Training and drilling is the most effective method for preparing a team, and it is more important than ever in this world of instant news. A team can be effective only when everyone clearly understands the goals and the roles they and others on the team must play in order to achieve those goals. Another way of putting it is to use the game analogy. A team can't win if it doesn't understand what winning means, and a team can't win if each member doesn't know what he or she must do as part of that team.

Much of my experience in crisis communications has involved the JIC model, or Joint Information Center. This model provides an excellent template for developing a fully staffed and efficiently operating crisis communication operation. The JIC was developed to flesh out the public information function of the Incident Command System, or ICS. ICS was developed in the 1970s by the fire service as a means of quickly developing an effective management structure to respond to out of control fires. It has subsequently been adopted and refined by most major federal agencies responsible for responding to major public crises, including FEMA, the EPA, the Coast Guard, the FBI and others. It was mandated by Executive Order in 2003 for use by all first responder agencies that receive federal funding. That means virtually every local police, fire and emergency management department now uses ICS and its communication counterpart, the JIC. This mandate makes it even more important for today's communicators to become versant in this communication tool.

The Incident Command System provides a ready-made organization structure to quickly and efficiently manage a large-scale event, such as a fire, a school shooting, an earthquake, oil spill, etc. It is especially useful when there are multiple government agencies involved, including federal, state and local agencies. It clearly defines the command structure and the entire organization plan, and eliminates the very real potential for mission-diverting discussions like, "who's really in charge here," and "what are the boundaries of my role." While it is especially helpful for a company (called the "Responsible Party" in ICS terminology) which finds itself at the center of an event in which government agencies are responding, it is also a very useful model to study, adapt and drill for companies who face reputation crises without the likelihood of agency involvement.

The JIC was developed out of the ICS structure as a way of coordinating public information when multiple agencies are involved. Again, even if your organization's most likely crises are legal actions or product recalls which may not involve police, fire, or federal regulatory agencies, the JIC model is still very useful as a means of efficiently organizing and managing a crisis communication team.

The Information Officer is the communication manager overall responsible for public information. He or she has a direct link to the Incident Commander, or in the case of a multi-agency response, the Unified Command, serving on the Command staff. Closely related to the Information Officer is the Liaison Officer whose role is to provide the link between the various agencies and, in some models, also manage communication with government agencies and officials. The major roles within the JIC include the JIC Manager, Assistant IO (Information Officer) for Internal and Assistant IO, External. The Internal manager is responsible for development and production of needed materials, communication within the response organization and communication to the employees of the organization. The External manager is responsible for communication with outside audiences such as the media, neighbors, local officials, and other key stakeholders. Further roles are defined to further divide the responsibilities under each of these key managers. The model is easily expandable and with even minimal training and drilling, the communication response team can be organized and efficiently managed.

Some of these specific activities will be explored in more detail in the chapter on crisis response. The JIC manual is published by the National Response Team, chaired by the Environmental Protection Agency, and can be downloaded from the Web at www.nrt.org and selecting "NRT Publications."

Whether the JIC model is adopted and adapted for use by the organization, or whether a custom designed model of crisis communication team organization is adopted, the key point is to develop the organization structure, and then train and drill.

Training involves getting the team members together, explaining potential crises, identifying desired outcomes and major tasks that need to be done and by whom in order to achieve the desired results. This can be done in a didactic method of telling people what it is they need to do, but it is more effectively accomplished through hands-on experience. Short of a real incident, which is not a good time to train, the best method of preparing the team is through a drill.

Drilling involves setting up a scenario and either walking through it in a tabletop exercise or running a real-time drill. There is no better method for preparing a communication team than a full-scale drill. This is particularly true if the communication response involves the use of technology unfamiliar to at least some of the team. In a full-scale, real-time drill, a group needs to be involved who will provide the inputs to the drill as well as be reporters, neighbors, executives, employees, investors, government officials, etc. Sometimes called the "Simulation Cell," or "simcell," these people should be experienced in crisis communications, and need to take their roles seriously, even as they become the worst nightmare for the communication team.

One of the key players to participate in a drill is the attorney. These drills provide an outstanding opportunity to work through the thorny questions of accepting responsibility, telling bad news proactively, protecting credibility, getting out in front of the story and other communication challenges known to drive attorneys crazy.

A major advantage of a drill is to identify the strengths and weaknesses of various team members. Some may be more effective at information gathering, drafting and editing of materials. Some may do well in media interviews, while others may be best in personal, face-to-face discussions with stakeholders. The CEO or executives who will be involved in making decisions during a real event, and those who will provide the "face" on the organization, need to be involved in these drills as well, and their strengths and weaknesses must be honestly assessed along with other team members. Given the seriousness of a real crisis to the future of the organization, this assessment of strengths and weaknesses and needed skill levels should be seriously undertaken. Hard decisions made at the drill stage or post-drill stage can have an impact on the organization measured in the millions or billions of dollars.

That is the most important point to be made about the people issue in crisis or corporate communication in this era. Quite frankly, there are some cut out for this kind of work and others who are not. There are some able to adapt and grow with the changes in the media environment, and others who will serve as obstacles. Communication managers and top executives need to constantly ask themselves, "what is at stake?" When the importance of a fast, effective information response is deeply understood, the tough people decisions will be made. As an observer from the outside looking in at some of the organizations and the unqualified people they have in key communication positions, I can only conclude that the leadership either does not grasp what is at stake for the entire organization or simply does not have the leadership qualities to make the difficult decisions involving people they may like or who have long tenure in the organization.

Platform

The technology for communicating has always been an important issue, but never more so than today. It has become a cliché to claim that "the medium is the message," and yet it is quite obvious in a reputation crisis how important this is. Take, for example, a family member of a person injured in an industrial accident. How they respond to and feel about the company's apology for what has happened will vary greatly depending on the medium used to convey that apology. If they receive a personal visit from the CEO who communicates warmly, sincerely and with genuine sorrow, their response will likely be considerably different than if they received a letter or fax. Much more so if their only message of condolence or regret was expressed by a news anchor on the evening news reading a statement from the company that says, "XYZ Company expresses its regret over this incident."

The hierarchy of communication should always go from the most personal to the most impersonal. If the CEO could communicate directly and personally with each and every person involved, and each and every reporter, that would obviously be the ideal. The reality is that such a response is impossible, so the challenge for the communication manager is to come as close to that ideal as possible given the media, the technology, the people and the resources available.

While personal is best, it does not follow that the more recent technological means are therefore most impersonal. This is where Naisbitt's insight has done us a bit of disservice. High tech is not always the polar opposite of high touch. The extensive use of email for tying families and friendships together, the use of the Internet for locating old classmates, and the replacement of the telephone (another tech/touch medium) with email and Web sites for locating missing relatives on Sept. 11, all illustrate the personal nature of the most high tech of all communication devices. In mid-2006, the driving application of the Internet is social networking. Referred to in some circles as Web 2.0, virtually every company and technology provider is scrambling to figure out how to capitalize on the socializing aspect of the Internet.

One of the things that makes this discussion difficult is, with current technology, we can mass personalize. When I sign on to Amazon.com, or some other advanced E-commerce sites, I get personalized information about my past buying history, recommendations on new products that I might like based on past purchases, and other helps personally designed for me. Is this personal? Hardly, because there was no person involved other than the one who designed the program. But neither is it as impersonal as a catalog, and it certainly cannot be described as a mass solution. I am treated as an individual and I know that the information is there uniquely for me and uniquely tailored to meet my needs.

I have already described the role of technology in creating the instant news world we currently live in and particularly the post media world we are moving into. A technology-driven information world requires that technology be part of the information strategy of any company or organization operating in this environment. The issue is not whether you will use technology in your communication plan, rather which technology platform will you use and how effectively will you use it.

While we will explore some of the basic technology issues here, the next chapter will discuss specific applications needed to meet the instant response demanded in today's public information milieu.

A basic assumption of communication technology involves the use of computers. In the most basic uses, computers are used to draft and edit documents, write reports, and store data such as facts about the organization and mailing lists. The main issue today isn't whether or not to use computers, it is how they are linked. George Gilder, in a *Forbes* magazine article in 1994, highlighted the Sun Microsystems slogan, "The network is the computer." Much more than an advertising slogan, this is a profound insight because how computers are linked together makes all the difference in their power as communication devices, and whether or not their true capabilities will be unleashed. From this standpoint, we can say today that the Internet is the computer.

As the Internet develops further and further, we can see the truth of this evolving almost daily. At first there were massive computers that held all programming and data, and accessed by "dumb" terminals. Then there were "personal computers" that held the data and programs necessary for that individual user. Eventually these were linked, first by Wide Area Networks and Local Area Networks, but eventually by the Internet. Now we are well along in the process of eliminating the personal computer and instead replacing it with the Internet that will hold the programs and the data for its users. Completely personalized, highly secured, but still sharing an enormous platform of interlocked processing power and data storage.

All but a very few executives and communication professionals currently are linked to hundreds of millions of other computers through the Internet. This fact is the most significant change in the emerging post-media world. It is essentially this light-speed linkage that creates this new public information environment. But when it comes to using this capability, most communicators are severely hampered. The obstacles to effective use of the Internet in public communication include fear, lack of awareness of the technology, budgetary constraints, and Information Technology policies. It is like a medieval king having available a machine gun or a tank to help him fight his battles, but he cannot use it because he either doesn't know how or the person in charge of weaponry simply won't make the tool accessible to him.

The Internet is the only realistic platform for communicating in this instant news world. More specifically, an Internet-based communication management application operating on a crisis-capable Web server is rapidly becoming an essential tool of today's communicator. As a platform, the Internet offers the opportunity for a team to work effectively together on a common desktop to create, edit, approve and instantly disseminate the information needed. Information can be mass customized. All types of information can be presented quickly and at virtually no cost for distribution – information such as audio interviews, video, all manner of printed materials and every conceivable kind of photographic or illustrative image. A virtual command center can be established instantly and new team members can be quickly incorporated by issuing passwords and security levels.

The first and, at this writing, only virtual communication center designed for crisis communications was introduced in 2000. By early 2006, it had been adopted by numerous federal, state and local agencies as well as leading global organizations in oil, airplane manufacturing, education, insurance, food, manufacturing and many other industries.

Today, there are a great many professional communicators who have at their fingertips the opportunity to instantly summon a global team of communicators. They can work together in real time or as their own clocks allow to draft, edit, review, approve, upload any kind of media and instantly distribute any information they desire to an audience of one or many thousands. And they can do this without a single Web programmer in sight and without the participation of a single person from IT. These communicators can command the full capabilities of the Internet for both team and external communication.

Communicators ranging from the Coast Guard public information officers during Hurricane Katrina to the crisis communication experts responding to a massive industrial accident at a refinery in Texas had this virtual communication technology in common. Because of that, they were able to communicate without hindrance even though, in the case of the US Coast Guard District 8, their headquarters were also inundated by the floodwaters of Katrina. And responders to the refinery incident were able to call on an experienced team from around the nation to respond virtually and instantaneously to media, family, government and other inquiries from across the town or the globe. These teams did not assemble in a designated command post, instead they assembled at their desks, in front of their computer screens, in their home offices or from wherever they could access the Internet.

But although communicators with access to virtual communication center technology are growing, they are still very much in the minority. Most communicators today, while certainly adept at computer skills, are limited because company policy operates around a LAN mentality. This is understandable since Information Technology managers see the work that people need to do as restricted to those inside the company and the LAN has traditionally offered a higher level of security. Add the opportunities now afforded by VPN or

Virtual Private Networks and the reach of the LAN can be extended through secured connection with the Internet. If they have extended beyond the LAN in some mission critical applications such as to facilitate a global supply chain, they likely have not gone beyond the LAN for reputation management. Crisis communications and reputation management issues are seldom on the front burner for most IT managers.

In simple terms the problem with the LAN, even with VPN, is that it does not easily provide universal access. The perceived problem with the Internet is that it does provide universal access and therefore is a security risk. The reality is that opening up the Internet as a platform for public communication challenges the Information Technology people to their very core: control of the resource. Security issues are relatively easily resolved. Turf issues are not.

Top executives of today's "at risk" companies need to be completely aware of this situation. Tools are currently available which will enable you and your communication team to respond quickly and efficiently and meet the "now is too late" standard. But making these tools available runs counter to the inherent control issues of most Information Technology leaders. Their power is gained by controlling access to technology when their role should be seen as power through providing access. There is no reason today's communicators should not be able to fully and completely command the capabilities of the most powerful communication implement ever devised even though the thought of programming or increasing technological knowledge is abhorrent to them. What keeps most people from making use of this is either their fear or internal obstacles relating to IT policy.

There are two major issues involved in this difficult situation. First, not understanding the value of an open but controlled access platform for team communication. Second, not understanding the criticality of crisis capable Web service.

On the issue of universal access, in a crisis situation today open but controlled access is essential. By open and controlled we mean using the Internet but controlling access through various methods including multi-tiered passwords. In an example based on a real event, let's assume you are the head of communication for a large hospital. You find out that a legal action is being filed and the attorney for the plaintiff is a publicity seeker. You get a call from "Good Morning America" or the "Today Show" who courteously inform you that the attorney, the plaintiff, and a physician friendly to them will be on their show discussing their lawsuit. You ask if you may be there also. They say no, but if you can get them a statement of response in a half an hour, they may use it on the air. The problem is the CEO of the hospital is on the other coast, one attorney involved is in Denver and the other in San Francisco. The attorney's reaction, of course, is to say nothing. But you press and get agreement to work out a statement that the attorneys can live with and the CEO will approve. But how? Email? Much better than letter. Fax?

With four or five different people involved, all making changes to your document? LAN-based application? Are these outside attorneys going to have access to your LAN, even with a VPN? The best application is one that is Internet-based, allows the communication manager to provide needed passwords that control access only to the portions of the application needed and one that allows real-time drafting, editing and distribution.

In this case, the company involved did have access to that kind of technology. Three different attorneys, the CEO and the communication manager all got their licks in on the document. The news producer on the other side of the continent got the response by email in 20 minutes and the statement was read on the program the next morning.

The other issue involves crisis-capable servers. There are very good reasons why companies and organizations ought to have their public communication technology including press room and incident dark sites on web servers completely separated from their regular operational servers. Most web servers today, except for companies relying on heavy traffic for e-commerce, are not capable of handling the bandwidth required for multiple millions of hits. Yet, we have shown that a great many companies and organizations are vulnerable to these kinds of hits in a major news event. The cost of upgrading can be substantial and few IT departments are willing to spend the kind of money needed for the remote possibility that they will need that kind of capacity.

At the same time, new services are being offered to share crisis capable servers across many users. Similar to insurance, these services offer multi-million hit capacity and share the cost across many at risk users. Is there a chance that a number of different companies in different industries would experience multiple crises or catastrophes on the same day? Yes, there is that possibility. But it is far more likely that each crisis occurs independently and the cost of preparing can be shared.

When using such a service, if the company's press room is hosted on such a server it will automatically take the hits in the event of a major news crisis. If not, traffic can be quickly diverted from the company's main site by using a crisis specific domain name on the initial release and all subsequent public information about the event. More and more companies are taking this approach and are setting up response oriented domain names that drive traffic to the crisis servers and away from the main business servers. Even without this, the company's main site can be protected by providing a link on the homepage that directs visitors to the incident site.

The primary obstacle to this is the IT department's requirement that any and all company sites be hosted on their own servers. Again, it's an easy pitch for the IT department to make to the executives. Why wouldn't we want that? Saves money, adds security, gives us control. Yes, and leaves the organization highly vulnerable to reputation management crises and highly vulnerable to a web service crash that will take the entire company's Internet operation down.

This situation can result in a kind of Catch-22 of rather ridiculous proportions. One high-level communication manager wanted to make use of Internet-based communication management technology for crisis management. But the large company he works for had a policy of no outside hosting of company sites. Why not put the software application on the company's servers then? Because the company's servers can only take a few thousand hits and if a crisis hit, the traffic would bring them down. OK, then why not make use of the service that hosts crisis information sites and relieve the company's servers of any hit burden? Because company policy won't allow outside hosting of company Web sites or services. This is a global company with very high risk of international level news interest.

There is good news to this particular illustration. Through the almost heroic efforts of crisis management "champions" within the organization, reason prevailed over the IT obstacles and the company has adopted virtual communication center technology on a global level. It is rapidly becoming one of the most well-prepared global giants in dealing with the challenges of instant news.

As usual, when the demands of various departments collide, it is the executive leadership that must decide. In this case, it needs to start with executive awareness of the issues and how important they are to the future prospects of the company. It is the responsibility of the communication professionals, either those inside the company or outside experts, to inform and educate the executives on what is at stake and what solutions are available. It is also their responsibility to make clear the internal obstacles that stand in the way of implementing the solutions needed to make certain the organization is fully prepared to respond.

We have identified and discussed four important elements of preparation and their related obstacles: policies, plan, people and platform or technology. The four-legged table has been set. Preparation is possible. That's the good news. The bad news: tomorrow will be different.

9.
The Role of Technology

New crisis management technology is transforming how companies and organizations manage public information. Technology created the challenging demands of the instant news world, and specifically designed technology is proving to be critical in meeting those demands.

Unalaska Island, Alaska, Dec. 11, 2004

A Malaysian ship carrying soybeans is off the Alaska coast. On Dec. 7, a report is received by the Dutch Harbor Coast Guard office that the ship has lost power and is drifting toward Unalaska Island. It is carrying nearly half a million gallons of heavy fuel oil and 21,000 gallons of diesel fuel. The Coast Guard proactively prepares to respond to a potential spill. Unfortunately, efforts to avert the grounding fail and the ship breaks apart. During the rescue, a Coast Guard helicopter carrying 10 people, including seven rescued crew members from the grounded ship, crashed on site. Six crew members were lost.

Texas City, Texas. March 23, 2005

Contractors working at the largest BP refinery were completing major maintenance activity and restarting production units. A unit was overfilled, vapor was released and the resulting explosion blew out windows seven miles from the refinery. Fifteen workers were killed and over 100 injured.

New Orleans, Louisiana, August 23, 2005

In New Orleans, Coast Guard crews began tracking the storm brewing in the Atlantic, watching as it grew to Category 5, one of the most dangerous storms on record. They prepared for the rescue work that would be needed, but also prepared to communicate with the world about the storm, its dangers, and the efforts the Coast Guard crews were making to save lives. When the storm hit the coast on August 28, the District 8 headquarters near the French Quarter in downtown New Orleans was inundated. With all their normal infrastructure gone, the performance was all the more remarkable. Within a few days, 33,520 lives had been saved, including 12,533 lives by air resources. And the Coast Guard continued to communicate without skipping a beat and despite the complete loss of their headquarters and IT resources.

What these three incidents have in common is that the communication managers responsible for keeping the public and media informed all used the same virtual communications management technology. With this technology, they were able to maintain a continual stream of proactive and interactive communications – both to internal teams as well as the media and the public. They were able to collaborate fully over the Internet with a dispersed team – allowing, for example, information officers in Washington D.C. to respond to media inquiries focused on Anchorage.

During the height of the refinery accident response, one communicator headquartered in Chicago was dispatched to the refinery in Texas. But his wife was due to have a baby any day. When he discovered that the virtual communication technology enabled him to perform his function regardless of location, he returned home for the birth of his child and continued to do his work as if he was in Texas. At the same time, members of the public, family members and others submitting inquiries to the communication team were assisted by qualified communication responders from around the country. A virtual Joint Information Center was established, increasing the speed and effectiveness of the response by tapping into a distributed team.

While local, state and federal agencies were roundly criticized for their poor response to the devastating hurricane, the Coast Guard stood alone as an exemplar not only of fast and dedicated response, but also of continuous and proactive communications. In evaluating their ability to maintain this constant stream of public information when the whole world was demanding it, and despite the total loss of IT infrastructure, the Coast Guard public affairs managers were fully functional through the the use of virtual communication center technology.

The new media environment requires that today's executives and communicators have a different picture in their heads about communicating with the public and the many stakeholder audiences. The old picture revolves around sending out press releases by broadcast fax and holding a press conference or conducting media interviews. The new picture is more like managing a control room in a highly complex industrial facility where multiple processes are occurring at the same time and everything needs to be carefully managed and controlled. Such a complex operation cannot be managed by sending runners out to check on this unit or that operation and having them report back to the office. Complex process management, in which speed is the driving element, requires all aspects to be networked together with monitors displaying real-time information about what is happening.

New communication management technology provides the means to manage the most challenging issue or crisis situations. Even a relatively small team can manage the quickly escalating demands of multiple audiences wanting immediate, direct and individualized information. This technology is entirely Internet-based, providing universal access but is highly secure and controlled with multiple levels of user access. The most important advantage of using the new breed of communication management technology is that it puts the full potential of the Internet as a communication tool in the hands of executives and communicators and removes control from technicians, web programmers and Information Technology managers who understand technology but don't understand the communication demands of the instant news world. You might note that in the scenario described above, not a single programmer or technician was part of the information team and there was no delay or additional steps required to make use of any aspect of the Internet.

The term communication management must be distinguished from the now commonly-used term "content management." There is a critical difference. Content management is focused on allowing a group of users with password access to jointly manage and control content on a Web site or Web sites. Communication management incorporates the content management function but goes considerably beyond it. Content management is aimed at "pull" communications where viewers come to your Web site when they want and view or download information that they are seeking. Communication management incorporates interactive communication and "push" communications. Interactive involves the give and take, input and response, of most human communication. "Push" means directing the information to specific individual users via email or other more traditional means such as fax, telephone or snail mail.

The many tasks to be managed by the communication team can all be supported by currently available technology. We'll break these tasks into various elements, understanding that in an instant news event, they flow seamlessly and simultaneously together.

Information Development

If we look at the task of the communicator as getting the right information to the right people, right now, the first job is the right information. Information development involves collecting the facts, data, comments, images and all other elements needed. Then drafting those elements into an appropriate form such as a press release, backgrounder, fact sheet, or other type of document. Normally, the draft needs to go through a review process and the more important it is in terms of the company's or organization's reputation and credibility, the more thoroughly it may be reviewed. The editing process may put it through many hands and eyes with a variety of people marking changes. It is not uncommon for people outside the organization such as attorneys, or consultants, or communication professionals to be consulted or to actively participate in this process. Finally, it must be approved. A communication manager may have approval authority over most such documents but when the company's present and future rests on what is said, the CEO or other top executive may be the final approval authority. In a crisis situation, this is most frequently the case and if the Incident Command System is implemented, nothing can go out without the approval of Unified Command.

All this can work relatively smoothly using the common computer and Internet tools used today such as word processing software and email programs. Documents are stored on network servers, outsiders participate via email and their changes are incorporated back into the drafts on the server. But, the problem with the normal way is the need for speed. In a crisis situation, the normal way of doing things is almost always too slow. The instant news environment and the expectations of Internet users require a process that takes just minutes rather than days or hours. The urgency of getting it out is matched by the urgency of getting it right because no other release or document may be more important to the viability of the organization than the first few releases going out after a major event has occurred. Equally important is the development and distribution of information inside the organization to employees, managers, and families.

The only viable solution today is to place the process on an Internet platform. Document and information development needs to be able to be accomplished completely on a common desktop made possible by the Internet. Team members can participate regardless of location providing they have password access. Current technology provides for virtual communication centers specifically designed for this purpose. Drafters can create new documents in advanced html editing tools that present a Word-like functionality. These same advanced editors provide users used to common word processing software the tools to place images, design pages and fully control how they want the information to look.

Images and files can be uploaded for placement in documents or on a public Web site simply be clicking a browse button and browsing for the file on a desktop or network server. Each person with appropriate password access who signs into the password secured management center can then see which drafts are available for editing and see what changes to earlier drafts have been made by other editors. Designated "approvers" are established by the control center administrator and only they have the approval buttons on their screens allowing them to move the document forward to posting onto the public site or automatic distribution via email, fax or telephone.

The very significant dilemma, of speed vs. accuracy, can only be effectively resolved by having a team prepared to work together instantly, and by providing a platform that makes that possible. Having document creation, editing and approving on a universally available but highly secured communication management center is the only practical solution for this problem. It has proven its worth in numerous crisis situations, demonstrating that it is possible to resolve this difficult dilemma.

In addition to providing an Internet platform for document creation, more companies and organizations are also preparing for the demands of the instant news world by preparing incident "dark" sites. Dark sites are fully prepared Web sites that are not available to the public but can be made available in very short order and when launched provide the information that the public and the media are looking for about the event. These sites are exceptionally helpful in getting a fast start in providing information and are one important opportunity to get ahead of the information curve.

However, most of these sites are built with common static html technology, which means they are dependent on technicians or programmers to keep them updated as the event unfolds. This may not be a problem for an event that has no changing information, but such events are quite unlikely. By building dark sites on a fully dynamic communication management platform the company has a better chance of staying ahead of the curve. Drafting, editing and approving information online is one critical element as is the ability to instantly post existing digital documents without needing technical assistance. The option, of course, is to have an exceptionally efficient and responsive web team able to keep up on a 24/7 basis for an indefinite period of time. The cost and inefficiency of this suggests the technology platform is a more suitable solution.

Information Distribution

Information distribution remains one of the most challenging aspects of high-speed communications. Many professional communicators rely on their email program such as Outlook to manage media contacts and in the event of a crisis will email releases from their desktop, faxing the ones that may not have email addresses. Others rely on outside news distribution services for all distribution of releases. These solutions represent significant problems in the event of a crisis event.

Crises simply refuse to occur during business hours when you are sitting behind your desk looking for something to do. If you are away from your office, getting access to your contact list may be a problem that delays the release of information from minutes to hours or even longer. As we have discussed, these delays can be very consequential. Additionally, in a crisis event, many of the reporters and other non-reporters seeking information (such as a US Senator or local state representative) may not be in your database of contacts. A large number of names, phone numbers, email addresses, fax numbers, etc., will need to be added. The new additions need to be kept in a place where multiple members of the team can access them. Using an outside service invariably means that while the service will distribute to their previously developed lists, the important names you collect during the event will need to be managed independently.

If you take the reasonable approach that these pre-developed contact names and the ones captured during the crisis should reside on a server within your LAN, you still have the very real issue of the access of team members to the LAN. Will they always be in a position to access that critical data? And, unless you have developed a means of capturing names off the public site and automatically having your LAN-based database updated, there is an important manual step that must be included in your planning and execution.

The rather obvious solution to this, just as in the document creation issue, is to put the contact database on an Internet platform. The contact database available to all team members via password access enables any team member anywhere, anytime to get at the contact names. When integrated with other Internet-based communication management functions such as Inquiry Management and automated distribution, the data management element becomes much more manageable and more importantly, contributes to the speed of response.

Standard data management capabilities need to be available if the data resides on the Internet. Communicators without technical skills beyond that required by basic word processing software need to be able to sort, find, organize and set up sub-lists of all kinds within databases. The data management system should also be able to easily accommodate not just media, but all potential stakeholders and audiences who may seek information including shareholders, employees, executives, neighbors, elected officials, etc. In other words, the data fields need to be flexible to handle the different types of data you may want to collect on each of these types. This is one critical difference between a system such as this and the many news wire services that a great many communicators use. To use only a media list and not an integrated list including all key stakeholders is strong evidence of someone operating in the media world of the past and not the instant news post-media world. Managing these contacts must be simple enough so that communicators can "slice and dice" the data on the fly without requiring an Access programmer or technical help that may not be available at 3:30 a.m. when you are trying to prepare and distribute information while on vacation in Bora Bora.

With both document preparation and data management available on the same password secured Internet center, the real power of the Internet as a communication tool becomes accessible. The Internet is the best platform for getting the right information out quickly to the right people. Current technology allows you to take the press release you created and approved online and distribute this instantly to databases of reporters and stakeholders managed within the same control center. A click of the button and the document is simultaneously posted to the public Web site and instantly emailed to the mailing lists you select. It is a simple one step process.

Faxing is accomplished in the same way. Currently available technology enables you to automatically fax the same document to any name you select that does not have an email address attached to it; or if you prefer for safety sake, you can both email and fax to each name on the list.

A third automated distribution option is also available: text-to-voice conversion and automatic telephone messaging. Voice engines take written documents prepared within the communications center and when approved, convert the words to synthesized voice in one of several languages. The phone numbers on the list are dialed and when answered either by person or answering machine, the system delivers the text message in a remarkably human-like voice. Voice options include male or female with even regional accents as options. Calls are made at a rate of thousands per hour.

The implications of this kind of currently available technology are quite significant. Fence-line neighbors for example want and have a right to know about activities within the plant that may affect their safety, security and peace of mind. The telephone notification system makes it possible for a communicator to quickly type up a message and distribute via mass telephone calls to the neighbors surrounding a plant. That message or a modified version can simultaneously be emailed, faxed or telephoned to reporters or anyone else needing the information immediately. In an earlier chapter we discussed how expectations and demands for information change when it is understood that technology makes needed information available. What becomes possible becomes demanded à la FedEx. The common sense reality of this situation means that every company and organization now needs to become aware of the technologies others are using to see what standards are being set and how that is adjusting the expectations of their audiences.

Interactivity & Response

The two-way nature of communication is often given lip service but not seriously addressed. Admittedly, most of the focus in this book has been on quickly getting messages out to specific people and audiences. However, the ability to listen is also greatly improving with technology and there is much evidence that, similar to the demand for information, the individual's demand to be heard also corresponds to their realization that the technology exists to facilitate listening. The surprising popularity of radio talk shows is one example of how in this media saturated environment, people are longing to be heard.

At the most basic level, a communication system today must allow interested people to register their interest. The easier and more inviting the better. A Web site that has no contact button or no email address to send questions or comments to, or does not encourage response is a Web site that subtly communicates "we don't care much about you." If a system is used that places the contact databases on a Web platform, it is a very easy step to have dynamic and automatic database development from the public Web site. This is done increasingly and helps eliminate a lot of double entry of names; more importantly, it helps communicate that you are eager to communicate with them. When this technology is used, visitors to a public site are encouraged to register themselves and those names are automatically added to the database managed within the Internet-based communication management system.

A second level of interactivity is to facilitate questions, comments and inquiries. A government agency found itself in the middle of a sizeable public controversy. It offered an 800 number for citizens to register their complaints or comments. I asked how those calls coming in were managed. I was told, somewhat sheepishly, that they were gathered on an answering machine and that the answering machine could handle 60 calls. I asked how many calls they had received. 1,400. When the machine had filled, they erased the calls and reset it to receive the next 60. No doubt, if the public calling in had an inkling that this is how their efforts to communicate to their government were being handled, their anger would have increased.

Since we live in a mixed media world, inquiries and comments can and do come from a variety of different media: telephone, fax, email and even by mail once in a while. Email is now the most important means of interaction, but it also represents significant management issues. By 2001, Congress was already receiving over 80 million email messages and the burden of those emails simply was beyond managing. Personal experience in attempting to contact federal level elected officials confirms that while they may have the automated response down, they do not yet have the ability to manage the email messages they receive. This same problem will plague any company or organization finding itself in the news.

While some email management technologies currently exist and no doubt will emerge to help address this significant problem, one of the best ways to manage inquiries today is to incorporate them into the communication management system. This is done by providing an inquiry function on the public Web site so those inquiries are managed on the team communication management center. Aside from the technology, which is becoming increasingly common, reporters and members of the public or other key audiences must be directed and encouraged to use the inquiry management system available on the public site. A public site inquiry form will ask the person inquiring to indicate if he or she is a member of the media or a member of another identified audience group such as elected officials. It will also provide a convenient form for indicating the topic, the specific question, the time the response is needed, what company, media, or organization the individual is with and other pertinent information that will help build a valuable inquiry history.

An inquiry that lands on a private communication team site without some notification is trouble. What if no one checks the inquiry list? Current technology alerts the communication team or designated members that an inquiry has been registered. As a user of such technology, I receive an alert on my text pager whenever inquiries land on certain client communication sites that I am managing.

A third level of interactivity is more directive listening. Questions can be directed to public site viewers or can be sent directly to specific individuals via email. Current technology facilitates this by providing simple survey building tools and the function of providing a viewer survey or poll on the public site, with the results monitored and analyzed on the private communication management center. Communication managers can select whether to share results with the public on a real-time basis or keep all results private. This technology also enables surveys to be "pushed" or published to lists managed within the system. Examples of this include use by government agencies or elected officials to get snapshot views of public reaction to new proposals or controversies and by companies to gauge public reaction to new initiatives, proposed actions, or even just to get a sense of how they are doing in communicating to key audiences.

Interactivity also includes tracking what the reporters write or present. There are many technologies currently available for media tracking from a variety of vendors, both as packaged software and as hosted Internet applications (sometimes called ASP's or Application Service Providers). Integrating these into a comprehensive communication management system has not yet been accomplished. However, current technology does facilitate linking articles and reports to the specific inquiries and responses provided to reporters, so the basis exists for a more comprehensive media tracking system.

Inquiry Management

Inquiry management can make or break a communication effort. Earlier we quoted a frustrated communicator who spent two solid days responding to reporters but the company was criticized in the news accounts for being unresponsive simply because the stretched communication team couldn't get back to everyone in a timely manner. We also conveyed the disturbing story of neighbors near a plant that had experienced an explosion and fire emailing the company to find out if they should evacuate only to have their emails answered two weeks later. The best of communication efforts will fail in the minds of those people who have asked a question and not received a response.

Technology has a very important role to play here, as does training and communication policies and plans. Technology can provide the means to collect, organize, track, and report on inquiries. Technology can facilitate getting the appropriate responses to the right people and also help a communication manager or company executive monitor the effectiveness of the response in real-time or in detailed reporting after the crisis has passed.

With the communication management technology now available, inquiries are captured from the public site as well as captured by members of the communication team recording telephone calls or email inquiries and adding them to the inquiry list maintained inside the private team site. By having all inquiries recorded and available on this site, all team members can work in concert to manage inquiries even if it is 2 a.m. and they are scattered around the globe on vacations or business trips. An effective inquiry management system will show which inquiries have been completed and which ones have not. It will also allow a communication manager to act as a sort of air traffic controller and direct specific inquiries to the most appropriate member of the team. It will enable each member of the team to see who is working on each inquiry, and whether they have responded and how they have responded. It will also allow a communication manager to view all inquiry activity to determine the nature of the questions, to see if rumors are arising, and to evaluate both the speediness and effectiveness of the responses. The system will also enable the communicators to write the responses, forwarded the drafts to others for review, and send directly from the system via email to the reporter or inquirer without having to exit the system.

In a large organization, such as a global manufacturing company, the communication team may be responsible for handling inquiries on a wide variety of issues from around the globe. Reporters are known to develop direct contacts with several of the members of the team and go from team member to team member, asking the same question. The problem for the communication team is the risk of inconsistent answers as well as the fact that multiple team members are spending time on the same question. The only way to improve efficiency, quality and consistency of response is to have communication management technology that allows every team member to share the information in real time. Today, that reality essentially forces the technology onto the Internet because of its accessibility; it also requires that the communication system be highly secure.

Another advantage of this available technology is record keeping. Where drills are required by law, such as in the oil industry, the documentation of drills can be very significant. In drills where this technology was used, the complete record of all communication activities including all inquiries and their responses was prepared simply by requesting a report from the system. The resulting printout recorded the full communication activity during the drill including all details on each inquiry and their responses. Even more so than in a drill, such automated record keeping can be invaluable as part of a debrief after a crisis event and can supply the highly useful training material for the communication team to better prepare for the next event.

Web site Control

The Internet is arguably one of the most powerful and flexible communication tools created. Yet, for most communicators that power remains largely leashed. With the current content and communication management systems available it is quite surprising that more communicators and communication managers are not rising up in protest against the restrictions that artificially limit their ability to make use of this vitally important tool. To gain control of the Internet means more than being able to fully and completely manage the content of public Web sites. But that is a basic starting point that the vast majority of communication managers have yet to get to. The company's public site is one of the most important faces the company puts forward in a time of crisis. To be forced to go through even one layer of personnel or policy to control that site, let alone multiple layers as is now quite common, makes the web a tool with limited usefulness to the communicator when it is needed most.

With the many options for commanding web content available today, there is no policy or security reason that should prohibit the communicators from taking command of the content. It should be clear when I say taking command that I mean being able to fully control including changing or adding content without requiring the involvement of any technical resource, even if the communicator is only able to perform the most basic of word processing functions. Today's Web content management technology allows this. The question is whether or not the company will allow it. That is a matter of understanding the critical role the Web will play in a crisis.

This role is better understood when executives understand how a reporter reacts to initial information about a story. The first and natural reaction now is to hit the organization's Web site. It is the fastest, most convenient source of basic information about the company including location, what it produces, numbers of employees, size, etc. Knowing that this is the behavior pattern of reporters will lead forward-thinking executives and communicators to realize that the telling of the story that is unfolding can be best facilitated through the company's public Web site.

That is not to say that the public site used by the company for general information or for conducting their routine business ought to be used in crisis communications situations. There are two good reasons why a separate information site should be used. One, is to avoid the dual problem of obliviousness and over reaction. And the other is to take the burden of public information traffic off the normal business infrastructure.

Let's say you are a food manufacturer and you have a serious problem with a batch of product requiring a public recall. When the news breaks the reporters will hit your Web site as will a great many customers or consumers who may be looking for details about which products have been recalled. What will they find? Business as usual? Nice statements about how long you've been in business and your long-standing reputation for safety and quality? That's obliviousness. It communicates a powerful message that the company just doesn't really get it. People directly and significantly affected by the incident can respond very negatively to this obliviousness and it is natural for reporters to interpret this as a lack of concern about the seriousness of the incident. On the other hand, if the Web site is totally subsumed by huge warning messages and all other information is lost in the information about this one particular product, the damage to ongoing business may be much greater than necessary. I went to one well-known national food manufacturer's Web site without knowing anything about a product recall. The site was completely dominated by safety warnings and the product recall information. If I had been a customer looking for some basic information, it would have seriously given me pause.

A related problem is the issue of traffic. In a major public news crisis there is a real potential for heavy traffic, as we have already discussed. Most companies' public sites are not designed for crisis communication traffic. A site that works well managing hundreds of thousands of hits will likely crash under the burden of millions. Even if it remains operational, significant slowing will result in viewer frustration and the use of other means to communicate, such as picking up the phone. Then, one of the most important and efficient tools will have gone silent both for ongoing business as well as communicating about the rapidly evolving crisis.

The solution to both of these is to have crisis communications managed on a separate site hosted on crisis-capable servers. This is the direction more companies are taking despite having to work through very serious obstacles raised by many IT departments. IT departments face the uncomfortable dilemma of having to commit precious and limited budget dollars to building crisis server capabilities or alter their policies to allow outside services to host these special purpose Web sites.

Having a separate site on separate servers manage the public communication provides the opportunity to divert traffic from the public site for both appearance and infrastructure benefits. An objection may be raised that people will go to the public site anyway and therefore you don't avoid the hits by having a separate site. The answer to that is when the initial information is submitted, it needs to include a URL or Web address specifically for the public information site. An increasing number of organizations are securing domain names to be used in the event of a major crisis event. For example, XYZP Consulting Services may have a regular domain name of www.xyzpconsulting.com and set up a domain name such as www.news.xyzpconsulting.com or even a simple www.xyzpresponds.com. Those receiving the initial information will know which site to go to; those who haven't – the majority – will go to the main company site looking for information. A link on that site directing them to the specific incident site needs to be clear, unmistakable, but it need not dominate the site nor significantly detract from the company's ongoing operations. Two problems are thus solved – the organization is seen as neither oblivious nor over-reactionary, and the Internet infrastructure of the business is protected.

The topic of incident "dark" sites was mentioned earlier. These sites are prepared in advance specifically for this purpose, and if built on the kind of Internet-based communication management platform described in this chapter, not only fulfill the public Web site function but offer fully integrated communication management. But, to meet the "now is too late" instant news demands, these sites need to be able to be launched by an executive or communication manager anytime, anywhere. To activate a Web team or to get the IT staff moving in the middle of the night to activate a Web site is neither kind, practical or necessary. Today's technology provides for launching such sites at the touch of a button by authorized staff with the appropriate passwords.

This ability to launch new and specific purpose Web sites is one important element of taking control of the Internet. Today's well-appointed press rooms have all the functional capabilities described in this chapter. They are fully loaded with background information about the company; releases can be drafted, edited, approved and posted online by clicking the right buttons. Information prepared in the press room can be instantly distributed to infinitely flexible contact lists via email, fax or even telephone. Databases of contacts are built at least in part automatically by viewers registering on the public Web site and inquiries are recorded and fully managed within the system. Now a crisis hits.

As an example, we'll say it is a legal issue involving a top-level executive. The story is not going to go away. No incident or dark site has been prepared for this particular eventuality. The communication manager launches a new site based on the existing press room site. She selects all the existing information to be transferred and all the existing databases. The new site is then built and launched with the selected information transferred automatically. Now, the horde of new reporters and other audience members who register on this incident specific site are captured in that database and do not taint the original press room database. Information specific to that incident is created, approved and posted to that public site. Team members such as attorneys who need access to that site are also given access to the inside of the press room site. The incident's communication activities can be managed and controlled much easier through a specific site dedicated to that incident. The ability to launch, transfer data, and independently manage this separate but related site and control center is a key part of today's communication management technology and is being effectively used by a number of companies, agencies and organizations.

Group Communication

Web sites are not just effective for public communication. Group communication or semi-public sites are growing in popularity. Communicators may wish to use Web browsers and Web sites to communicate with specific individuals or groups while keeping the public out. Some public relations managers wish to keep media communication from the public (although in my mind the policy is questionable since knowing the information is also available to the public helps reporters treat the information carefully.) Group Web sites are appropriate for associations or for private communities, or for internal communication. Communicators need to not only be able to launch and fully and completely control the content of all of these sites without technical assistance, they need to be able to determine whether or not they want these sites to be public, private or semi-public. The communication management technology available does allow communication managers with the highest levels of security to determine if each site they control is to be public, available to a limited group, or kept private to authorized users only. They can also designate certain data in a public site for access by authorized persons only.

Internal Communication

One of the most discussed items coming out of major disaster events such as Sept. 11 and Hurricane Katrina was the need for effective internal communication. Many became very concerned about what systems and policies were in place to inform employees within the organization about what was going on, provide instructions on what actions to take and locate employees to make certain they were safe. Even minor events such as the Nisqually earthquake in Puget Sound of February 2001 demonstrated the cellular phone system is easily maxed out. In the first hour after that event you were quite fortunate if you were able to check on family or friends by either landline or wireless phone. Yet, the Internet remained very much intact. Company officials from the rest of the country resorted to email and internal Internet communication such as through the communication management system to ascertain condition of employees and operation of the facilities in the area impacted by the quake.

The communication management technology described in this chapter is used for business continuity as well as public information. One leading national firm installed the virtual communication center technology as a backup system to be able to maintain contacts with literally thousands of offices and agents around the country in case of catastrophic failure of its headquarters IT technology. The headquarters was located in Chicago and within months of establishing the backup technology, the entire mid-west region experienced a large scale blackout that took out the servers and standard communication systems. With the virtual communications center technology, the company was able to continue serving customers throughout the nation without skipping a beat.

Internet technology needs to be part of the comprehensive plan for employee and leadership communication in case of large-scale internal or external crises. The Internet-based communication management system described here can play a key role because of the ability to launch new sites on the fly and the ability to control access to any site. An internal only site can be launched to keep employees informed and a different site can be launched exclusively for the management team. One user of such a system uses a site specifically for employee information related to weather conditions. During bad weather episodes, employees can check the site to determine if there are changes in work locations, work hours or if they are just to stay home. Of course, they need not check the site for the information because the same information can be instantly pushed to them via email and telephone.

It is becoming common practice with users of such systems during drills and actual events to establish secured documents on the private site for executives only. Different security levels can control who can see which document which means that Incident Status Reports containing raw information not yet confirmed can record events as they unfold. Images such as helicopter overflights or photos or videos of the activities can be loaded and retained for internal use only. As executive leadership is increasingly dispersed in this global economy, making use of these communication tools simply to provide management with the information needed to make fast and effective decisions is extremely important.

A user of the technology described here is the communication manager for a global oil company. A large tanker carrying gasoline ran aground in a sensitive environmental area on the East Coast. It occurred after work hours at night and the communication manager launched a site using a prepared incident dark site from his computer in a spare bedroom. Built within that system was a database of more than 1,800 reporters. He used a template to complete an initial statement release that described the grounding and what was being done. The information site used a special incident response domain name that was registered in advance for just such eventualities. Company executives in London were able to view this site from their homes or offices and keep up with the very latest information. A widespread release was never sent because the tanker, a new double-hulled ship, was floated off the bar at high tide and no fuel was spilled. It was a potential nightmare that ended happily. Particularly for the communication manager who demonstrated to executives in the company that he was exceedingly well prepared to manage not only communication with them, but with the entire world if needed.

User Access

References have been made to multiple levels of user access in such communication management systems. There are a couple of different business models used by suppliers of Internet-based communication tools. Many providers of Internet-based software price their service on a per month per user basis. They sell what is sometimes referred to as "seats." This limits the number of users who have access to the tools appropriate for routine day to day communication activities. A problem arises when a sizeable incident happens because at that point a number of people from the CEO or Chairman to outside contractors may be quickly pulled into the communication team. Only technology that is made available to an unlimited number of users can be effectively used in the time of a crisis. Other business models are simply not intended for crisis use and are not appropriately scalable. This is an important consideration when evaluating potential Internet-based technologies for crisis management purposes.

Because a large number of users can be provided access does not mean that you want all functions of the communication system to be accessible to all users. Certain functions such as signing in new users, assigning passwords, creating secured documents, posting information to a public site and launching whole new Web sites need to be accessible only by the highest level communication managers. These communication management systems accommodate this by providing multiple levels of access, in some cases providing grids of functions that can be assigned to specific users, in other cases assigning functions to multiple levels of access codes. A user assigned access level one, for example, may only be able to view and edit certain documents or be able to view and respond to inquiries. Where a person with access level 10 can launch new sites, assign system administrators, change basic site information, and manage other such high level uses.

Hosting

All Web sites, including the virtual communication center sites, must reside on a server somewhere. Hosting of communication management systems is an important element of the infrastructure. This issue is one of the most common reasons why communication managers who wish to implement the functionality of these advanced systems within their companies or organizations are prevented from doing so. IT policies may prohibit outside hosting and even though the software may be available for licensing on company servers, the company servers typically are not suitable for crisis communication applications and present access issues in a multi-agency response. Having a neutral site, a Switzerland of sorts, allows all appropriate agencies to come together quickly to develop unified messages.

The ability to absorb a heavy load of traffic is the essential element. Traffic really consists of the number of people attempting to get information from the site and the type of information they are viewing or downloading. One user viewing streaming video will absorb much more server and bandwidth capacity than a number of visitors viewing static pages. As an example, when the US Coast Guard rescued football hero Larry Czonka from Alaska's cold water after a fishing accident, they posted video of the rescue on their public information site using virtual communication center technology. Fortunately, the system was hosted on crisis-capable servers since the large video file took considerable bandwidth to download. It wasn't a significant issue until Sports Illustrated ran a story on the rescue including the Web link to the Coast Guard video. The thousands of readers trying to simultaneously download this compelling video would have brought most organization's servers to a grinding halt.

Companies and organizations today need to be serious about their ability to take the hits and deliver the information. IT departments and executives alike must be informed, probably by their communication managers, that in today's instant news environment in which the Internet is moving us into a post-media world, communication ability depends on servers. Whether ultimately they take the approach that they will absorb the cost themselves by building crisis-capable server capacity or decide to share costs by using outside hosting services, the decision needs to be made to provide for the potential demand.

How many hits? The heaviest load of hits on Web sites in early 2002 measured in excess of 10 million hits per day. By 2006, more than half of the US homes were equipped with broadband and the potential traffic on a high-visibility Web site has grown tremendously. The use of the Internet in the 2006 winter Olympics in Turin, Italy, provided a great case in point. With over 300 million page views, this Olympics blew past the hits during the Athens games just two years earlier. Although TV ratings for the games were down considerably, officials and sponsors concluded that exposure did not decrease – just shifted from the TV screen to the computer screen.

No company or organization with the potential to take center stage in the instant news world can leave itself unprepared to deal with the potential of millions of hits they would receive in a major incident.

Earlier we said that there were four important elements to effective communication in the instant news world: policies, plan, people and platform. The technology platform exists to enable communicators to take much greater control over the Internet than ever before. The issues come down to people, plan and policies. Are the people prepared to make use of these technologies? This question is more about willingness to change than it is about technical ability. Resistance to change and ignorance about the changes in the world around them are the biggest obstacles to implementing needed changes.

Most significantly, does the company policy encourage or prohibit the use of such technology to enhance the ability of the organization to communicate quickly and accurately? As we have seen, there are many obstacles within organizations that prevent the changes that are needed. Leadership is the key. Today's organizations need leadership that recognizes the new demands and is willing and able to push through the obstacles to put into place the policies, plans and technologies needed to protect the organization's future.

10.
Before the Crisis

For companies or organizations that have the potential for reputation damaging public issues or crises, communication strategy can be viewed in three parts: Before the Crisis, During the Crisis, and After the Crisis. This may seem a bit negative or pessimistic, but in reality it is not. If you do those things needed to best prepare your company or organization to withstand a crisis of organization-threatening scope you are doing the best possible job of routine public relations or image building.

Having significant crises in mind when constructing a corporate communication effort is one of the best ways to focus the strategy on those things that really matter. It may seem overly negative or morbid, but it can be as helpful as walking through a cemetery as you are contemplating life's decisions. A deep understanding of your mortality and the shortness of life help concentrate the mind on those things and relationships that matter the most. A deep and realistic understanding of the very real risks to an organization's reputation and relationships can help concentrate the mind on what needs to be done to protect and enhance those. It is a wonderful way to focus, see what is truly important and help make important decisions.

We know what it looks like when a crisis occurs and the company is not prepared or does not respond well. The brand value is destroyed, key employees leave in droves, recruitment is difficult, stock value hits bottom, customers defect, and others in the industry shake their heads in a sort of "there but for the grace of God go I" sense of relief, pity and bemusement.

We also know what it looks like when a company emerges from a crisis stronger than ever. Johnson & Johnson emerged as a highly respected company in the aftermath of the Tylenol scare by using a textbook case of crisis management. Haggen, a Pacific Northwest food retailer, emerged with its reputation very much intact after its aggressive, proactive stance following a Hepatitis outbreak linked to an employee. In early 2002, Alaska Airlines was reported to be the only major air carrier experiencing significant growth in a very troubled travel economy. The remarkable story here is that Alaska had been seriously criticized in the national and regional press following the January 31, 2000, crash of Flight 261 off the California coast. There were serious allegations and some genuine problems that were identified in the intense scrutiny following the crash. Yet, Alaska's reputation, while threatened and damaged to some extent, was neither destroyed nor sufficiently sullied to require re-branding or large-scale retrenchment; in fact, within two years the company has emerged as a bright spot on the travel landscape.

A case can be made that these good and bad stories coming out of crises depend entirely on the response during the crisis. But a stronger case can be made that the brand or reputation equity held by companies and organizations will have much to do with how well it emerges from a major reputation crisis. Haggen enjoys an outstanding brand reputation as a quality food retailer enjoying strong sales for a retailer with a high price position. Alaska's safety record was one of the best in the industry and matched by a reputation for quality of service that led them to advertise that their outstanding service did not equate to high prices.

A stellar reputation depends on much more than effective communication. Product and service quality must be excellent and consistent and the entire organization must operate, plan and market to maintain and build that reputation. But the communication manager or executive responsible for communications has a key role to play in making certain the operational excellence translates into desired perceptions held by customers, industry influencers, stockholder and employees.

We are going to make the not unreasonable assumption that the crisis you need to plan for will involve accusations of wrong doing in some form. Certainly not all crises involve this, but a vast majority does – even those involving accidents. Our society has evolved the notion that there are really no such things as accidents and that inevitably someone will be found to have intentionally caused the damage at worst, and at best was seriously negligent. In preparing for such a crisis, the most critical element will be credibility and, as we will see, not necessarily your credibility but the credibility of those who stand in support of you. That being the case, the most effective preparation is to focus pre-crisis communication efforts on those people whose relationship to the company is most critical now as well as those whose relationship to the company during a crisis will determine its viability.

To illustrate some of these key points, let's use a hypothetical example. One Saturday morning you wake up and pick up the morning paper and read that an acquaintance has been accused of masterminding a scheme to bilk his company out of serious money. Your immediate natural reaction is to weigh the evidence that is presented and pronounce him guilty or not guilty. What process do you use? There are three basic questions: How well do you know him, and do the accusations fit with your knowledge of him? How well do you know his accuser or accusers, and do the accusations fit with your knowledge of the accusers? Finally, what are others whom you know well and greatly respect saying about this person or the accusers?

If you know the person well and have had enough experience with him to believe that you are in a good position to judge his character, you will base most of your opinion on that personal knowledge. If your personal experience strongly contradicts the charges, a higher level of evidence is required to overcome your skepticism. Match that against your knowledge or perception of the accuser. If you also have some knowledge of the accuser and know him to be a drug-abusing, wife-beating habitual liar, it will have a serious impact on your judgment on the charges. If, on the other hand, your experience with the accused leads to you to believe that it is entirely conceivable that he would do such a thing, relatively flimsy evidence and the lack of credibility of the accuser will not likely dampen your judgment that the accusations are most likely to be true.

However, if you do not have direct personal experience or strong perceptions about either the accused or the accuser, you will likely suspend firm judgment until you have heard from others. If someone close to you, whom you know to have direct and personal experience with the person accused, and whom you know to be an honest and trustworthy person, tells you that he believes it is true then your judgment will most likely quickly go against the accused. Similarly, if the person you know and trust says the person making the accusation has a personal agenda or other reasons for making the accusations and is not to be believed, then you will likely assume innocence for the accused.

This simple parable provides a basis for exploring many of the key issues relating to communications programs aimed at positioning the organization to withstand a major reputation crisis.

It's All About Relationships

The underlying philosophy of this approach to effective external and internal communications is that business and life is all about relationships. It is not unreasonable to say that the economic value of most companies is related to the relationships they have and their ability to leverage those relationships into new ones in the future. For example, an accountant will value a company by looking at its assets and liabilities. A manufacturing company may include equipment, inventory, raw materials, cash, receivables, etc. What are all those items, particularly the manufacturing equipment, raw materials, finished goods, etc. good for? They are only valuable in the potential they offer for someone to employ them as a means of developing valuable relationships. The products and the potential to create those goods have no economic value without the willingness of people to buy them. The stronger that buyers/seller relationship is, the higher the economic value of those relationships. Loyalty, also defined as resistance to price-based competition, translates to economic value. An office full of the latest high computers and networks is of no value in itself without the ability of someone to take those tools and with people, build working relationships with others that are valued by those served.

Certainly the same is true of non-profit organizations and even government agencies. While government agencies may appear to some to have a life untouched by performance, accountability or meeting expectations, the reality is their existence depends on those who vote budgets and who approve funding requests. Non-profits live or die on the perception of those whose contributions make their existence possible. Relationships are at the heart of virtually every enterprise.

This reality makes the communicator's job easier to understand. Communication, after all, is primarily about building relationships. That may come as a surprise to some who view communication as providing information. But what is the end purpose of providing that information? In most cases it is to create, enhance or protect the relationship. Certainly this can be seen on the personal side, but it is equally true on the business or organizational side. This is frequently forgotten when there is bad news to communicate. Bad news to stockholders will result in loss of share value. The real bad news for the company is when the stockholders lose confidence and trust in management. This may be lost for performance reasons, but it is far more quickly lost when there is a perception that management is hiding information, covering up problems or in any way being less than forthright – even about bad news.

Many women instinctively understand the real nature of communication better than many men. John Gray pointed this out in his book, Men Are From Mars, Women Are From Venus. Women tend to view a conversation about a problem as relationship building. The information conveyed and the potential solutions discussed can often be secondary to the value of having discussed them and shared the problem together. Men tend to view the information content as primary and want to get quickly to the solution, viewing the value of the conversation only in terms of its problem-solving effectiveness. That women are more right about this than men is evident in the response to listening. Listening is the most powerful key to relationship building. In part because it does provide the information content needed to serve effectively. Perhaps more importantly, genuine listening demonstrates value and communicates respect in ways that cannot be replicated by anything else. Listening is unique in its power to establish and build relationships. As a result, listening ought to be at the very heart of most corporate communications programs. Unfortunately, this is frequently not the case.

If the executives of an organization view at a fundamental level that their success in leadership will be measured by the quality of the relationships of the people whose perceptions are vital to the organization, it changes in profound ways the understanding of the job. Put another way, a CEO's primary task is to enhance loyalty within the people who matter most to the organization. This concept should also change to some degree how the success of the enterprise is measured. Financial measurement is one very important indicator, but it is not the only important one. One big disadvantage is that it is all backward looking. Relationship valuation measurements are forward looking. Current relationships are the best predictor of future performance. The ability of the organization to develop and strengthen relationships and leverage strong existing ones into powerful new ones is perhaps the most critical factor in evaluating the future prospects for an organization. In this view, the role of communications manager becomes highly strategic. The Chief Communication Officer ought to be, and in some cases is, the executive with overall responsibility for translating the organization's operations, administration and all other elements into strong, long lasting relationships and leverage those into the appropriate new ones.

That job may seem overwhelming until it is understood that for the vast majority of companies and organizations, their business depends not on relationships with millions but with a relatively small number of people who are critically important to the organization. In our consulting business we have come to call these "the right few." Much to my surprise, when I began focusing on this element of business success, I discovered by accident that there was an exceptional concentration of strategic relationships in most business. Business volume can normally be traced to a very low percentage of key customer or key customer referral relationships. While we used to talk about the 80/20 rule, in reality it is more concentrated than that so we could reasonably talk about the 90/10 rule or even the 95/5 rule. But this doesn't just apply to customer or external relationships. When I have asked the question, "How many people does your business truly depend on so that if you were to lose those it would cause serious risk to your business?" I discovered a very common answer: from five to seven. This was true of businesses doing volume in the hundreds of millions as well as one-person businesses.

Whether this formula applies to your business or organization is not really the point here. What is important is that if you do a careful evaluation of the people whose positive perception of your enterprise is vital to your future, you will almost certainly find that those people are both fewer than you thought and more significant to you than you thought. Clearly, if those people are the right few, it becomes critical for the communication manager and the top leadership to focus on what can be done to strengthen, improve and leverage off those important relationships.

Building Reputation Equity

In the example presented above about the accused swindler, it is clear that the judgment of those reading about the accusations will be based primarily on their experience. This is the key to building reputation equity. An organization with strong reputation equity has put positive perceptions "in the bank" that can be drawn on at those times when the credibility and reputation is being questioned. The more equity in the bank, the better able the organization is to withstand serious accusations and even serious wrongdoing. But it is not just a general, positive perception that matters most. The most important element of this effort is the direct, personal experience of the relatively few people on whom the company's credibility will rest at the time of crisis.

The most important people are those whose opinions about the company matter to those who matter to the company. In other words, people who have strong influence on those individuals whose opinion about you is important. It is simply not possible to have direct and personal relationships with everyone whom you wish to think positively about the company. But, for those people who may be neutral on your character and therefore don't have a basis for making a judgment on the accusations they read in the paper or hear on the news or read on an Internet page, the most important basis for making a judgment is the opinion of those they respect.

This phenomenon is what makes celebrity endorsements so powerful in advertising. The public tends to believe that they know celebrities personally. Witness the general grief when a well-known person such as Princess Diana or John F. Kennedy Jr. dies tragically. These celebrities are also accepted and respected and therefore their opinions carry weight. Certainly, there are exceptions to this respect idea; for example heavyweight boxer Mike Tyson may have been respected for his boxing skills but his incredibly poor behavior has diminished his respect to the point where his opinions on matters of ethics or behavior would bring amused laughter rather than respect. The "borrowed credibility" of celebrities is sufficiently powerful to even overcome the public's natural skepticism about paid opinions. The public seems willing to suspend their disbelief about people such as Michael Jordan and Paul Harvey, preferring to believe they would not represent a product they couldn't endorse no matter how many millions were offered to them.

This is not to suggest for a moment that public relations managers for pulp and paper mills or micro-processor plants using toxic materials need to go out and find a sports celebrity to say good things about them. What they need to do is to figure out who the people who do not know the company well will turn to for an opinion on the crisis and the accusations. As an example, let's say the mayor of a smallish community is well liked and respected, serving her third term. The natural gas supplier encounters a serious problem with gas delivery during the height of a winter storm and long time critics are complaining the executives are incompetent, or worse, they are cutting costs to preserve their profits at the risk of poor people freezing in their homes. If the gas company has a strong reputation and is well respected among its customers and throughout the community, it can quite easily withstand those kinds of attacks. If not, judgment will rest with those whose opinion counts in the minds of the public. If the well-respected mayor stands up and says, "I have worked with Nelson Blothmore, the CEO of Blothmore Gas for many years and I know that he is doing everything he can to meet the needs of these people," that opinion will carry weight. At that point in time, the mayor is perhaps the most strategic relationship for the future of the company.

Building reputation equity, the essential task of the communication team in the pre-crisis mode, depends on identifying the strategic relationships, the right few, and focusing communication and relationship building efforts at them. Every situation is clearly different. But, every communication situation involves the process of identifying the right few and focusing efforts where they will create the most significant results. Strategic relationships are ripples in a still pond. The right few have enormous influence.

Flying Under the Radar

In the past 15 to 20 years, the public information and news environment has changed significantly, as we have already discussed. Environmentalism, consumerism, public health activism and activism of all sorts have become the most potent forces for change in our society. This is true not because of some vast conspiracy but because both activists and the media have noted that people care about these issues. This environment of political and media activism and heightened public concern, has led many companies with activities that have potential environmental or public health or safety to concerns to adopt a stealth strategy wherever possible. When talking to a number of executives about their community relations efforts the most common explanation I have heard for why there is reluctance to put relationship development programs in place is that "we prefer to fly under the radar."

This is an entirely reasonable concern. To actively promote the fact that you want to place a fuel pipeline through a community, or run new 230,000 volt power lines through local farmland, or that you want to build a high tech plant that uses no less than 20 materials considered toxic by the federal government and that could cause serious problems in a worst-case scenario, is risking attention and opposition not desired or needed. However, there is a big difference between going out and asking for attention on these issues to putting in place an appropriate corporate or community relations communication program.

In a situation repeated many times, one company sought a state permit on a quiet basis. By doing everything to meet the permit requirements they had every reason to believe they would receive the permit. They didn't count on the politics of it. Rabid opposition mounted, quietly at first but suddenly in a burst of zeal and misinformation that built huge momentum over a year's period of time. The activists' intentional emotional characterizations of the issue and their supposed evidence of extreme public risk played well to the media's need for a good story with white hats and black hats. The strongly negative media coverage blossomed quickly into rapidly escalating public opposition. The permit was denied by a body specifically put in place to prevent NIMBYism (Not-in-my backyard), and not on the basis of failure to meet conditions, but with squishy words that clearly revealed the political nature of the decision. The company reapplied but now with huge political opposition and an understanding of the potency of activism and media support for activism. While opposition could not have been prevented, if the company had been prepared with solid if quiet community leader support, if it had been prepared to counter the rapidly rising accusations, and if it had laid the groundwork to gain solid public support, the story would be different. All those things happened, but under the extremely trying conditions of vociferous and effective opposition, which makes the support-building task infinitely more difficult.

The company did not need to fly above the radar to prepare. But it did need to prepare, primarily by quiet and judicious relationship building with the right few strategic individuals. It also needed to prepare by being more equipped to counter the opposition in the public with effective presentation of the facts and effective countering of the misinformation.

Goal Setting & Measurements

Communication efforts are very measurable, and need to be measured. That may come as a surprise to many executives and perhaps a few communication professionals. There is some comfort in operating in an environment without accountability. But that environment also has serious risks. As a communications professional, I want the leaders I am serving to have a clear idea of what their investment will produce in terms of results. I want to know what "winning" is from their perspective. If an effort or campaign or project is completed and I consider it highly successful but the executive doesn't it has to be because we did not start with an agreed-upon clear and concise definition of winning. Communication managers (or for that matter, all professionals) who work toward ill-defined or undefined results are taking serious risks with their reputations.

We discussed communication goal setting in a previous chapter. Building high value relationships is the goal of most organizations and is also the goal of most communication efforts. A general goal states what winning is, such as: "We want to be able to emerge from a serious crisis with our reputation for credibility enhanced and able to continue and grow our business." Beyond that, measurable objectives need to be put in place. What does it mean to emerge with reputation intact? Ability to move forward can be measured objectively in business sales or profitability, but what about the relationships?

Perception measurement is an essential element of practically any communication effort. Since we are talking about focusing on the right few, we are not necessarily referring to large scale, scientifically accurate perception surveys. These have their place but typically not in the kind of relationship-oriented reputation equity effort we are discussing here. People answering questions posed by zombie-sounding college students with minimal training and where it is obvious they are simply filling in a form to be entered into a computer do not consider this nor treat the experience as real listening. Typically, such surveys have neither the benefit of providing valuable relationship information nor the benefit of communicating to those participating that they are valued. Objective perception measurement is much more effectively done by focusing the questions on the right few and doing the interviewing in person or, if personally isn't convenient or cost-effective, by a conversation-style telephone interview.

Goal setting is not just about perception evaluations. In specific campaigns, setting specific objective goals can be very helpful. In the situation described earlier in this chapter where the industrial firm found itself with strong opposition in gaining a facility permit, specific goals were set to gain community support. Those goals included the number of letters written by community leaders to the governor of the state, the number of cards indicating support sent to the state committee, the number of prominent community groups providing public endorsement. The goals even included the numbers of people speaking at upcoming public hearings including a diminishing number of people speaking in opposition to the project. This was important because a considerable effort was expended at dispelling misinformation with a primary purpose of countering the efforts of activists to secure passionate opposition through emotional accusations and misinformation. Those goals were also important because a public permitting process is unpredictable. It was important to establish objective goals in addition to the overall definition of winning which was to secure the permit. Failing to secure the permit would constitute failure of the effort, but by meeting all the objective support-building and opposition-diminishing goals, at least a moral victory could be gained by achieving those goals. With them, there was great clarity of strategy and purpose between the communication team and the organization's leaders.

Strategic Relationship Development

The natural inclination of many in public relations when the go-ahead has been given to build public support is to mount an advertising campaign. This natural tendency is one reason why executives tend to be leery of giving the green light to the communication team to attempt to build support. A highly public campaign can have potentially negative effects such as heightening opposition, opening the organization to accusations of using "slick, Madison Avenue techniques" to gain government approval, and highlighting issues that may otherwise remain dormant. There are definitely circumstances when a public effort involving paid advertising is advisable and even necessary, but it should always be seen as a support method to the fundamental task of building reputation equity, which is strategic relationship development.

The first step is to identify the who. Who are the people whose perceptions are vital to the current business and future health of the organization? Who are those people with whom you ought to have strong relationships, but do not? On a global corporate level these people are going to include high-level elected officials from many countries. They will include major customers, customer referral sources, key industry reporters, key stockholders, executives, industry influencers, labor leaders, policy makers, regulators, etc. On a local level, strategic relationships may include neighbors, local elected officials, local reporters, major customers, owners, key employees, consultants, etc. Whether global or local, the basic principle remains the same: a relatively few people carry the present and future value of the organization around in the perceptions they hold about the company, the benefits it offers and the perceived value of their relationship with the key people in the enterprise.

The truly strategic individuals are strategic in part because of the position they hold, but also usually in part because of their personality. Personalities come into play in how influential one person is over many others. Are they "connectors" – do they naturally put the people in contact with other key people around an issue? Are they "mavens" – people with recognized expertise that has considerable influence over others. Are they talkative and persuasive? These personality factors in addition to position held in the community or network have much to do with how influential they will be and how strategic they should be considered in the relationship building effort.

The next step is listening. As mentioned above, listening does two critically important things. It tells you what you need to know to meet the needs and expectations of those important people; more importantly, if done right it communicates that you respect and value them. Listening is the most important element of effective relationship building. However, there is a risk. Listening without response can be deadly. To create an expectation of value and of meeting needs and then to not effectively respond with communication and delivering the goods can mean the positive results gained by listening can turn to negative results in the relationship. Another way of saying it: listening and responding are both essential.

Effective listening will result in a much greater understanding of the benefits the "right few" either receive or wish to receive from the existence of the organization. Sometimes the benefits are entirely predictable. For example, employees are likely to want good pay and benefits, opportunities for growth, stability, and pride in their place of employment. Shareholders can be expected to want a competitive return on investment, but they may also seek involvement, participation, recognition, influence, etc. Sometimes, the benefits are not as obvious. In evaluating what it takes to establish a high value relationship with community leaders for a sizeable industrial facility we discovered that they wanted assurance and stability. The jobs and taxes this facility provided for the community were critical for their futures, but with frequent ownership changes they did not feel certain that the facility would be there for the long term. This valuable piece of information was extremely helpful in crafting messages that, while not promising that which could not be guaranteed, provided information that helped reassure them based on what was happening in the industry, facility performance, and insights about ownership changes.

One of the other important information items gained by the community leader research was their desire to have personal contact with plant managers. Community leaders have influence in part because they are perceived by others in the community to be "in the know." This perception is considerably enhanced when they can mention casually in conversation that they had lunch or coffee with "Mr. Smith" or happened to run into him a cocktail party and they discussed "such and such." This desire doesn't always correspond very well with a busy executive's schedule that is focused on problem solving and operational issues. However, when executives understand how important these relationships are to the present and future of the organization and how vital they can be during a reputation crisis, a small amount time can usually be set aside providing it is judiciously administered by the communication manager. In this particular case, a monthly "Coffee with the Manager" was instituted and community leaders were invited to participate by invitation. Those conversations with a group of 10 to 12 diverse community leaders provided the opportunity for continued listening as well as the opportunity to address specific concerns or issues. Nearly everyone invited eagerly attended and the comments filtering back through the community as well as the annual perception survey validated that this approach was highly successful in creating the high value relationships that were the goal. Without conducting the listening in the first place, it is highly doubtful if this strategy would have emerged or have been supported by a very busy management team.

This "Coffee Meeting" further illustrates a key point in strategic relationship building. Start with the most personal and work downward from there. In this high technology world, a premium is placed on personal and face-to-face interaction. There is great power in this in developing a strategic relationship program.

The listening processes ultimately will result in having solid information on which to build messages aimed at specific groups and individuals. Those key messages should form a consistent whole and should directly address the "What's in it for me?" question of every strategic relationship. This is the next step in the process: formulating and disseminating key messages. These messages must above all be true, they must be as personal as possible, and they must be relevant (that is, address directly the sought after benefits). How to communicate them? We have already suggested one method that is both efficient and personal meetings with groups of people who share some common interests. If personal time with managers is not feasible, as it will not be for the vast majority of those whose positive perceptions are sought, then other methods need to be chosen with a priority on those that are the most personal. For example, a letter from the CEO personally signed is considerably more personal that a beautiful four-color newsletter that addresses the same issues. A presentation at a service club is more personal than a videotape or an interview on local TV. An email directed at an individual, addressing specific concerns and inviting interaction is more personal than a Web page. Even Web sites, however, can be used in more intimate forms of communication through the use of private sites or private areas on Web sites where certain people are allowed access to non-public information.

Reporter Relationship Development

Reporters are important people, too. For most public relations practitioners, it seems silly to treat reporters as almost an after thought. They are their reason for existence. A primary theme of this book has been that in the post-media world in which direct communication is becoming more and more common, reporters become not the end all and be all of communication, but one more very important group requiring effective relationship building.

The methods for building relationships with reporters are not fundamentally different than any other group or any other person. First, prioritization. Who is most important? To whom should most effort be directed? Second, listening. What are their needs? What do they want, need and expect from you? What benefits can you offer that support important personal and career goals they may have? Finally, response. What messages are you sending, not just by what you say, but by what you do?

Reporters get to keep their jobs if they get the information needed to present to their editors and audiences and do so with the credibility and balance expected by their editors. They have the opportunity to excel and advance if they prove extraordinarily effective at capturing and presenting information – particularly unique information – of high public interest. The communication professional's job is to help them do just that. I'll put it even more strongly: as much as possible, given the absolute necessity to advance the cause of the organization for whom he or she works, the communication professional's job is to help reporters succeed.

A communication manager's job description ought to include making life easier for all reporters who seek information from them. Credibility is the major tool and major goal. The best way to damage or destroy relationships with reporters is to be disingenuous, to lie, to mislead, to break promises, to be untrustworthy. There are times in the course of normal interaction that you cannot provide information that you possess. Reporters understand that, but they also understand that it is their job to do their level best to get that information, if not from you then from others. This situation does not threaten credibility. Telling them one thing when you mean another or not showing up when you said you would meet them or suggesting that you can give them something greater than what you can – these things cause loss of credibility.

One public affairs leader for a large government agency said it was their goal to be the first and best source of information about events where they were involved. That is a highly appropriate goal for each and every communication manager for companies and organizations. You want reporters to understand that there is no faster, better, more accurate or complete information about what is going on than what they can get from you. They want to know that you will be proactive; that you can be counted on to deliver information to them rather than waiting to be asked.

This position has caused some raised eyebrows when practiced in tradition-bound organizations who normally exercise the "don't ask, don't tell" policy of public information. A small-scale event occurred at a facility. Emergency notification procedures had been activated which was standard for even minor events such as this. Because the local media were tuned to emergency radio frequencies, they would know that something was up. I opted to proactively send a short press release explaining the circumstances, what was happening, the nature of the event, the response, etc. While top management approved this decision, lower level management who saw absolutely no point in alerting the local press to something they might not even notice strongly attacked the decision. They certainly had a point. No one goes out of their way to seek out press coverage of accidents or other events that could harm a reputation. But the point I made to management was that I wanted these reporters to trust me. I wanted them to know that for any event or situation that may be considered newsworthy I would be a reliable source of fast information and that I would do everything in my power to get the information they need when they needed it. Most importantly, I wanted them to understand that when a major event happened that they could trust me to help them do their jobs while doing my job. Since this was a considerable change from the previous management of public information, the reporters were initially surprised and skeptical. But it wasn't long before the nature of the relationship between the local media and the facility began to change. In the case of the minor event where we issued a release, not a single local media saw it worthy of coverage, which I considered a victory.

In building relationships with reporters, it is helpful to understand that they have unique needs as well. Print reporters have different requirements from local TV reporters who in turn have needs different from national cable and network reporters. Trade publication reporters have different needs than general news publication reporters. Of course, reporters themselves are individuals with individual quirks, personalities, expectations and pressures. It is also true that communication managers may not always be dealing with qualified, experienced reporters. Local papers, even dailies, are training grounds for rookie reporters but as the news business continues to change, many substantial publications have reduced their staffs of experienced reporters, replacing them with lower paid reporters with much less experience. These circumstances can make the communication manager's job more difficult but also provide opportunity since the basic rule is to help the reporter do the best job they can.

Responding to Minor Events

The minor incident described above illustrates another point. The best opportunity to build relationships in the communities or networks in which your important audiences live is when a relatively minor crisis occurs.

In a previous book, Friendship Marketing, I explored the concepts of loyalty and trust in more detail. Trust is built when someone perceives that the other person in the relationship is willing to sacrifice their own interests, needs, desires, and self-centeredness for them. The opportunity to observe this most clearly is when there is a problem. Billing problems, quality problems, expectation problems all provide the opportunity for one to observe the behavior of the other. Since we all understand our intensely self-centered nature, when I demonstrate to you that I am willing to place my interests second to yours or you demonstrate that to me, trust is established. This does not mean that one should go out and cause problems with customers, or supervisors, or strategic relationships in order to build trust. But it does suggest that one should view those problems as unique opportunities to emerge with a stronger relationship. That may indeed be the meaning behind the Chinese character for crisis that simultaneously means risk and opportunity. Each crisis, particularly minor ones, should be viewed as opportunities to build relationships and reputation equity.

A minor crisis provides the opportunity to demonstrate to the strategic relationships you have identified the character and nature of the organization. Quick, effective, comprehensive, proactive, personalized and direct communication with those people about something that has gone wrong with the company or organization can communicate a tremendous amount about the trustworthiness of the organization.

Assume for a moment that you are a strategic relationship of another organization and they encounter an internal problem that may not see the light of day. But you have been made privy to the information and the company has explained what happened, why it happened, the culpability of the company in it, and what is being done to prevent future recurrences. Now assume that this same company is involved in a far more significant crisis and they are accused by reports in the press of stonewalling or covering up or outrageous malfeasance. These accusations counter your experience with the company whom you perceive to be honest, forthright and willing to confront problems directly. This is the equivalent of the example that opened this chapter where you read about an acquaintance that is accused of swindling. Your previous experience with this person will largely determine your judgment. Those minor crises provide the opportunity to establish a record of proactive communication that reveals the character, values and principles of the company or organization.

Use of Technology

So far, there has been nothing in this chapter that hasn't been applicable to the old world of slow news and media exclusivity. But we are now in a world of instant news, entering a post-media world. In this world the fundamentals don't change. Relationships are all important. Character, truth, honesty, values, virtue and principle all matter. Knowing the people who are most important to you is critical, but it has always been. Listening and responding remain the bedrock of relationship development. But, something has dramatically changed. The tools by which these tasks are accomplished have changed tremendously and with them the expectation of how people communicate and interact.

The same technology discussed in the previous chapter used to communicate rapidly and effectively in a crisis event is also being used daily as part of community and strategic relationship development programs. The demands are the same. The only thing that really changes is the extreme urgency and overwhelming multiplicity of tasks that characterize a communications crisis. But in understanding that distinction is where the power of Internet-based communication tools resides.

There is probably not a single communications department or operation in a company or organization today that does not believe the demands placed on it are greater than the resources available to meet those demands. The suggestions about thorough evaluation of all potential strategic relationships and establishment of proactive programs to communication with them were likely met with some audible groans by communication managers struggling to keep up with the demands of the media alone.

Communication management technology designed to effectively manage crises is aimed at one simple goal: doing the most with the limited resources available. There is no guarantee in a crisis that a fully qualified web team ready and able to meet your every whim will be available on a 24/7 basis. As a result, the technology described in the previous chapter requires no technical expertise, enabling even confirmed Luddites to easily manage Web content, distribute to email lists, upload and post images, and even launch entire new Web sites. Similarly, in a crisis, there is no certainty that a room full of seasoned veterans with adequate telephones, computers and faxes will be able to handle the potentially hundreds of calls from reporters and others seeking information. The technology is aimed at limiting calls by instant and proactive distribution, feeding inquiries into an inquiry management system, simplifying responses and sharing information to improve quality of response. In a real event, this kind of technology has demonstrated that much more work can be done by fewer people – exactly the point of technology in the first place.

The same productivity tools aimed at improving crisis communications can be and are effectively used in routine day-to-day communication. The primary result is that fewer people are doing more effective communication. While some in the communication profession may take this as a negative, executive leadership will welcome this increase in performance and productivity. For those who fear this change, I would remind them that a few years ago when graphic design was done with wax, X-ACTO knives and drawing boards, the computer threatened the occupation of graphic designers. "Everyone will be able to do this stuff," some complained. Yes, it has proven true. Everyone's design quality and production has been dramatically improved by desktop publishing technology. Yet, there are far, far more people employed in the graphic design profession and doing graphic design at all levels than ever before. The real skills of graphic design are in more demand than ever. However, if your communication skills are the equivalent of operating a X-ACTO knife safely, you do indeed have reason to be concerned about the new highly productive communication management technologies.

The same technology designed to help speed press releases via instant and integrated email, fax and telephone distribution is also being used to connect ever-larger groups of individuals into closer intimacy with the company or organization. The same tools designed to increase interactivity are being used to build the bonds needed for reputation equity. The same listening tools can and should be used to support the listening process of strategic relationship development. In this case, when speed is not so much the issue, productivity is. So much more can be done. As FedEx and Intel have proven, if more can be done, more will be demanded.

Reputation Equity Summary

There very well may come a time when as a CEO you need to turn to people outside your company for help in order to survive. The help may be in the form of letters addressed on your behalf to U. S. Senators, or it may be in submitting op-ed pieces to the newspapers. You may need good and respected people in your community to say to their fellow citizens that what they are reading in the paper about you isn't true. You may need key stockholders to come to your defense and you may very well need the strong loyalty of managers and employees. At that time of great need, the reputation equity you have in the bank will be worth the gold in Fort Knox. More than that, since the very life of the organization may well depend on those important friends whose trust has been cultivated in advance.

But that equity does not appear on its own. Too many executives busy with their operational issues assume that the world knows all the good things they are doing and the communities in which they operate understand the benefits of their existence. People who enjoy the benefits of your organization's existence every day do not necessarily think about it or are even consciously aware of those benefits. The taxes you pay that support the school district are largely invisible to most parents. The contributions you provide to charities and local causes impact only a few if only the organization knows about it. The benefits of good jobs and the multiplier effect in a community are forgotten by most whose lives are enriched by those benefits.

In 2001, Boeing shocked the Seattle community by announcing it was leaving Seattle. The local TV news reporters hit the streets to get public reaction. Some expressed dismay, but one young man, with sheer delight on his face said, "Great! I hope they all leave so we can have this city to ourselves." The selves he was referring to no doubt had trust funds or independent means to be unconcerned about the potential loss of thousands of jobs and the economic devastation of a city. He imagined a city filled with beautiful buildings, well-tended streets, overflowing coffee shops without the burden of major employers. To him, there was no benefit to a company like Boeing providing tens of thousands of well-paid jobs. Suffice it to say, he is not likely to become one of Boeing's, or any other major employer's, strategic relationships.

Now, we turn to the reason for all this preparation – the organization-threatening reputation crisis. With a solid base of strategic influencers loyal to the organization, with a track record of fast, direct communication with reporters and stakeholders, and with the policies, plan, team and technology in place, you are ready for the challenge.

11. What to do While it is Happening

"While it is happening" means while the white, hot glare of news cameras are on you, and you wake up each morning knowing you face more headlines in the paper. A crisis is not a singular point; it is a continuum that flows out of everything you do, and who or what you are. After the moment in the spotlight has passed, the crisis flows on, usually remaking you and redefining your future. But here we will focus on that flash of time when it seems the whole world has focused its brief attention span on you and your organization.

We will follow two different crisis events, both very loosely based on a combination of real situations and drills.

Notification

It was late on Thursday afternoon when the owner of a small public relations firm got a call from an on-again-off-again client. The client was the CEO of a fast growing chain of dermatology clinics that had established a strong reputation for leadership in a popular new form of aging treatment. Women and men were flocking to the small clinics for the laser treatment and the results in almost all cases were outstanding so that the vast majority of new patients came by referrals. Nevertheless, the company advertised heavily and the brand name was becoming well known as the leader, and also viewed as more commercial than some felt comfortable with for a medical clinic.

"We've been hit by a class action lawsuit and I need your help," Aaron, the CEO, said. Steve, the crisis management consultant called in, took some small satisfaction in this, in that he had been unable to establish a solid, ongoing public relations or crisis communications plan with this client.

"I just got a call from the producers of the 'Today Show' and Matt and Katie are interviewing two ladies and their attorney who are claiming we botched their procedure," Aaron explained.

"Is it true?" I asked.

"Yes and no," he replied. There were some problems, relatively minor problems but the ladies refused treatment to fix the problems, which could have been addressed by more treatment but instead went to an attorney. The attorney was well known for taking high profile cases and noticed an opportunity in this new procedure. He needed to build a class of victims and to do that he needed publicity. He'd been through this route before and he knew the right people to call.

"Will they allow us on the show with them?" Steve asked.

"No, but they are putting a doctor on with them who is a supposed expert in this field and who has a large but undisclosed investment in one of our competitors. Not only that, but the attorney has sent out a press release and my assistant is fielding calls right now from reporters from all over the place."

"What is she telling them?" Steve asked.

"What our lawyers told us to say, that it's a legal matter and we can't comment on pending litigation."

"Oh, boy," Steve said under his breath, or something to that effect.

"What did you say?" asked Aaron.

"Uh, never mind."

The fireball could be seen for 50 miles making it plainly visible to many residents of the nearby large city. The well-placed bomb had taken out the refinery's distribution center including the pipeline that fed avjet fuel to the nearby international airport that served the entire region. The fuel pipeline was the only source of fuel for the airport, and laws passed in the previous years had restricted fuel truck tankers so that without the pipeline, flights would have to be seriously curtailed.

The explosion was loud enough to rock the house of Mark, the refinery's assistant human resources manager and designated information officer. It was 3:30 a.m. but he jumped out of bed and stared in disbelief at the huge orange glow coming from the refinery. He was booting up his computer at home when he got the page. Full-scale response was underway with all required agency notifications taking place.

"What happened?" Mark asked when he got the Safety Manager on his cell phone.

"Don't know, but security did grab three guys who were trying to get out who didn't have any business being there."

"How'd they get in the fence?"

"Don't know."

"Anyone hurt?"

"Yes, we know there were several workers near that area at the time and we haven't accounted for them yet. I'll let you know as soon as I hear more."

"Wait, one more question. What about fence-line neighbors? Any homes damaged or need for evacuation?"

"We have no reports of neighbor damage or injuries but we have notified the local department of emergency management that we want everyone along Franklin Road evacuated."

"I'll send the telephone alert to that area," said Mark and the manager agreed.

Command center would be established in pre-designated area in the Visitor Complex with the Joint Information Center in the trailer behind the medical office. Based on the sketchy information from the Safety Manager, Mark guessed this would be treated as terrorist activity with the result of much higher press attention than if it were an accident. Before heading to the command center, Mark turned to his computer, entered the inside of the prepared incident Web site and typed in a quick announcement to the neighbors living along Franklin Road. He selected their names from the database in the system, clicked the "urgent" button, and ran a quick test telephone call. When he received the test call on his cell phone confirming the message, he clicked the button to call those neighbors and phones along Franklin Road immediately began to ring with the request that they immediately evacuate to the designated Red Cross shelter.

That completed, he filled out the initial release template with the minimal information available. After entering the appropriate site title and basic information, he made the prepared "dark" site public, now with specifics about this incident. A public Web site specific to the incident was now available to reporters, neighbors and the world. He posted the initial statement on the public site and distributed it by email and fax with a few mouse clicks, after securing approval of the Incident Commander. After he launched this new incident specific site, everyone would be directed to use this site rather than the refinery's regular Web site. For those people going to the regular Web site looking for information, a button on that site directed them to the new incident site. He alerted the communication team with email, text page and telephone messages using the text-to-voice feature of the communication management system, quickly dressed and drove the 10 minutes to the plant.

For Mark, it was now that the policies, plans, people and platforms that had been prepared came into play. The communication team could work effectively if there was clear policy direction established in advance; if there was a simple but effective plan that would tell various people where they needed to go, what tools they needed and what they were to do; if the people who were to help manage the response had been trained and had a good idea of what was expected of them and what would unfold in the coming hours; and if the communication management platform had been put in place to facilitate group communication leading directly to public communication.

Golden Hour

The Golden Hour is golden because much is determined about how the story will be told happens in that first hour. As the old saying goes, you have one chance to make a first impression. A slow response is, unfortunately, too quickly interpreted as "we don't care." This is a new concept for many in public information and crisis communications because many do not understand that with the trend toward instant news and the new technologies used by broadcasters that news coverage of an event begins the instant broadcasters become aware of the event. Not just broadcasters, either, because with the Internet everyone becomes a broadcaster which means that all newspaper outlets also report news much faster on their Internet sites.

The goal of the most enlightened communication managers is to be the first and best source of the news. That goal can only be realized by putting in place the processes that will allow them to gather needed information quickly and then distribute it at the speed of light.

Preparing the Clinic's Response

Steve's challenge was to get a reasonable response to the producers of the "Today Show" in very short order. He got the names and email addresses from the clinic CEO of the four attorneys working on this case. Two were in one office, but one was in a different city and the other was out of town. She needed to be included in the decision of what to say as well. Steve logged on to his agency's virtual communication management system, established for the purpose of assisting clients – even on-again off-again clients – in their time of need. He assigned all of the attorneys and his client passwords and got all of them signed into the system by alerting them by phone or email. Once inside, they used the secure chat room to discuss options. Several attorneys did not want to give any statement. Steve argued that a no response in this situation would likely be reported on the show as saying the clinic declined comment, which would be tantamount to accepting guilt. Steve drafted a statement that said this was a legal matter and the clinic was not able to discuss the details, however the allegations are without merit and the clinic looks forward to the opportunity to demonstrate that in a court of law. The statement also declared that the procedure was one of the safest medical procedures used today and that this clinic had one of highest success rates of any clinic performing this procedure – a statement the CEO said could be verified by readily available data. Each attorney reviewed the draft and marked it up with their comments. Everyone was online working on the same "virtual desktop" and so could review the changes made in each draft as they were completed. A lively discussion took place between attorneys and Steve with the clinic CEO making a final determination based on what he was willing to live with. Once agreement was reached, Steve clicked the button that said "Post this draft" so it appeared on the public Web site and clicked another button that emailed it from within the system to the "Today Show" producer. Steve called the producer immediately who said she had just received the email with the statement.

The Refinery Incident Evolves

On the short drive from his house to the refinery, Mark got another call on his cell phone from the Safety Manager. He got a quick briefing on scope and status of the fire, information that two bodies had been recovered but there were still three missing. He also found out that three young men caught by security were now in the hands of the police and that they were of mid-eastern descent. He was told that Jack Wyles was now the Incident Commander. In his car, Mark dialed the number of the Houston Crisis Center who had already been alerted by the response team. He confirmed a full-scale response from the information team was needed and confirmed they would arrive by company jet in six to eight hours.

When Mark arrived at the command center he quickly grabbed one of the laptops, logged on to the virtual communication center, edited the initial statement draft with updated information and printed it out. He quickly found the Incident Commander, told him he was serving as his Information Officer and had an updated statement ready to release. The Incident Commander held off the others clamoring for his attention long enough to carefully read the statement, initial it and hand it back to Mark. Mark walked back to his computer, clicked the "approved" button noting who approved it and when, launched the site, posted the release, selected the full database of 1,249 reporters he had prepared for a full scale media alert, and hit the button that emailed and faxed it to all reporters on his list. Elapsed time from explosion: 43 minutes. A fully loaded public Web site was available for the public and the press and a release prepared and distributed to all reporters in the greater region. During this time his cell phone rang four times with reporter calls. In each case he quickly told them the information would be available at the refinery's press room on their Web site within a few minutes and that he would email the release to them and that he could speed future inquiries if they submitted their questions about the incident to him through the public Web site. The inquiry management function of the virtual communication center enabled him and his slowly expanding information team to track inquiries, speed email responses, and verify information that was being provided by new communication team members as they arrived.

Organization & Personalities

With the task for getting an immediate response completed, both communication managers needed to move quickly to the task for putting in place a communication team that will enable them to respond quickly and communicate proactively in the coming hours, days and weeks. Steve's task was much simpler than Mark's because the scope of media and public attention would be considerably less. But Mark's task was made easier by much more careful and thorough preparation and by the fact that government-mandated oil spill drills had prepared a response and communication team to deal with events of this magnitude. Steve had been suggesting quite vigorously to his friend and client, the clinic CEO, that some preparation should be put in place including an incident "dark" Web site that would contain the information reporters would want to know about safety and effectiveness of the procedure. Also, they should identify media spokespersons and do some media training to prepare for this kind of public attention. But, those suggestions had been placed on a lower priority list as the clinic moved forward with major technology investments and rapid growth.

Steve would manage the communication function but he needed a spokesperson. The clinic CEO was simply not the right person. Steve's recommendation to the CEO was the chief of the medical staff should represent the business. Steve had immediately asked that all media calls be referred to him and by now he had fielded several. He was serving as the media gatekeeper, fielding the calls, determining deadlines and story slants, and used this position to help prepare his client to respond effectively. In the meantime, when a reporter called he got the contact information and told them the clinic had just received the complaint and were reviewing it and would provide a response to the media as soon as the review was complete. It bought precious little time because he understood the regional press would be running with the story soon. He drafted a quick media statement and question and answer document to be used by the head of the medical staff, and sent a notice to the attorneys and CEO that it was available on the password-secured communication management site for them to review. Then he called his spokesperson to discuss what could and could not be said. He found an argument. The medical staff person was in no mood to take instructions from some outsider who didn't know squat about dermatology.

"This isn't just about dermatology, this is about legal issues and protecting your clinic's reputation," Steve argued.

"The hell it is," said the doctor.

Steve ended the conversation and called the CEO. Either the doctor would get with the program and participate with the communication team or Steve would have to serve as spokesperson. About 10 minutes later the CEO called back saying his medical chief understood the situation better now and would support Steve.

By now the attorneys had worked over the statement. A brief chat room conversation within the communication system resolved a couple of wording difficulties and the statement was ready to go. Steve approved it for release in the system, posted it to the public site in a moment, emailed it to the medical chief and phoned him to prep him for the first interview.

Mark's challenge involved many more people. The first three members of his communication team were assigned roles immediately. One would be JIC manager, setting up all the logistics needed for a full scale Joint Information Center operation. The communication team would soon consist of public information officers from various agencies such as the Coast Guard, the police department, probably the FBI, the state department of environment, local emergency management staff, etc. These people needed computers, desks, phones, and some of them likely needed brief training to participate fully in the Internet-based communication system. Mark assigned one person to be Assistant Information Officer, External and another Assistant IO, Internal. External would manage inquiries coming from the outside including media, government, neighbors, community, etc. Internal would handle employee and in-company communication and also coordinate with the Incident Command staff, locate, prepare and update information about the incident and the response, secure approvals, etc. They knew these jobs from previous drills and they got to work immediately. When a more senior or experienced communication team member arrived, Mark would quickly make an assignment change. Each of these managers in their turn took in newly arriving communication team members and made assignments to help collect status reports, draft the next release, or hunt down answers to new questions as they emerged.

The state department of environment public information manager arrived about 90 minutes after Mark began the process of establishing the communication center. By now two releases had been put out, a press conference scheduled and inquiries were being managed with dispatch. Sandy was intent and officious.

"My boss, the on-scene commander for the state, has requested that I serve as Information Officer," she announced.

"I will take it up with Unified Command in a few minutes," Mark said. "In the meantime, would you be willing to help out with media inquiries?"

"'Afraid not," she said. "I'm to take over. I'm not taking direction from anyone else."

Mark finished reviewing an early draft of the next release, marked a few changes and then went to discuss the situation with the Unified Command. In the ICS system, the Incident Commander is god. When an appropriate authority for the lead federal agency shows up, he or she automatically becomes part of the Command team, now called Unified Command. The lead responding agency for the state also has a position on the Unified Command team, as does the lead local responding agency such as police, sheriff or local emergency management department head. But the Incident Commander for the company involved, known as the "responsible party" always has a place in Unified Command. Tribal leaders, when their land or property is affected, also become part of Unified Command. Should an impasse occur, final authority rests with the FOSC or the Federal On-Scene Commander. Mark conferred with Jack Wyles, the Incident Commander for the company who said he would confirm it with the other members of Unified Command. At this point the FOSC was the Environmental Protection Agency representative. At the point it was determined to be a terrorist activity, the federal command position would switch to the FBI. Mark observed a brief discussion among the Unified Command, the state commander shrugging his shoulders, shaking his head and turning away. "Carry on," Jack told him.

"I've been confirmed as Information Officer for now," Mark told the woman. "Now, if you would be so kind, please help out with media inquiries. Sally here is the JIC manager and Al is Assistant IO, External so he will get you caught up on inquiry responses." The woman glared and then walked away.

Turf wars, power struggles, personality clashes and all the weaknesses of humans working together in tight quarters and stress-filled circumstances play a role in crisis communications. The most important element in managing these difficulties is strong, competent, experienced leadership. The second is preparation and an organization structure that is prepared in advance and is understood prior to the incident by everyone on the team.

Mark was strongly aided in his difficult task of having Incident Commanders who understood the vital role of public information in a crisis situation and who also understood the absolute need for speed. The commanders recognized that they could be major stumbling blocks. I have personally observed one incredibly officious and uncooperative state official block vital public information in real situations and drills, in some cases for up to two hours, for the only apparent purpose of demonstrating that he had the power to do so. The fact that he was successful in doing so demonstrated first of all that his primary concern was establishing his own power position rather than contributing to the team effort, but also that the other incident commanders did not demonstrate the requisite leadership needed to put an end to the frustrating nonsense.

Prioritization

Within an hour of the explosion, Mark's communication team was settling into their tasks and the JIC was beginning to function relatively smoothly. Mark decided he needed to take a few moments so he stepped outside where he could clearly see the bright glow of burning fuel and the news helicopters circling overhead at the prescribed distance away. Priorities, he thought. Employees' families. Company leadership. Government officials. Neighbors. Community leaders. Oh, yes. Reporters. Local, regional, national, international. He jotted a few notes and returned to the Joint Information Center.

He called a brief meeting of his management team, which now included the Assistant IOs for Internal and External, the JIC manager and their deputies.

"We've probably got eight hours before the team from Houston arrives," Mark told them. "I want to get maximum information out to our various groups to help minimize the inquiries coming in, or else we will get buried in a hurry."

Mark was focused on a key issue for information officers. How to manage the potentially overwhelming deluge of media inquiries from around the world. What was top priority? Preparing the information and pushing it out to the rapidly expanding email list of reporters who were adding their names onto the list via the incident Web site? Or slowing that process and using more team members to respond to the expanding group who were gathering at the facility? Mark decided that both were necessary but if he kept up the proactive flow of information, it would be the best way he could minimize the questions being thrown at his small team. "Feed the beast," he thought. "Or get eaten alive."

Mark directed that a private Web site be launched for company leadership with a direct transfer of the reports inside the main crisis site that would allow them to follow incident status as it changed. All appropriate company officials would be alerted by email and some by phone of the general password used to enter this site. Employee's families would be provided the approved public statements as soon as they were distributed to the media by email and those without email addresses would get a text-to-voice telephone message. Neighbors in the five-mile radius identified in eight different sectors in the database would be similarly notified. All government officials and community leaders would get a modified version of the public statements emailed or faxed to them concurrent with the release of media statements.

"Critically important," said Mark, "is to include the incident URL, www.fairawayrefineryresponse.com in all messages going out including the phone messages. Also, please request that if they have questions to enter them through the inquiry function on this site. If we can maximize use of this, we'll limit phone calls and cover the most ground."

Mark understood there are two important realities to prioritization in crisis communications: everyone is a priority, and there are still priorities. So he gave one final instruction to the assembled communication team. "We want those whose opinions matter the most to understand that this refinery, this company, these agencies working together are unified in their efforts to minimize danger to people and damage to resources, and that they can count on us for the fastest, best, most accurate information about this event."

With the approval of the Unified Command, Mark's team had been posting digital images, even a short video, of the response team at work. Mark took a call from the CEO of the company. "Wow," he thought, "I've never talked to the CEO before." The CEO congratulated him on doing a good job and then told him he had received a call from a lead attorney for the company vigorously complaining about the images on the public Web site. "I think we need to take those off," the CEO said.

"We certainly can and I will be happy to comply after confirming with Unified Command," responded Mark, "But you need to know that the result of that will be that reporters and members of the community will go this local online news site that has pictures and stories of what is going on. Check it out at this Web address," Mark said, giving him the URL. The CEO checked it out. The question was, did the company want this small independent news operator with great photos that everyone was screaming for to become the primary and best source for information about this event. That job is what the JIC was established for, but if company attorneys are fearful of how the images might be used down the road want to pass control of the information to people outside the JIC, then the CEO needed to understand that the company attorney was changing company communication policy, Mark explained. The policy clearly stated the company or the JIC in which the company operated was to be the first and best source of information about the incident.

The CEO said to leave the images up for now and he would get back to Mark if and when he needed to remove them. "Keep up the good work," he was told. He never heard back.

Broadening the Clinic's Message

After the "Today Show" statement had been received, Steve also turned his attention to priorities. He was fielding media inquiries and working with the medical officer who was now much more cooperative in providing the approved and appropriate responses. For those inquiries coming in via the public site about the legal action, Steve handled those himself quoting the medical officer as the source. There was more that needed to be done. Steve was very aware that the clinic's tens of thousands of patients would shortly be getting news of this action and they would get it in time to tune in to the "Today Show" and see what Steve fully expected would be a hack job. The black hat would be placed on the clinic's head. Steve saw that the CEO was still online in the private communication system intranet site, but also that one of the attorneys – one of the least public relations sensitive attorneys – was also still online. Steve decided not to use the chat room but phone the CEO.

"Aaron," Steve said, "I want you to consider something." He went on to explain that he felt it would be a good idea to email a letter to all 43,219 patients who had been served by the clinics owned by the company in the past four years.

"Let me get this straight, Steve. You want me to tell my patients who represent 85 percent of my business through their referrals that they should watch the "Today Show" tomorrow while we get hammered?"

"Uh, yes," said Steve. They would get the story eventually, through the press reports, through watching the show, or hearing about the show from their friends and neighbors. "We have the chance right now to tell the story to them first. Tomorrow we won't have that chance. Yes, there is a downside risk in that you are drawing more attention to what may very well be a negative story. But the upside is their understanding that you are communicating directly, honestly and truthfully with them."

"What about the attorneys? I can see where they would be concerned that this could hurt us in court?"

"Losing the confidence of your patient base may very well be the end of your business, Aaron. It's your call, of course, but even a significantly increased risk in court doesn't compare to the risk of negative opinions of those people who are most important to your future."

"I get your point. Let's get on the phone with the group."

The email was sent. Unfortunately, only 50 percent of the patients in the database had an email address so a few went by fax and the rest went by mail. They would not hear from the clinic prior to the show, but they would know the clinic had communicated with them as quickly as they could.

In the instant media world, decisions about priorities go far beyond the question of which reporter's call to return first. Those people who control the future of the institution by the positive or negative perceptions in their head are all important. It is absolutely true that while we are moving toward a post-media world, we are still very much in a media world so that reporters, editors and producers are still of vital importance in opinion making. But that is shifting and with the Internet, the opportunity to communicate immediately and directly is shifting that balance. The ability and willingness to use that capability determines whether or not a company or organization will trust their future to the media or will take at least some control in their own hands.

Inquiry Management

If Mark did not have the option of communicating quickly and directly to the various non-media groups, or if he decided to wait for later to communicate, the burden of inquiry management would have taxed the ability of even the most well-prepared and well-managed information center to respond. In the second and third hour of the refinery explosion, Mark's workload would be reaching a climax. Inquiries would be pouring in at accelerating rates via email, telephone and from the growing number of reporters, videographers and producers in the satellite trucks arriving at the refinery main gate. The governor's office, US Senate and congressional offices and the White House would be calling in for briefing updates. The airport manager would be expecting a call. The CEO of the company that owned the refinery as well as the entire executive level would be pressing for ongoing information. Neighbors, the mayor, the county executive and assorted other elected officials and community leaders would be emailing and calling.

Even if the latest Internet technology is used and the most proactive communication actions are taken, the inquiry burden will be very great. Reporters will be flying overhead, driving up in satellite trucks and certainly calling every landline and cell phone number they have in their PDA's (Personal Digital Assistant) to get the answers they are looking for. Mark made sure that his JIC manager understood the importance of getting every inquiry logged in the communication management system no matter how it made its way to the JIC. This provides communication managers the opportunity to review what questions are coming in and provides some measure of quality control over the answers provided. The standard two-part form used in most JICs simply cannot match the functionality of available Internet-based inquiry management.

Inquiry management is not just a crisis communication problem, but it is a part of everyday life for communicators in most larger companies and organizations. This function is certain to grow in complexity and demands as we continue to move to a post-media world where growing categories of stakeholders will have the same high expectations for direct, instant and accurate communication as reporters now have. The demands are higher today than they need to be because of inadequate technology platforms used. For example, one large corporate communication team recently explained that it is very common for a reporter to contact different members of the team with the same question. These people may be scattered in different parts of the country. Two problems occur: a loss of productivity occurs because now perhaps two, three or even more communicators are working on the same issue or response. Secondly, if the answers provided are not entirely consistent, quality control becomes a concern. Aggressive reporters can have a field day with reporting on even moderately conflicting information provided by different issue managers or spokepersons. Internet-based inquiry management technology solves that problem by allowing all members of the team to work as a team on a common desktop enabling them to view the inquiries each member is working on in real time. This avoids duplication of effort as well as inconsistent responses.

With this technology, inquiries are instantly logged as they come in. Inquirers are encouraged whenever possible to log the inquiries themselves using the public Web site which is directly linked to the secure inside communication management site. Either way, contact databases are automatically kept up to date by direct link to the inquiry system. Inquiries coming in from the external site trigger an email notification which means that designated team members will see an email pop up in their regular email or on their text pager or email-capable cell phone. Inquiries can be directed to the members of the team best positioned to answer them, and when a response is completed, it is emailed directly to the responder from within the system, avoiding an additional step of re-entering the response into regular email. The system records all details including date and time of inquiry and date and time or response as well as what the response is and who responded. The inquiry management screen alerts the team to all the uncompleted inquiries as well as giving them shared and easy access to all past completed inquiries. This in itself adds greatly to efficiency as a responder can quickly check to see the same or related questions and see how those questions were answered. WiFi technology and the increasing use of fully functioning PDAs equipped with keyboards means that communication managers on the move can maintain full and constant contact regardless of location.

This technology provides communication managers and executives far greater oversight of the inquiry management process than ever before. They can view in real-time the questions and answers, spotting emerging trends in questions, misinformation or rumors. They can also quickly identify when any member of the team is supplying inconsistent, inaccurate or inappropriate information.

While productivity and quality of communication response are the primary advantages, this new technology can also decrease administrative burdens in other ways. In industries where response drills are required by law, detailed documentation of the drill is also required. Since every detail of the inquiry function is maintained in databases, these systems usually provide detailed reports that meet or exceed all regulatory requirements.

Steve was also using the inquiry management function of his Internet communication management system. While the call volume was insignificant compared to Mark's challenge and he and the medical officer plus an assistant in his office were the only ones actively managing the function, he found it very helpful to review the inquiries and responses with Aaron and the legal team in the days following the "Today Show." One thing the reporters' inquiries demonstrated, is that they had some level of understanding that the aggressive press effort orchestrated by the attorney was an attempt to create publicity needed to generate a victim pool to warrant class action status. As a result, Steve noted to the CEO and the attorneys that the press coverage of the story was far more muted than what they might have expected. The attorneys too were surprised by the relatively low-key response of the media. Reluctantly they agreed that being proactive in communicating the clinic's response may very well have impacted the reporters' understanding of the story and therefore their coverage of it.

Mark was relieved of his position as Information Officer 13 hours after first hearing the explosion from his bed. The Crisis Team from Houston arrived nine and a half hours after receiving notification and the experienced Information Officer from headquarters assumed Mark's role after a two-hour transition which enabled her to get fully up to speed on what was happening. By that time, his team had released five public statements including various versions for the stakeholder groups, and had conducted two press conferences. One he had conducted because the Unified Command got tied up on critical operational issues just prior to the announced briefing time and one in which three members of Unified Command participated. Mark hung around for a half an hour or so to make certain things were running smoothly and went back home. He had managed to get a couple of calls in to his wife who was understandably concerned and as he pulled into his driveway he could feel the burden being released. But, he sensed his work wasn't done.

Rumor Management

Nearly every student has played the communication game in school where a story is whispered to one student who must whisper it to the next until it passes through the class. At the end of the line, the story is almost always unrecognizable. Person to person communication passed through many ears and mouths is notoriously inaccurate. Add to that the reality that not everyone wants the information to be accurate. Negative twists and turns are not always entirely innocent.

Rumors and rumor management are a necessary part of communication management and particularly so during a crisis when a reputation is on the line. Rumors have sometimes been likened to cancer: detected early they can often be treated but left to spread undetected or without response the damage can be very severe. That means that the first and best line of defense is early detection followed by aggressive response. Part of preparing the team needs to include instructions on how to recognize rumors and then when spotted the rumor should not be laughed off but reported quickly to the information officer or communication manager.

Steve encountered the rumors very early. They involved the clinic's past legal history. Steve soon detected that the reporters asking questions about the legal history were on more than a fishing expedition; they had some information that the company had a history of legal actions. An email and response to the CEO clarified the situation. The clinic had never gone to court. However, there were two instances where a patient experienced some difficulties, hired an attorney and reached a settlement with the clinic. The agreement included re-treatment. As is usual the rumors had a portion of truth, but the truth was stretched or distorted almost beyond recognition. Steve drafted a statement in the communication system that explained clearly that in two previous situations where patients had been less than satisfied with results the patients had agreed to re-treatment and their complaints satisfied. In this case, the patient had refused re-treatment. The holding statement also made clear that the clinic's patient results were among the highest in this area of medical practice and that while legal action in this area was growing due to the rapidly growing number of clinics providing the procedure, but the action facing the clinic was the first legal action of this nature it faced. After brief legal review and the obligatory wording changes, Steve approved the holding statement and released it only to those three reporters who had asked the question. He did not want to raise the question of legal history if it wasn't necessary, but now he and the medical officer serving as spokesperson were fully prepared to respond if and when a question should arise.

Mark's problems with rumors involved the question of injuries or fatalities. The initial report he received was that two bodies had been recovered. Later information revealed that only one was dead but the other was rushed to the burn center in the nearest large city and was in critical condition. There were still at least three missing. Injuries or fatalities trigger the portion of a crisis communication plan that everyone dreads the most. The shock, horror and disbelief of losing co-workers is combined with the great difficulty of relaying the information to family members. This burden is exacerbated in the era of instant news because the families need to be notified by company officials, usually the highest-ranking company official available, and not by the media. That's one important reason why extreme caution in dealing with public information about deaths and injuries is an absolute must. Perhaps the only thing worse than having a family member find out about the death of a loved one on TV is to have that death reported only to find out later it wasn't true. The West Virginia mine incident of early 2006 also demonstrated that false good news that is not quickly corrected can be devastating to families as well. Accuracy is critical and speed here refers more to the speed of getting verified information directly to the families as soon as possible.

Whenever he had a spare moment, Mark was monitoring the inquiry screens. The fact that his team was putting out updated releases whenever new information became available was keeping the inquiry load down and the number of routine, predictable questions down. Mark first noticed a couple of inquiries coming in that hinted at some knowledge about who the dead and injured may be. Then he was handed a phone by one of the media responders who whispered he needed to hear this question. The reporter told him he had it on good authority from an employee he interviewed as he was leaving the plant that a senior manager, possibly the operations or maintenance manager was among those caught in the explosion. Mark knew it wasn't true because he had seen both of them in the command center.

But he also wasn't absolutely sure that a senior plant manager wasn't involved.

He conferred with the Unified Command and they concurred with his recommendation. He amended the next release to explain that the information they had available indicated that as many as five workers involved in distribution center activities may have been in the area at the time of the explosion. One worker was seriously injured and had been sent to Mercy Hospital by helicopter. The status of others who may have been in the area has not yet been confirmed. He also decided that at the next press conference which was coming up in an another hour, he would ask the plant manager, the operations manager and the maintenance manager to attend and have the Incident Commander for the facility introduce the senior managers for the facility. They would not take questions but they would be visible.

While writing this chapter I watched a local all-news cable channel seriously blow it. For almost two hours they offered up the blaring "Breaking News" headlines. A prominent politician in the state was in a coma following a skiing accident. They showed file pictures of the handsome state senator at work in the senate and repeated the story at least every 10 minutes. Then, suddenly the report changed. It was not the well known senator who was injured but someone in his family. The misinformation was blamed on a hospital employee who told the news crew that the injured person was the senator. But, what responsibility did the reporters have for verifying the information? There was no apology, no explanation, no attempt to explain. Just a simple change in the story. A troubling aspect of such a story is that many people viewing the news during those two hours saw the story but didn't hang around to hear the rather quiet correction. An injured family member doesn't warrant continued breaking news coverage, so after the very short announcement of correction the story was over. That means that the majority of people who watched that channel believed that the senator was in the hospital clinging to life.

Responsible journalism and responsible communication requires a great concern over accuracy. Communicators today need to understand the tremendous pressure news reporters are under, particularly to find and report on breaking news. Everyone needs to take a deep breath and remember that real lives, real heartbreak, real careers, real futures, and real pain are at stake.

Negative Reporting

Rumors are one thing. Negative reporting is another. The two may be connected when a report is released that is critical of the company or organization involved and the report is based on false or highly distorted information. But much negative reporting is true. It may be spun heavily to fit the "black hat" mold, but when based on undisputed facts and not misinformation or the 10 percent truth, it's simply a negative story that is damaging.

Lindi Diaz, the experienced communication manager from Houston, took over for Mark and immediately faced a growing concern. She was forwarded a call from a media responder in the JIC who felt the Information Officer should hear the question directly and respond. A report was circulating, said the reporter, that the refinery had failed miserably in a recent security check undertaken by the National Guard and the Coast Guard and that the presumed terrorists had walked through an unsecured gate near the plant's electrical generation facility. The reporter said he had the information from a reliable source and would put the story on the wire in a half hour but wanted confirmation or a response from the refinery. Shortly after she told the reporter she would get back to him as soon as she could, she noticed three new inquiries logged on the system with similar questions. No question, a story would break soon with these accusations.

As she walked to the Unified Command area, Lindi's thoughts cleared. She had no idea whether there was substance to the information. But, this was not a Joint Information Center issue; this was a refinery and company issue. She spoke for a moment with Hank Peterson who had replaced Jack Wyles as "responsible party" Incident Commander. He agreed with her approach and she left while he informed Unified Command of the pending story and how the JIC was going to handle it. Lindi got the refinery manager on the phone and suggested he be prepared to handle media inquiries related to the plant's security. She briefed him and a communication assistant who would help the plant manager, then she drafted a statement and secured approval for a general release to the media. The statement said the Joint Information Center was there to provide information about the event and the response and would not be in a position to provide information related to cause including questions about security. Such questions could be directed to local police, the FBI or the refinery. She briefed her Assistant IO's on this statement who in turn briefed the responders and the statement was distributed to all reporters.

Ron, the communication manager now working with the refinery manager, went to work on the refinery's pressroom Web system that used the same online communication management technology now being used by the JIC. They hammered out a quick statement that said the refinery had passed all security inspections and that information was not available regarding the cause of the incident nor could terrorist activity be confirmed. However, the refinery already had a team in place doing an investigation of possible causes including the possibility of terrorist activity and a security breach. This statement needed legal approval from the corporate attorneys in Houston. Time was running short. The attorneys were online and reviewed the statement, discussed some wording changes, expressed concern about even recognizing the possibility of a security breach and agreed on a statement when the plant manager said time was up. Because the JIC communication management system and the refinery's communication management system were operating on the same platform, databases of reporters –

including all those who had recently inquired – were transferred over at the click of a button. An email went out with the refinery's statement.

Both Lindi and Ron soon noticed a shift in the general pattern of inquiries. Focus started turning from the response to the fire and potential impacts on area fuel supplies to questions about terrorism, security procedures, points of entry, identity of the suspects etc. While Lindi and succeeding Information Officers in the JIC focused on the unfolding events in the response, providing status on fatalities and injuries, coordinating information about impacts on fuel supplies, the security questions were referred to police agencies and the refinery. The FBI had been participating in the JIC nearly from the beginning but had not replaced the EPA as Federal On-Scene Coordinator and did not until two days later. The shift signaled a confirmation of terrorist involvement and further moved the focus from the incident response to investigation. Five days after the explosion, the JIC was shut down, in large part because the media coverage was related to the terrorism aspect.

The first question about security problems at the refinery had set off a firestorm of debate in the offices of corporate headquarters in Houston. Ron was communicating within the virtual communication system and on the phone to his counterparts in Houston. The head of public affairs for the company assumed the role of communication manager for the company and the CEO became directly involved in the response. Despite the warning, the team was still shocked to find the banner headlines: Security Failure at Refinery Blamed for Explosion. The main source providing the serious accusation was the deputy director of the local department of emergency management. He had been interviewed by a newspaper reporter, and, although he was not directly involved in the security procedures or reviews, he had heard his boss say after the last inspection that the refinery was dragging its feet on some important new security measures. This offhand comment was now the basis for damaging accusations.

The fact was the refinery management and the EPA and National Guard had been discussing new and very burdensome changes in security procedures. There was a dispute about what the refinery was able and willing to do. Some new requirements involved very significant costs without any real apparent benefit and none of those items were involved in this situation. It was also a fact that the terrorists' planning had been outstanding. They created a diversion that drew the refinery's beefed up security team into a high response and enabled them to cut through and enter the refinery fence at a strategic point far away from the diversion.

Ron suggested on a conference call that it was probably pointless for the refinery or the company to defend itself against the rumors and accusations about security problems. They had a good relationship with the local people from the EPA office and the National Guard despite the fact they hadn't agreed on every procedure. It was agreed they would hold a press conference at the refinery with the local EPA and National Guard leadership to discuss security procedures. The ground rules of the press conference were established that limited the questions to security precautions, measures taken and compliance issues. Those responding to questions would not nor could not address the cause of the explosion, which was now a refinery, police and EPA matter. Ron introduced the spokespeople present including the refinery manager, a colonel for the National Guard detachment and a regional manager for the EPA. The refinery manager spoke first explaining that details about security precautions and new measures could not be discussed for, well, security reasons. However, the company and the refinery understood very well the strategic importance of the nation's fuel supply and the role of the company and refinery in providing that and therefore took its responsibilities to added security very, very seriously. The refinery had cooperated fully with all agencies involved in security measures and was never out of compliance. Not all measures that had been identified were completely in place because there was an ongoing review of procedures and a constant process of adding new ones. The two people from the agencies echoed what was said and took a number of pointed questions, but at no time were the reporters able to get the agency representatives to point a finger at the refinery and blame this incident for a security lapse.

While the issue did not go away, reporting on it diminished greatly. The deputy manager of the department of emergency management was suddenly unavailable or unwilling to talk to reporters anymore. Without getting agency representatives willing to point to specific lapses or specific problems, it slowly became a non-story.

Steve had a similar problem and solved it in a similar way. One aggressive reporter was able to identify one additional past patient who seemed less than thrilled with the treatment and made comments about running a "cosmetic factory." The clinic was an active participant in the dermatology association linked with this procedure and Steve was able to get the active involvement of the head of the association who had very positive comments to make about the clinic, the quality of the medical staff, the strong record of safety and effectiveness and the unfortunate trend of unjust legal action against this new and very helpful procedure. Now it would be seen as the complainers against a respected industry leader – not the poor victims against a prosperous clinic bent on protecting its reputation.

Ahead of the Curve

A journalist laughed when I suggested the goal of effective communication response was to stay ahead of the curve. There is a sense of playing fast break basketball. Just when you think you've done your job and won the point, the other team is three quarters of the way down the court and impossible to catch. The only way to play this kind of game is to anticipate the break and think through the next step before you're even done with the last.

During one of the most significant news stories I was involved in, new information came to light that would set the reporting off in a new direction. It was significant news and while not positive to the company, not particularly damaging either. Being a junior member of the team I urged them to release it.

"Why?" the veteran communication manager asked me with a smile. "That's their job to do. Why do their job for them?"

Why? Because that's what I thought this was all about. About providing good information, about building trust, about letting the reporters know that we have nothing to hide and will not hide anything. Because if we provide it first, not just to the reporters, but to all those people who care about us and this situation, we get ahead of the curve. It was clear the communication manager and I were playing a different game.

One of the most difficult and important decisions to be made during a crisis event is whether or not to be proactive in communicating the bad news. Yet, it is this proactive communication that does more than anything to build trust and confidence and to lay the groundwork for moving forward with even greater strength in the future. While writing the update to this chapter, I received an email from a recent client who had accepted my advice about sending an immediate notice to families of patients in a senior care facility which had experienced a tragedy. This is what she wrote:

"Several resident family members called or stopped by my office to thank us for the nice letter and how much they appreciated the timing of having a letter in hand before they read about the incident in the paper. It made them feel like they were in the know and weren't just part of the public."

That is precisely the intended affect of such proactive communication.

Steve anticipated a shift in focus toward more medical field statistics about safety of the procedure. He had discussed the need for this type of information before with Aaron, the CEO, but nothing was readily available. Steve took a few minutes from media responses to contact the three medical associations with some relationship to the doctors who practice this procedure. Information was sketchy, but he combined it with some quick Internet research into a fact sheet on dermatology procedure fact sheet. While some outlets continued to focus on the complaints of the two patients involved and the sound bites offered up by the media savvy attorney, others began more in-depth reporting of the safety record of the procedure. They even compared this record against other comparable medical procedures such as eye surgeries, liposuction and other elective procedures with some risk. The results showed favorably and the stories began to change.

Mark returned to duty after much needed rest. But he returned not to the JIC but to the refinery where, unlike the JIC, things were beginning to heat up. The FBI had begun to take a stronger role and had released the identities of those who had been arrested by the refinery security people. An FBI spokesperson had also said innocently, "We don't know how they got into the refinery but we know they did because the bomb was placed well within the refinery's security perimeter." Absolutely true, but it set off another firestorm of questions aimed at finding out exactly what happened and who was to be blamed. What was even worse is that the public was being warned that flights leaving the regional airport may be curtailed because of the possibility of fuel shortages. The legislature was trying to decide if they should pass emergency legislation to put an exemption on truck traffic, but the well-practiced truck opponents were grabbing lots of space and time in the media talking about the frequency of accidents and the numbers of fatalities expected from increased truck traffic. Now there were three confirmed dead and three injured, two very seriously. A prominent local attorney who also served on the board of several important civic groups announced that two of the victim's families had retained him and he had information from refinery employees that security procedures at the refinery were "a joke."

The fire was out. The mess was being cleaned up. Workers were going home exhausted. For a day or two the main headlines in the papers around the region carried stories other than the blast. It was time to start thinking about recovery after a major incident – the next chapter.

12.
Reputation Recovery and Issue Management

In a serious crisis, a company's credibility is often seriously compromised. Reporters write their stories assuming the public franchise has been lost and the news stories become self-fulfilling prophecies. When the company leaders or spokespeople try to speak, their words sound weak and defensive, and the organization's leadership begins to adopt a "bunker mentality." However, an explosive crisis is not the only situation that causes this loss of credibility and resulting weakness in communication. Companies actively engaged in controversial public issues such as permitting new facilities, fighting legislative or regulatory battles, or combating ongoing activist's attacks share similar circumstances with those who have just come through a major crisis event.

In the first few years of the 21st century, an entirely new kind of reputation threat has emerged: the online reputation terrorist. It is not a crisis in the sense that a major accident or a major executive crime is because the attack may never reach the mainstream media. But that does not mean such attacks aren't potentially very serious and even deadly. In fact, they are dangerous because they can do immense damage while seeming innocuous enough as to not raise a response. Experience has now shown that even large companies with solid reputations can see substantial damage including loss of sales, share value, and morale as a result of just one or two highly effective reputation terrorists taking full advantage of the Internet and search engine technology.

This chapter addresses how to communicate and rebuild a reputation when your standing in the public has been damaged or called into question, or when you are under continual, long-term attack that is eroding public or customer confidence. It's been said repeatedly that credibility is everything. Credibility means the audience inherently believes you or at minimum gives you the benefit of the doubt. So, what happens when that belief is gone and your words are considered suspect? How do you speak and what do you say when no one will believe you?

There are three phases to this process:

1. Getting Out of the Bunker
2. Restoring Credibility
3. Returning to Normalcy

How soon you can go from one to three, or whether or not you can get to three at all, depends on the seriousness of the crisis, the culpability of the organization in causing the crisis, and the effectiveness of the communication response and recovery strategy.

1. Getting Out of the Bunker

Sometimes company leaders under attack do adopt a "bunker mentality" and other times it only looks like that. That is one of the key issues in reputation recovery in the instant news world because it can look like the company is unwilling to respond simply because its communication process is operating too slowly. In the weeks and months following the revelation that an Arthur Andersen partner in Houston destroyed key documents needed in the Enron investigation, there was a strong suggestion that the leaders were hiding out somewhere. The appointment of former Federal Reserve chairman Paul Volcker to an oversight board, the resignation of Andersen CEO Joseph Berardino, the decision to separate the audit business from other Andersen activities, the launching of a campaign to help protect the jobs of thousands of innocent employees – all these were taken in incremental steps over a four-month period. Because they always seemed late, slow and in response to the ever-deepening crisis, they never had the intended impact. Neither did they help the company to emerge from the appearance of hiding out. None of these steps were certain to put an end to the reputation crisis Andersen faced. But because each step was seen as "too little, too late," and leadership was not as visible or as loud as needed, these actions were almost certain to have minor impact, if any at all, on the continuing slide.

The bunker mentality was quite clear in the weeks following a tragic industrial accident. The company's leaders were tired of the media. For weeks they had been tracked down, and hounded, and they had become somewhat accustomed to seeing satellite trucks outside their office door. When the immediate furor began to die down, it was understandable that they were not eager to spend any more time talking to the press. After all, they did have a job to do and they had been distracted from getting back to business by the incessant and insistent press of reporters. But to those on the outside, to the key influential leaders in the community, this understandable desire to get back to the job at hand can and did look very much like a retreat to the bunker.

This tendency to keep one's head down when under attack is true for long-term controversies and public issues as well as in the aftermath of a major news event. When confronted with activist opposition during a permitting process, it seems the natural tendency of many companies today is to delay a public response until the heat becomes nearly unbearable. Instead, they tend to focus on preparing their pitches to the regulatory bodies holding the public hearings believing that the only thing that matters is meeting regulations and convincing the regulators of that.

Experience has shown in the past few years that the perception of public opposition – even when created by just a handful of dedicated opponents – is enough to delay or even kill otherwise fully acceptable projects. The bunker mentality in these situations proves to be very expensive.

Another example of the bunker mentality at work is a large international sales organization that faced two or three online critics. They knew they were there but largely ignored them despite the seriousness of the attacks. The company leaders forgot one basic principle: a lie repeated often enough becomes the truth. They also forgot that in today's world, most people consult the Internet prior to doing almost anything – including buying from someone or joining a home-based sales organization. What these people found was devastating. The bunker mentality applied to online reputation assaults can be particularly costly.

Following a crisis, or when opponents have turned up the heat, the temptation to quietly get back to business after the media storm has passed has to be fought. When credibility is at stake and when the attacks have stung, it is critical to move aggressively, publicly and with considerable visibility. In the instant news world, with the tools of the broadcaster or publisher at hand, this job is made easier regardless of whether or not the mainstream press has moved on to another story or another "breaking news" crisis.

There are two very important reasons why it is important for the communication team and the organization's leadership to venture out into the light of day as the immediate pressure of the crisis is beginning to ease. One is to get an objective measurement of the damage done to the public franchise. The other is to make certain those who are still observing the company and its action, understand that there is nothing to hide and no reason to hide out.

Measuring the Damage

When a company or its leaders have been attacked and damage has been registered, a response is required. But what level of response? How do you make certain you are not adding to the damage by over-responding? Time, effort and money spent on repairing a reputation is wasted if the attacks or negative stories have not significantly impacted the standing of the organization in the perception of the public or stakeholders. A crisis, attack or extended public controversy almost always requires a measured response. The question is what measurement will the measured response be based on? Leaders and communication managers who have been through this will most likely admit that the guide used to measure the sense of where the public response is at is their own gut instinct. This is gauged by reading the news reports, letters to the editor, op-ed pieces, and what is overheard on the street on the way into work. These same leaders, when confronted with this, would likely agree that they are in no position to accurately gauge public or stakeholder opinion at this critical time. They are too close to the events, too emotionally involved in all the happenings and too boxed in by others who are also too close to it. There is too much of a chance that those around them will tell them what they want to hear or at least color what they are saying to minimize the reality. At the same time, it is quite possible that by reading the newspaper reports or watching the TV news, those inside the events could come to the conclusion that the public is horrified and has turned completely against the company. Reading public opinion through news reports can often lead to over-reacting and potentially increasing the damage. A measured response means measuring perceptions and not relying on gut instinct or the insider-only perspective.

The best way is to get out and find out what people are thinking. As I mentioned earlier, this does not usually involved a large-scale sophisticated survey. There are times when such an effort is essential. But in starting the discussion about how the public and stakeholders are feeling about the controversy or events, some simple structured listening can go a long way.

Whose opinions really count? Are you concerned about how the County Executive feels or a key City Council member? Call them and ask them. Are you concerned about how the average investor might be responding to the news? Call a dozen and ask them. If you get 10 different answers, you might want to keep calling. If the answers are pretty consistent, you have at least a small measure of how investors are feeling about all the news reports.

If you're a member of the communication team or company leadership and your face hasn't been plastered all over the local newscasts or newspapers, get out into the community and listen to what people are saying. Catch people in casual conversation, or engage them yourself. Assign a few members of the team to call out to randomly selected people from some of the target groups. A picture will begin to emerge that can help in evaluating what public and stakeholder response is and can serve as a helpful guide to the communication response and ongoing reputation building strategy.

Keeping Visible and Vocal

In the instant news world, a major story usually hits with remarkable speed and then, almost as soon as it appears, it can fade away in the burst of another major story. The company leaders at the center of the story assemble their crisis response team, confer with all the experts, discuss a strategy, and launch a response. They may set a press conference only to find that no one is interested any more. The storm has passed and while they were cooking up their response, the public has already concluded that whatever has been said negatively about them must be true because they were "not available for comment."

The lack of visibility demonstrated by many organization leaders in the immediate coverage of a major event is usually not because they are hiding in the bunker, but merely that they haven't realized that they are living in a "now is too late" world of instant news. Maintaining high-visibility is critically important in the early going of a crisis and it is also critical after the initial media wave has faded.

The question about visibility is relatively easy to answer when the reporters are calling and seeking interviews. What about when the media wave has passed, or when the opponents are creating momentum of public opposition but the press hasn't really taken much notice? This can be a much harder question because now you are not responding to the demands for visibility but proactively seeking it.

Two questions need to be addressed: when do you proactively work to enhance visibility and two, how do you do it when the media is not of a mind to pay attention?

The answer to the first one is in the measurement. If the assessment is that the damage to the organization's reputation is significant and the company has gained a perception of being less than open, honest and transparent, visibility becomes an essential element of restoring confidence. If there is no real damage, it is slight, or continued exposure could cause unnecessary damage, the decision will be to do the needed reputation recovery work without proactive public visibility.

The answer to the second question is in remembering we are entering the post-media world. You, too, are the broadcaster. You have the tools and technologies at your disposal to communicate with key stakeholders and influencers regardless of media interest. You also have the option of communicating your message through email, direct mail, and even buying advertising to speak directly to the news audience.

It's an important, and frequently difficult, call to make. But if transparency and openness are at the core of public concern, the answer is usually simple. Be visible and vocal.

2. Restoring Credibility

Credibility is gold and is a terrible thing to waste. In reputation recovery and issue management we have to assume that it has been damaged or destroyed. Put in terms of the instant news world, the black hat has been securely placed on your head. The question now is what to do about it?

The Need for Speed

Two well-known American companies faced significant reputation crises in the early going of 2002. For one, the story erupted quickly in the news, had all the makings of an extended and very damaging problem, but quickly dissipated and now is forgotten in the public consciousness. For the other, the story resulted in the end of the history of a well-respected brand and world-wide enterprise. While these organization's crises were quite different and the difference in outcome was dependent on more than how they responded to the crisis, nevertheless the approach they took in defending themselves and recovering their reputations is very instructive. The company who emerged unscathed demonstrated that it understood the need for speed, aggressiveness and that the black hat had to land somewhere. The other responded slowly and always from a defensive position without any apparent or effective effort to remove, replace or re-color the black hat.

On Christmas Day, 2001, a Secret Service agent of Arabic descent was heading to join President Bush at his ranch in Texas. He was refused entry onto an American Airlines flight apparently because he was carrying a gun and he appeared to be mid-eastern. President Bush was absolutely livid as all the national news broadcasts demonstrated. He struggled to find the words in his anger. There was good reason for his concern. All the efforts to gain support among moderate Arabs and Muslims in the fight against terrorism were dependent on demonstrating that America is friendly to the Arabic people, non-discriminatory, and that America abhorred the isolated acts of violence against Muslims and people with Arabic appearance in the aftermath of the Sept. 11 attacks. The message that a major American company was apparently engaging in racial profiling – even against a person working for the president of the United States – could be seen as an embarrassment to the president and his efforts at coalition building.

The agent immediately hired an attorney who repeated the claim of racial profiling vigorously and often in the news stories that followed. A lawsuit meant the story would have a long shelf life, and, if past history was any indication, the issue would be tried in the media with only the prosecution being heard from. What was expected was that American Airlines would not respond publicly but reserve its defense for the courtroom. After all, it was a legal matter and lawyers on the defense don't like to publicly comment on legal matters. American Airlines had the black hat securely on its head; the whole world had seen the president's fury aimed at the company and an angry victim with a well-spoken accuser was getting maximum media attention. But, in less than a week, the story went away so that now few even remember it. The reason is simple. American Airlines moved the hat. The day after the agent's racial profiling complaints were aired nationwide and an Arab-American group expressed its outrage, the airline responded. The pilot was quoted by American Airlines spokespeople as reporting that the agent was angry, his

Secret Service documentation was faulty and he was abusive. There were very few in America, including the president, who would doubt the pilot's judgment that it was not prudent to allow an angry, abusive man carrying a gun on an airplane, particularly when his credentials don't check out. Especially when only a couple of days before another terrorist attack – a shoe bomb in this case – had been narrowly averted in the air.

When there were no vociferous denials on the part of the agent relating to his demeanor or paperwork problems, the issue was dead. The Arab-American groups who loudly howled after the initial reports had lost some credibility. The attorney working for the agent would have to go in search of another high-profile opportunity, and it is pure speculation, but the agent was probably advised by his superiors that it might be in his best interest to show a little temperance in these tense times.

If the airline had decided to wait to respond to the charges, if they had been convinced that the time and place to present the evidence of the agent's behavior was in the courtroom, the airline would likely have experienced serious reputation damage. As it was, they responded quickly, aggressively and effectively defended themselves against what could have become a major business problem.

Arthur Andersen LLP did not escape the black hat. Given the seriousness of the consequences to many of the Enron bankruptcy, Andersen's role as auditor, and most critically the actions of the Houston partner in shredding vital evidence, there is no question that the company faced very serious reputation challenges. However, the misdeeds of one partner ought not to be a death sentence for a company of Arthur Andersen's size and stature. Although its problems were more severe than the airline, it is clear that Andersen leaders could have communicated much more quickly, aggressively and proactively than they did. They did not do what American Airlines did. They did not maintain visibility, accept the responsibility the public expected of them, question the placement of the black hat, and commit to open and honest communication regarding the now visible problems. As mentioned earlier, they did take a series of strong and much needed actions such as appointing a well-respected national leader to chair an independent oversight board. But these actions all fell under the "too little, too late" category. Their only hope was to take strong and decisive action early.

In talking to one crisis management expert who had counseled the firm well before the incident, it became clear as to why the company succumbed to the bunker mentality and refused to respond effectively. He reported that his conversations with senior management about preparing for a major reputation crisis revealed a level of hubris and confidence about the strength of their brand that they felt essentially untouchable. Their refusal to consider the kinds of disasters that could occur and their vulnerability proved fatal in the end. A classic case of "pride cometh before the fall."

Replacing or Re-coloring the Hats

Both examples discussed above demonstrate the value of the old and highly useful adage about getting on the offense. Being on the defensive means the black hat is securely attached. A company cannot succeed in protecting its reputation with a black hat on its head visible to everyone on the outside and totally invisible to everyone on the inside.

Going on the offensive can be a very difficult proposition, particularly when the accusations are justified. When actions or inaction by company employees or leaders have resulted in genuine harm to innocent people, the environment or some other aspect of the public good, the black hat is there for a very good reason. But, an organization wearing a black hat needs it removed if it is to operate effectively in its marketplace and in the eye of the public. Time heals most wounds, but the time it takes for reputation damage to fade can be very costly. The best course of action is to take strong, positive, aggressive steps to restore a damaged reputation and the earlier the better.

There are several approaches to going on the offensive from most extreme to most conservative:

A. Attack the attacker

B. Shift the ground of debate

C. Focus on public benefit

A. Attack the attacker

As noted earlier, we are in an era of public debate that is often raw and unseemly. Negative or attack ads are the predominant form of political communication. It seems Americans have become a people who are quicker to anger, eager to blame, and open to seeing the worst in people and situations. Negative ads have become predominant not because politicians have become more mean-spirited, but because attack ads work. Research has demonstrated repeatedly that people don't vote for someone as much as they vote against a candidate. Today's elected officials seem to have an understanding that they are in office not so much because they are loved and supported by their constituents, but they were the least bad of all choices offered at that time.

Former President Clinton demonstrated, much to the amazement of even his closest aides, his ability to recover his reputation from near collapse, not just once but multiple times. This remarkable ability, detailed in George Stephanopoulos's book <u>All Too Human</u>, demonstrates that this was based primarily on Mr. Clinton's willingness to attack the attacker. Mere denial was not enough to defend against the accusations of a Ms. Flowers, Paula Jones or Kenneth Starr. The response would come down to an issue of credibility and Mr. Clinton was very successful in undermining the credibility of those who attacked him, thereby helping to limit the damage to his credibility. If he hadn't needed to resort to this very aggressive tactic so often, it is unlikely that his reputation would have emerged largely intact. This is due in part to his many contributions and strong support from many quarters; in other words, without positive public benefit attacking the attackers is not enough. The negative aspects must include the positive aspects for there to be any hope of success.

While this strategy of launching very personal and very aggressive attacks as a means of defense has been proven to be effective in some cases, executives and communication leaders are wisely reluctant to employ it except in perhaps the most extreme circumstances. It is almost always better to attempt to elevate the debate than be the one to bring it to new lows. This is true despite the all too common situation of facing highly personal attacks by opponents who feel passionately about the issue. Those attacked by the "true believers" must remember in a mud fight with a pig, as the saying goes, everyone gets dirty but the pig enjoys it. It should also be pointed out that although negative campaigning has proven distressingly effective, all elected officials have become victims of the general disgust that most Americans feel over the political process and the declining respect for politicians in particular.

Attacking the attacker refers to waging battle over credibility. Who is to be believed? Far too often companies and organizations under strong attack seem unwilling to engage the battle and point out when accusers are wrong. There certainly are times when the best policy is to ignore the other voices and carry on with a positive message. But a lie repeated often enough becomes the truth and too many companies seem willing to allow the accusations to be made without answer. One does not need to resort to ad hominem (against the man) attacks to undermine the credibility of the accusers. Usually, there are sufficient overstatements, hyper-emotional language and flat-out factual errors to provide evidence that the truth is not being told.

Attackers, including the new breed of activists, "bloggers," are especially adept at the 90 percent lie or even 50 percent lie. They base statements on fact, but so distort the underlying fact as to make it look damaging. Exposing the method by simple but careful explanation of the fact in its proper context can make it clear to the more objective audience that the attacker is engaging in a dishonest and unethical tactic.

This strategy proved its effectiveness in a hotly contested public battle over permitting an industrial facility. The company attempted the "stealth" approach first, working only with the regulators and doing little to gain public support. In the meantime, the strong activist opponents, including an elected official, built an exceptionally solid base of opposition, flooding public hearings with passionate voices. The opponents used hyperbole, misinformation, emotionalism and personal attacks. They were remarkably effective, resulting in a decision by the permitting agency clearly based on political pressure and not on any determination of meeting requirements. In a second effort to gain approval, the company took on the opponents directly. A publication was prepared that used direct quotes from the opponents including the accusation that the company intentionally was setting out to kill people. Each statement of the opponent was carefully examined and facts countering their position were offered. The publication created a storm of controversy when published in the very newspapers that took a strong editorial position against the project and the publishers found themselves in the position of defending the right of advertisers to have their voices heard. While the opponents howled, they could find no factual errors or misstatements to destroy the credibility of the publication. The results were seen in the next public meetings in which far fewer opponents spoke and, except for the extremist leaders, most were far more cautious and judicious in their remarks.

The opponents were not attacked personally. The publication boldly stated that this was to address a campaign of misinformation. The attackers were accused of being dishonest, not by the company, but by the exposure of their statements contrasted to the clear and indisputable facts.

A similar approach was used in another highly charged public issue in which an activist was very effective in whipping up a highly emotional public frenzy. It resulted in repeated public votes against the company despite the clear idiocy of the policies. Few elected officials today have the courage to sit in front of a hostile council room and make unpopular decisions. But, when the supporters of this activist received a multi-page document detailing the many public statements of this activist and clearly showing the distortion, misinformation and hyper-emotionalism displayed, only a few die-hards were willing to publicly speak at the next public hearings.

Many grassroots organizations have achieved a level of credibility with mainstream media that far exceeds the credibility granted to major corporations and even smaller for profit organizations. There is a strong sense that because these frequently involve volunteer effort and are not motivated directly by stockholder demands or the profit motive that they are inherently more believable than for profit organizations. At times it is appropriate, however difficult, for companies attacked by these groups to show they do not have the purity that they may pretend or that may be offered to them by the public and media.

An "environmental" group was the spearhead of a campaign to prevent a pipeline company from gaining needed permits. However, the primary funding for this citizen's group came from a fuel barge company who stood to lose millions if the pipeline permit was granted. The interesting thing was that when the newspaper editors were made aware of this, they could not bring themselves to expose it and lose the very convenient accuser who was providing the basis for the stories they printed about the negative aspects of the pipeline. The company left it at that. In retrospect the issue was important enough that it would have been worthwhile for the pipeline company to become the broadcaster and let those who cared about credibility know about the clear agenda behind their environmental attacks.

A more moderate form of taking the offensive is to create alliances around a common foe. Restoring credibility, like politics, can make for strange bedfellows. So does war. The unlikely alliance of the Western democracies and the Soviet Union could only have come about because of a common and very powerful foe. Reaching out and finding even unlikely alliances is important when under sustained attack.

The activist community is very adept at forming virtually instant alliances, particularly in the Internet age. It should not be presumed that the leaders or members of the various groups would agree with each other very much. Some are far more extreme in their values and methodology than others. Nevertheless, when they identify a project or a company that represents something they both agree is bad, there is no time for quibbling over disagreements. An alliance is formed based on their shared opposition to the project or company. They have found a common foe.

Could Andersen have re-colored the very dark hat it was wearing by attacking the attackers and finding common cause with the public? Possibly. Members of Congress were quick to jump on the attack and express their outrage at Andersen, as they have done in many other such high-visibility situations. While accepting full responsibility for the shredding and remorse for the lapse in ethics and judgement it represented, Andersen could also have strongly suggested that this situation showed that it is time that Congress thoroughly examine accounting practices currently permitted by law. If it is true, as I have been told by accountants, that at least some of the accounting practices adopted by Enron were legal but highly suspect, then this becomes a matter of regulatory and legislative concern. Andersen or any other accountant cannot be expected to coerce a client into doing what is right when what they are doing is legal. By making deceptive but legal accounting practices the culprit, it starts to become much more of a question as to who is the accuser and who is the accused.

It should be noted that Andersen's ability to carry out this kind of strategy was essentially nullified by the shredding. If the controversy was only about accounting practices, the reputation risk would be serious but manageable. As it too many critical reputation crises, the cover-up becomes the crisis.

B. Shift the Ground of Debate

There is the accuser and the accused. The one on the offensive and the one on the defensive. If the black hat is securely placed on your head and you are the subject of unremitting attacks, how do you even the score – without appearing nasty, unlikable and without character? One key is to shift the ground of debate and become the accuser instead of only the accused.

Before President Clinton launched his attack on Kenneth Starr, the independent prosecutor appointed to investigate first the Whitewater issue and then the sordid Monica Lewinsky scandal, the entire controversy revolved around the president's personal morality and honesty. By making Kenneth Starr the poster child for the "vast, right-wing conspiracy" he shifted the ground of debate. He made common cause with all those who feared and distrusted the far right and said, in effect, this issue isn't about me, it's about politics. It's about future direction of policy. He said, in effect, "You and I and all those concerned about the right-wing taking over this country and the damage it would cause are in this together. That's what this Ken Starr thing is all about. If he wins, we all lose." It was perhaps only the egregious nature of the moral problems at the heart of the story that kept this strategy from being fully effective. As it was, it succeeded in significantly undermining the moral authority of the special prosecutor.

The "Destroy Starr" strategy could be seen as an ultimate example of attacking the attacker, but it also demonstrates the value of shifting the ground of debate. This can be effectively done without resorting to the inherent risk and nastiness of personal attacks against those attacking you.

In the example of the public permitting controversy involving a very strong opposition group discussed earlier, the ground of debate was established by the opponents. It was about protecting the environment. Strong accusations were made about predicted environmental damage. The company was continually on the defensive: "No it won't, no it's not true, our impacts will be minimal, blah, blah, blah." But when the publication referred to earlier was launched with the bold headline that the company was addressing a campaign of misinformation, the ground of the debate was changed. Were opponents intentionally misleading their supporters? Were government officials failing to take notice of the facts? Is it possible in our democratic society that important public decisions can be made based on completely false information? Using their own words rather than attacking them directly, the company put the attackers on the defensive. They had to answer the questions about the truthfulness of their statements. When the accusers are on the defensive, white hats and black hats get very confused. The ground of debate on this issue was changed from environmental concerns to the question as to how should public debate be conducted.

Once that new ground of debate was established, when opponents launched new attacks on the environmental consequences, the response was, in effect, "There they go again." Because their only rhetorical tools were misinformation and hyperbole, their attacks were turned against them.

In a different battle, the opponent was extremely effective in controlling the debate. Operating from a base as an elected official provides great advantage for populist style activists, as many are discovering. The willingness of the local paper to print the colorful accusations, the passionate, if outrageous, statements combined with the unwillingness of the company to do much to counter these made it a one-sided debate with the black hat firmly fixed. However, a quiet but nagging issue was raised: what about the cost of all this? The government involved had spent hundreds of thousands of dollars in foolish legal actions, all destined to fail, but the elected officials did so willingly rather than vote against the angry crowds. The fiscally conservative council members became increasingly ill at ease when the issue of the cost of continuing the legal battles was consistently raised. It was a ground of debate on which the activist opponent could not possibly win. Although it did not end the debate nor did the company ultimately succeed in the issue, the strategy created a two-front war. It provided the grounds for creating public support and counter anger – that is anger that countered those who were angry about the accusations against the company. And it made the situation more complex for the elected officials who needed to make decisions in the public eye on the issue.

c. Focus on the public benefit

The strategy of taking the offensive is always a matter of a two-front effort. One effort may be aimed at countering the accusations, claims or credibility of the accusers or opponents. The other must always be to present the positive side. As mentioned in the discussion on former President Clinton, his very aggressive attacks against his opponents would not have had the least chance of success if there weren't a great many people benefiting from his leadership and policies. His efforts at taking the offensive were at least somewhat successful because the two critical elements were there: undermining the credibility of those who sought to undo his presidency and reinforcing the benefits he was delivering.

In the public permitting debate, the positive benefits in terms of taxes, employment, construction costs, products produced were all continually communicated even while the debate was focused on the campaign of misinformation. The battle involving the wasting of public funds ultimately was unsuccessful in part because there was no real compelling story of public benefit to counter the myths of public risk promulgated by the opponent. But this situation is somewhat unusual. When a company or organization is attacked and its existence or operation is put at risk, there usually is a cost to that and frequently a cost not considered while the debate is raging on another topic.

A construction executive whose company had a remarkable record of negotiated work with excellent clients reflected, "Our clients would miss us if we weren't here." That's a strong statement in a crowded marketplace such as construction. It is what every company and organization needs to be able to say: "The people important to us would really miss us if we weren't here." Companies or organizations whose reputations have been tarnished need to think about who would miss them, who would lose if they disappeared. If the honest answer is no one, it is probably a good thing for the organization to go. But if there are individuals, groups, markets, networks, governments, communities, families that would be affected and would miss them, then the benefits involved become the basis for a strong and positive message.

Going on the offensive then comes full circle: it starts with those strategic relationships and a clear understanding of the basis on which they value you and what you offer them. But when under vigorous attack, the benefits message can't be heard; or put another way, it sounds quite different when coming from a person wearing a ten gallon hat that is very dark. Efforts must be made to remove that hat or at least change its color while at the same time, strongly reinforcing the reasons why they want you to be here.

Borrowing Credibility

When it is fully understood how difficult it is to operate in the public sphere when credibility has been significantly compromised, organization leaders and communicators will do just about anything to protect that credibility. Speed, as has been repeatedly mentioned, is one of the most critical elements in this era of instant news.

When credibility has been lost, almost everything that comes out sounds defensive. Even the efforts to shift the focus of attention can appear weak and desperate. Frequently, the very best approach is to allow others who retain credibility to speak on your behalf.

In the wake of the highly criticized performance of FEMA in Hurricanes Katrina and Rita, the director Michael Brown, was replaced. Michael Chertoff, the more highly respected leader of the Department of Homeland Security became much more visible in relation to FEMA. But no credible, highly respected leader became involved in overseeing the agency, speaking on its behalf or was named as Brown's successor. As a result, a year later the reputation of the agency is still very much in tatters and its performance is continually criticized in the media.

In one of its better moves (although still under the "too little, too late" category),

Arthur Andersen leaders appointed former Federal Reserve chairman Paul Volcker to head an independent oversight board. Now the media attention focused on him. He was not involved in any of the actions that caused the problem; he had respect; he had independence. He could clearly identify problems and suggested solutions, but he could also present the case for the existence of the company both for the benefit of the thousands of employees and the country and economy as a whole.

Following the Exxon Valdez disaster, a citizen's committee was established to help monitor the policies and plans of the companies operating in the Alaskan waters. While some in the oil industry remain skeptical of this approach and suspicious of the groups, it is clear that such a group is highly beneficial when the credibility of the companies have been lost.

The forestry company operating in South America established the position of Land Steward. A highly respected expert in environmentally sound forestry was named the Land Steward with full freedom to evaluate all planned operations and to speak freely, openly and independently about what he observed.

Another forestry company, in a situation illustrating unusual alliances, gained the vigorous support of a strongly environmental group by negotiating a joint venture project that enabled them to manage a prime forest parcel near their communal farm. They were obligated to manage it as a commercial forest, sharing profits with the forestry company. In turn, the company would protect this land from the clear-cutting practices that its permits allowed. As a result, this environmental group became a solid supporter for the company on other issues involving the environment.

The leaders of Arthur Andersen were essentially without credibility after the shredding stories had been played out. The forestry company with a tainted environmental record was essentially without credibility. Exxon, in the aftermath of the staggering environmental loss, was essentially without credibility. Even without major crises and in the best of situations, there are people with whom your company or organization has very little credibility. The answer to them must be, "Don't believe me, believe them." Finding the people who can be believed and who will speak on your behalf is essential when the ground on which you stand has turned to sand. Now is the time when all the hard work done in building solid, loyal relationships pays off. If your longtime friends who retain credibility and believability with the audiences won't speak on your behalf, you know you are in deep trouble.

3. Returning to Normalcy

Deciding when it is time to return to normalcy and officially declare the crisis over is often much harder than determining whether a crisis exists or not. One thing is certain in this instant news era: it's not over just because the headlines have shifted to a new topic. One of the rules of the instant news and post-media world is that the traditional media no longer have complete control over the length and content of the story. As long as "publishers," (now called bloggers) even those operating from their spare bedrooms, continue to distribute information, launch attacks, and carry on the debate, the event goes on. Legal issues resulting from the incident will also help make certain the crisis has a much longer public life than if it were only a news story that quickly came and went.

In one sense, after a crisis or a vigorous public battle, nothing is ever the same. Major crises are frequently defining moments for organizations in the same way life crises are defining moments for individuals. They become touchstones by which everything succeeding it is measured. They can deepen resolve and make an organization stronger and more sensitive to its surroundings. But, it can also weaken an organization and leave it listless and drifting. The difference, as in people, is to be found in character; in the case of an organization, it is to be found in the character and strength of the leaders.

The real question in returning to normalcy is when does the company return in the public eye to the business of brand building and business as usual? The danger of quitting too soon is that the company will be perceived as insensitive and oblivious. The danger of waiting too long is that the public exposure is unnecessarily prolonged.

A damaging crisis or public controversy means that credibility has been lost. Normalcy is then defined as that time when credibility has been restored. That can only be determined by measurement. The only real way of determining what the best course of action should be is through listening. The organization needs to reflect where the various audiences are at in the process and whether or not the company is believable. If mistakes are made either in carrying on too long or appearing insensitive, it is because the communication loop of listening and responding isn't there. The simple answer then is to let your audiences be your guide and make use of the direct communication tools to respond appropriately to each audience. If, despite your best efforts, credibility is still missing, leaders and communicators cannot and should not rest. The work must go on.

Identifying strategic relationships and building one-to-one high value relationships was the primary work identified in the chapter "Before the Crisis." It is appropriate that we return to that after the crisis or public controversy has ended. When a considerable part of the communication team's focus is building or re-building those critical relationships, normalcy has returned. Yes, the conversation may very well be about the events and their impact, but the pre-crisis work is being done. The circle is complete. When those personal and direct conversations no longer revolve around what is happening or has happened, you will know that life is going on again.

13.
Blogwars: The New Battlefront

As of January 2005, Pew Internet and American Life Project reported that one out of six Americans regularly read blogs, and one out of 20 were writing blogs. Eighteen million Internet journalists spending time out of their days or weeks to throw out to the world their thoughts and ideas about just about anything. Journalist has a double meaning – someone who writes a journal, and journalist in the contemporary sense of someone who reports on the events of the day and publishes for mass consumption and entertainment.

As of mid-2006, more than 50 million Americans are actively involved in providing content on the Web. Something like 20 million are bloggers in the sense of regularly contributing to their own Web site dedicated to expressing opinions or sharing ideas and information. Have you made enemies of any of these? If so, even one or two of those bloggers or other providers of Web content can potentially cause you and your organization untold damage. (For simplicity sake, we will lump all ongoing Web content providers into the overly general category of "bloggers" in this discussion.) One or two have proven the capability of causing billions of dollars in damage in loss of sales, share value and brand value.

All one has to do to see this phenomenon at work is go to your favorite search engine and type in the name of a few of the world's most prominent brands. Try Starbucks, Microsoft, Coke, Nike, Wal-Mart, etc. In most cases you will find "NameBrandSucks" sites only a few from the top listings. In some cases, they will even be on top! And if they don't show up with the brand wording alone, all you have to do is enter "Brand critic" or "Brand hate" in the search and your screen will fill.

Microsoft may well be one of the most targeted sites by blog critics. In the book Naked Conversations, co-written by the official Microsoft blogger Richard Scoble, the authors reported well over a million search engine returns when keying in words such as Microsoft+sucks, Microsoft+critic, and Microsoft+borg.

The venom of many of these corporate critic blogs can be staggering. One of them, Walmart-Blows.com even proudly states on their homepage that they were listed by *Forbes* as one of the top ten corporate hate sites in 2005; certainly a grand distinction. There is competition between the reputation terrorist sites and it appears that the competition is based on the degree of blatant hatred that can be expressed.

The Internet has become the vast public square for the digital world. It is also quickly becoming the "Cheers" bar of the world, where "if everyone doesn't know your name" they certainly can find you with a click or two. There are still multiple millions who are not participating in this global water cooler, but that is changing daily. More importantly, the people most likely to determine the reputation and brand value of your organization in the future are the ones most avidly hanging out online.

As someone interested in or involved in protecting or enhancing the reputation of your firm, you are in one of two camps: Either you are aware to some degree that you are vulnerable to an online reputation assault, or you have already experienced such an attack. If you have experienced one, perhaps it was a minor nuisance and not a major disaster, but you are now more aware than ever of the vulnerability to a serious reputation attack.

Understanding Vulnerability

Every day the evidence grows for the vulnerability of the large and powerful to the determined blogger. Intel, Microsoft, Apple, CBS and many other companies and organizations have seen market share drop and brands weakened by blog attacks. The blogs operating only in the blogosphere, or which remain on the Internet, have increasing power because of the capability to connect to literally millions in moments. But when the blogs go outside the Internet and connect with the mainstream media, the damage can be multiplied. The discussions about CBS's inaccurate story about President Bush during the 2004 election campaign existed for a number of days in the blogosphere before mainstream media picked it up. When it did, there were hundreds of thousands or perhaps millions who were already familiar with the facts, accusations and issues involved. The result was the end of the careers of some of our most prominent journalists and the CBS eye was blackened in a way that will take years to recover.

The more your organization affects the lives of others, the more powerful it is, the more well-known it is, and perhaps most importantly, the more it dominates its space, the more likely it is to be the subject of numerous blogs. And the more likely it is to be the target of a vicious and intentional reputation attack.

In the late 1990s and early 2000s, Microsoft clearly dominated its space. During Hurricane Katrina, FEMA dominated its space. NASA, after the space race anyway, dominates its space (literally and figuratively). A local daily newspaper without competition from another daily dominates its space. The single grocery store in a small town dominates its space. There is a price that attends this monopoly or perceived monopoly position: animosity. And these days where there is natural animosity, there are blogs and there is a ripe field for reputation terrorists who feed on the natural animosity.

Blogging analysts look at Microsoft, and its improving image, as an example of the power of corporate blogging. There are now well over a thousand Microsoft employees who blog about their work at Microsoft and the company publishes its own blogs, most famously Channel 9 (taken from the open channel on airlines where you can listen in to the pilot's conversations). Microsoft, to the astonishment of countless corporate attorneys, steadfastly refused to adopt a corporate policy on blogging. The fact that it has no policy is a policy itself that speaks very loudly for the confidence the management has in employees and the belief that anything that appears to hinder transparency is potentially deadly. But, have the unofficial and official Microsoft bloggers really turned the corner on the company's tattered reputation? Perhaps to some degree. But it is likely that Google had far more to do with Microsoft's improving stature, particularly in the technology world. The reason is simple. Instead of being the behemoth it still is, Microsoft is looking increasingly vulnerable to a company that clearly has designs on its dominate position and may very well be taking advantage of the limitations placed on Microsoft to rapidly extend unprecedented power. And companies that appear vulnerable do not generate the animosity that monopoly companies do.

There are other factors that determine vulnerability in addition to a powerful market position.

Here are a few that contribute to critical blogging activity and intentional reputation attacks:

Size – as we noted earlier, there is a general negative view of large corporations, fed in part by insistent media bias. Not a whole lot can be done about this, but it is important to understand that this is the public perception environment large corporations operate in. To ignore it or pretend it isn't there is to weaken the response strategy and the communications right from the beginning.

Bad behavior – organizational leaders do bad things. People working for companies and organizations do bad things. Not just the criminal activity that has been so much in the news, but even little things which show they don't care about customers, or are insensitive, or less than completely honest. When this bad behavior is experienced or observed by a blogger, the natural result is to use the blog to respond. The more the observation or experience affects the life of the blogger, the more that will be reflected in the tone and longevity of the blog and the commitment of the blogger.

Promising without delivering – most businesses seem to understand that it is not good policy to promise more than you can deliver. But these days it is more dangerous than ever because of bloggers. Expectations raised and then deflated cause animosity and these days that animosity gets relieved through a keyboard connected to the world. The hard sell pitch in which life changing results are promised for everyone who will buy your product, engage your service or buy into your business model might have been acceptable in the optimistic 1950s. But today, in a much more skeptical, and connected world, the disappointed and disillusioned find common cause easily and their criticism and anger becomes visible to all.

Environment or health-threatening industries – businesses and organizations engaged in activities that are viewed to be destructive to the environment are also particularly susceptible to blogging. Oil, energy, forestry, agriculture, real estate development, chemicals, pharmaceuticals, automobiles – the list will get very long in a hurry. The fact is there is little that we do that doesn't impact or disturb the natural environment in some small way, but companies or organizations identified as the worst culprits have huge bull's-eye targets painted on them. BP's efforts to re-brand itself from British Petroleum to "Beyond Petroleum" can be seen as both smart and cynical. It is crystal clear that people in developed nations where their concerns can go beyond the basics of food, clothing, water and shelter have adopted sustainability as a primary value. Companies and organizations have responded and are continuing to change to meet the new standards in order to protect their public franchise. But, it doesn't change the fact that if you are in an industry that has been damaging to the health or the environment in the past, you already have a wellspring of animosity in place just waiting for a specific incident to become the focus.

Employee morale – you might be doing just fine with your customers and even the financial analysts, but if employees within your company are experiencing a "downtime," your vulnerability increases. Employees and former employees can be particularly damaging as bloggers because everyone loves an inside story. A behind the scenes look at a company that is projecting an image in the public, very different from what is actually going on, is very vulnerable. Blogging has almost come to equate to transparency. All companies operate now in offices with nothing but windows, without shades or curtains. The whole world can see. Whether it has any interest in paying attention has a lot to do with the factors mentioned above and how eager those inside are to draw attention to the ugliness.

Blogging's Power: Fueled by Search Engines

The power of blogging is not derived from its ubiquity. We have been gathering around the water cooler and drinking beer with our friends at Cheers bars around the world for years. And when we do, we talk about what is on our mind. Sometimes, what is on our mind involves the reputation of companies and organizations we deal with. Blogging simply takes this kind of conversation and person-to-person interaction into a new realm. It is as if you could survey literally millions of conversations going on at once and within two seconds decide which group at the party you wanted to join. It is this ease of filtering through the irrelevant to find the relevant in such a vast pool of thoughts and ideas that makes the search engines so powerful and potentially dangerous.

Stated another way, without search engines those people making comments about your organization would be doing it quietly and in small groups, and therefore with little impact. With search engines, the lies, criticism, accusations, revelations and animosity can spread like a wildfire powered by the speed of light. The impact can now be fatal. There are five reasons why search engines give blogging its power.

- Their widespread use continues to rise
- Algorithms favor bloggers
- They facilitate community building
- They create an accessible long term record
- They are consulted frequently by mainstream media

Widespread and Increasing

Search engines have been around almost since the beginning of the World Wide Web, but it is only in the last couple of years that they have become one of the most influential forces in our world. The Pew Internet and the American Life Project reports that in 2005 use of search engines for all US Internet users on a typical day rose to 41 percent. That compares to 30 percent in 2004. In late 2005, an estimated 60 million Americans a day were using search engines.

The reason for search engines is very simple. With billions and billions of pages of information on the Web, the challenge is how to find what you want. Your "Favorites" or "Bookmark" tab will only handle so many sites. When you want to find something, you want to find it fast. The search engines, while far from perfect, do a remarkable job of sorting through the billions of sites and pages to find the information you are seeking. As a result of their efficiency, many users don't bother with capturing the URLs of sites they return to over and over. They know that simply by typing in a few key words in the search engine box they can find the site they are looking for in just a few seconds.

The other night at home was a great example. We were sitting in the family room casually watching TV with my wife, daughter and son-in-law. As most young men of his generation, my son-in-law appears to be permanently wired to the Internet. In this case, he is sitting on the couch watching TV while browsing the Internet on his laptop. The conversation turns to a woman my wife met at work that day who owns a restaurant in Vancouver, B.C.

"Check it out," she says to my son-in-law who quickly does a search and finds the restaurant. He reads off the menu and we all agree we need to go there soon.

A few minutes later, I mention the challenge I am having trying to schedule a summer vacation. We discuss several of the resorts we are considering in the Methow Valley of Eastern Washington. As we talk about the options, my son-in-law, almost before the names are out of my mouth, has located them and is showing us pictures of the rooms, the facilities, the rates and the availabilities.

It became very clear that the incredibly vast store of useful information is right at our fingertips. It also became clear that today's young people, let alone the next generation, will expect nothing less than being completely connected on a continuing basis to that vast store of information. And it is the Internet, made useful by search engines, which makes that possible. What becomes possible becomes essential, as we have seen over and over.

It is now commonplace, particularly with younger people, that before a decision is made to engage with your organization in any way, you will be "googled." Before someone buys from you they will, in effect, look at your ratings as a used book buyer on Amazon or any eBay customer routinely does. Before investing in your public company, they will see what they can find about your record. Certainly, before coming to work for you they will see what the search engines bring up. Before committing a contribution to your non-profit organization, the search engines will be consulted.

The biggest mistake you could make at this point is to assume that when you are "googled" that it is your own professionally crafted and carefully controlled Web site that will be consulted. Actually, given the way search engine algorithms work, it is more likely than not that your worst critics will be consulted before you even have a chance to make a first impression.

Algorithms Favor Bloggers

Search engine owners guard their algorithms – the formulas which determine where Web sites appear in their rankings – very carefully. But the way in which search engines rank sites is pretty well known. Key factors that determine where your Web site will show up or where the blog critical to you will show up are:

- keywords used in the text
- how many times the site is updated
- how many times it is linked to by other sites
- how many visitors it has

Search engines, unlike our own brain, do not distinguish on the basis of credibility. They do not decide when placing Web sites (blogs are Web sites) in order of rank that one person has more legitimacy than another. That means that a blogger with a personal or corporate vendetta with a proven track record of outright falsehoods gets the same treatment by the search engines as the CEO of a multi-billion dollar company. The influential role of search engines and their algorithms may be changing our views about credibility. One of the first things we do when confronted by information or an argument that challenges us is to ask the question: "Is this person credible? Should I believe or trust him or her?" But a high search engine ranking, while based on none of the traditional factors of credibility or trust, carries with it its own credibility. "Wow, look at that high ranking. This site must be important because it certainly is referenced often or a large number of people certainly must be linking to it in order to get that ranking." And therefore, though there is no "credibility filter" in terms of anyone evaluating the truth of what is being said, the high ranking alone counts for significant credibility.

When you look at the key factors in search algorithms, it is easy to see why search engines favor bloggers. The most important factor is the frequency of changes. Most large corporate sites today have become critically important sources of information for a variety of audiences, but most midsize and smaller companies simply don't have the resources or haven't committed the resources to maintain site content. So their sites get updated perhaps weekly, monthly or sometimes not even annually. Bloggers, on the other hand, frequently update daily. Some hourly. After all the term "blogger" is derived from "Web logger" or someone who regularly records what he or she sees on the Web.

Very active blog sites have lots of words, which contributes to the search returns; with more words, and more frequent use of key words, the search engines will deliver more returns. Active blog sites also have lots of links from their site and to their site. It's one thing they love to do. The bloggers community site, Newsvine, launched in early 2006, features "seeding" where site visitors provide the content to the site by "seeding" it with stories or links of interest. Then other viewers can comment on the seed that has been submitted. It's like one big party with all these discussions going on and anyone can start a new little group in a corner by throwing out an intriguing tidbit they found on a Web site.

Organizations who find their own Web sites overwhelmed by blogger sites on the search engines are beginning to adopt the strategies of bloggers in order to claim the ground that they believe is rightfully theirs. After all, it is Microsoft and Nike who own their respective brands. But in the most important party going on in the world, it is easy for a brand to get subsumed by others who not only do not have a right to it, but have personal reasons for damaging or destroying the brand. The options available for response do not include leaving the party. The party has simply become too important. The only option is to learn the rules of the party, invite more of your friends into it, and throw yourself in with all your energy. Corner lurkers will lose.

Search Engines Facilitate Community Building

The party analogy may be particularly apt when it comes to bloggers and search engines. Parties bring people together in a geographic location. It may include only friends or strangers. It may be for the sheer enjoyment of social interaction or around a particular issue, common interest or cause. The difference between the traditional party and the Internet party is the geography. Search engines make it far easier to collect people together around specific questions or topics, and that is one of the main things that feed bloggers.

The social benefits of the Internet were brought home to me within the past year in an intriguing way. My father was born and raised in The Netherlands, in the northern province of Friesland. He was almost 10 years old on May 10, 1940, when Hitler's army moved through the countryside and occupied the peaceful nation. For the next five years, my father and his family hid escapees, used a contraband radio to keep in contact with the Dutch government in exile, and harbored a contraband pistol. Any of these actions would have meant instant death for the whole family if they were discovered – and discovery was easy given the turncoat family in the small village who traitorously had villagers killed by the Nazis. One of the most memorable events of the war for my father was observing the death of one of the thousands of bombers who flew overhead. It was a crippled B-17 Flying Fortress returning from a bombing mission with one engine smoking. Overhead the small village where my father lived, the stricken plane was attacked by two German fighters. In moments, its wings came off and the plane plunged into a nearby field killing seven young American flyers. My father saw one parachute open.

He wrote about his experiences in a book titled The Way It Was. Someone living in Toronto, who was from the same village as my father, somehow got a copy of the book and read it eagerly. That person, probably using a search engine for some purpose, came across a Web site where a person was asking if anyone had witnessed a B-17 crash near Opende, Friesland, on a specific date. The Toronto reader noticed it was the same date that my father reported. He contacted the person asking the question and before long my father and Harold Adams, the now 80-something former flier who had floated down onto the fields of Holland near my father's farm were talking. Sixty-three years after that memorable event took place, the two elderly gentlemen could share a searing memory that meant more to them as each year passed.

That kind of social connectivity seems virtually impossible without the search engines we use every day and without the interest and willingness of people to put their lives, questions, and interests out to the entire world. It is that same connective capability that makes blogging so powerful. The interest in a specific life-changing event many years earlier is one compelling reason to go to the Web, but anger, bitterness, disappointment, or injustice at the hands of a large corporation can be even more compelling reasons. Now it is just far, far easier to find those people who share your passion – positive or negative – and to create a powerful connection and community. Geography doesn't matter much in that process.

The Permanent Record

As long as sites remain up and available, they remain searchable and contribute to the record. We discussed earlier the use of the Internet by journalists to research your company and that the record of press coverage available will color their stories. Let's say your company was involved in a scandal 35 years ago, which was widely covered. The people have long gone, the company is far different, and it's a different world. But when a new journalist writes about you, there's a very good chance that he or she will make reference to the old news because that is part of the journalistic record that is easiest and most accessible. This is why paying attention to what can be found in your journalistic record is important and seeking to create the best record possible is also important.

The same is true of bloggers. Search engines have made finding arcane tidbits of titillating information incredibly easy. When a blogger goes to write about you, the absolute easiest source of information is through the search engines. Blog critics seem to have the time, inclination and familiarity with search engines to make full use of their deep-diving capabilities.

The Web can be viewed as a very large file cabinet that is accessible to everyone. And it is not unusual for users of the file cabinet to fail to clean it out. Domain names have to be renewed and the fees for their use paid, but the fees are now pretty nominal and even if they do die, there are now Web services to provide Web sites that are no longer active. If you are wondering why a top new recruit decided not to join the company, or why your share price has been falling despite excellent performance, you might do a thorough check of that file cabinet.

Blogging and Mainstream Media

There are those who write about blogging and the new media who suggest that the traditional media have no impact. Indeed, when I started this book originally in 2001, one of my strongest goals was to demonstrate to executives and communication professionals that a massive power shift was underway. The original title for this book was "Post Media World." There is no doubt whatsoever in the six years since that the shift is massively underway. Mainstream media are doing their best to adopt new media as part of their mix and convergence is very much the name of the game today. Coverage of the 2006 Winter Olympics is a good example in that TV audiences were down from previous Olympics, but visitors to the NBC Olympics' site were very strong.

Even though that shift is underway and the primary message here is about the power of the new media, blogging in particular, it is when convergence happens around your reputation that things get most exciting.

For all the reasons listed above, journalists find blogs as a powerful new aid in writing their stories for traditional print and broadcast media, as well as their news Web sites. With the help of search engines, they can find colorful sources, background information, details that help flesh out a story, little known facts, and the temperature of the discussion around a company or a specific issue. Bloggers typically comment on the news. In fact, it appears that one news site, Newsvine, was designed specifically to facilitate bloggers and commentators to gather around the stories that interest them. One of the most important roles bloggers play is in helping keep the mainstream news media truthful and credible. If a mistake is made in a traditional journalists' story, bloggers have been quick to point out the errors. But increasingly, bloggers become the source of the news that finds its way into the mainstream media.

One of the most well known cases where both of those blog uses came together was in the CBS debacle. Longtime news anchor Dan Rather reported on the evening news that President Bush, then in the middle of a tough re-election campaign, had lied about his National Guard record. It was a stunning story. But it wasn't true. The bloggers dug deep and before long the errors in reportorial judgment were obvious – at least to those following the story through the blogs. But from there it was only a small mouse leap to the mainstream media. The blogs had done the investigation and it is doubtful if the other media would have dug anywhere that deep – in part because no doubt they are to some degree protective of their own kind. But the evidence was clear and now they would have to answer the question about why they weren't reporting what was clearly a major journalistic faux pas. They did report it. The result was the resignation of one of the last of the old guard nightly news anchors and the producer of the show who had a distinguished record in TV journalism.

Blogs teaming up with mainstream media is already an every day event and certain to grow in importance. It is especially true if the blogger writing about you is not a casual blogger with an attitude, but instead, a true activist or a reputation terrorist. The difference will be explored below. When an activist finds that his or her blog is no longer accomplishing the desired result, they will go directly to the media. This was evident in one case in which I was involved. The strategies employed against the blogger were having an effect, and so his activism took a new direction.

He found, possibly through search engines, reporters friendly to his position and made contact. Then his blog became a useful tool for conveying information to the reporter who turned it into just the kind of story the activist would enjoy.

It is important to understand this vital, symbiotic relationship between bloggers and mainstream reporters. There is no wall between the reputation threats coming from bloggers and reporters. What affects one affects the other. The relationship between the two means that a strategy to respond to bloggers has to keep in mind that there is always the distinct possibility of the conversation going on in the virtual Cheers bar of the Internet spilling over into the real bars and parties of our geographic lives. And that the spillover will be accelerated by stories they read not just online, but in their newspapers.

Winning the Blogwars

Assume for a moment that you are the communications manager for a large, multinational non-profit. Your agency has representatives around the world who are responsible for beating the bushes to find new donors. Word has been trickling in for some time from various parts of the world that new donor recruitment rates have been falling off. Then the quarterly results come through and show a significant drop in contributions. The cause is clear: your organization is in a blogwar. Or more specifically, it has been under attack for several months and there has been no organized defense. The senior executive team looks to you. We have to fix this problem, they tell you.

Here are ten strategies to consider as you march toward the battlefield:

1. Distinguish between blog critics and reputation terrorists
2. Correct it: problems, misperceptions or misinformation
3. Get out of the bunker and start talking
4. Talk to the saveables
5. Bolster credibility
6. Be human
7. Build rapid response capability
8. Take back the search returns
9. Move the black hat carefully
10. Never stop telling your story

1. Distinguish Between Blog Critics and Reputation Terrorists

Before rushing headlong into the blogosphere with the idea of taking out all the blogs who are damaging your organization, stop and think about who they are and what their motives are. Some people may have been hurt by your organization and are using this public forum to express their pain. Some may be casual observers quick to form and express an opinion and who are testing this strange new way of sharing thoughts and ideas with the world. But some may be out to get you. They may have had personal dealings that have hardened into an unchangeable passion. They may have the activist psychology discussed earlier in this book. It may be driven by a deeply held political position and they have adopted the "true believer" approach which tells them that their cause is righteous and therefore they have the moral right – no, the moral obligation – to do anything and everything to take your organization down. Lies, innuendos, half-lies, stealing, Google-bombing, cyber-squatting and every other disruptive strategy is justified in their eyes because of the evil you, your organization and its leaders are perpetrating in the world.

Different blog critics require different responses. Some critics may actually be helpful. One of the great liberal western values being spread around the world in this era of globalization is freedom of expression. We treasure it in the United States and in most Western democracies, but it runs counter to many cultures. While this freedom of expression can be unpleasant and challenging if you are the target, to suggest that it should be limited or halted in your particular case will immediately put you and your organization on the losing side of the free speech debate. You just don't want to go there.

At the same time, to allow individuals who are determined to undermine and destroy the good work your organization does using unethical and illegal tactics is simply irresponsible. Look carefully at the online records of the various critics. Google them. Find out what you can about them. I'm not suggesting here that you hire a private investigator, but try to understand what is motivating them and whether or not they should be classified as a disgruntled and cranky person who doesn't like your organization or a true reputation terrorist intent on destruction.

2. Correct the Problems

Accusations, whether from an online source or via a media story, fall into one of three categories: They are true, they are based on misperception, or they are intended to harm.

If the accusations are true, deal with the problem. In the example we are providing, it is possible that some of the agencies' representatives were overly exuberant in their fundraising methods and made statements that were exaggerations of the organization's performance. If this sort of activity is the source of some of the blog critic's complaints, find out the reality and then fix it and communicate about it. What do you think the response of blog critics and those who are observing will be when they see the organization respond like this: "We appreciate those who have brought this problem to our attention. We recognize that it is a serious problem and apologize to the people who have been hurt by the unauthorized actions of some of our representatives. We have launched an investigation and we are reviewing our policies to help identify those who are involved in this activity and we will take strong action to keep this from happening again."

Frequently, the accusations are a complex mix of some truth, exaggeration and biased interpretation. These fall into the second category. It is harder in these cases to take a completely non-defensive position as advocated in responding to the first category, but it must be attempted. Identify what truth there is in their accusation and deal with it. But also clearly identify the misstatements of fact.

A response to this kind of critic might be: "We appreciate the comments because they have been helpful to us in identifying some problems that needed to be corrected. We have taken action against three individuals where it was demonstrated that rules had been violated. However, the suggestion that this problem is very common and that most of our representatives engage in these improper activities is not true. After careful investigation we have found that the vast majority of our representatives do an effective and ethical job of presenting our organization and its accomplishments. We encourage anyone with specific, verifiable information about improper actions on the part of our representatives to contact us immediately."

The third kind of accusation calls for a different strategy. It is essentially the same as dealing with any other activist who is intent on harming your organization. Start with personal contacts – both to understand the motives and strategies of the activist but also to engage him or her directly and personally. It is not uncommon for this kind of personal attention and face-to-face contact to substantially change the attacks. It is hard to hate people who are going out of their way to listen to you and validate you. But the hardened critic will only turn those efforts against you. Be aware that everything you do will be the subject for frequent blog postings.

If the personal efforts do not create change, then you enter into a credibility battle. And whoever emerges as believable, trustworthy, and likeable will win the war. Everything that follows assumes that that is the kind of blogwar you are in.

3. Get Out of the Bunker and Start Talking

Recognize above all, you do not win this war by failing to engage. The field belongs to the attacker. The true reputation terrorist knows there is great risk for you to enter into the battle and they have a certain confidence that you will not deign to stoop to their level. They usually believe, and have reasons to believe, that you will let them say and do what they please without response. Mostly, because this is the kind of response that has been adopted when the criticisms of the past have not been elevated to the level of the mainstream media. Now that the Internet is the medium, blog reputation terrorists have to be dealt with more as if the media is involved rather than a strictly non-public attack.

You wake up one morning, do a Google search on your organization's name and you find that "Your name sucks" sites have multiplied. In fact, your organization's site is almost hard to find in the morass of hate sites. Now you have a problem. Your first problem may in fact be the difficulty of getting senior management to agree to address the problem. They may still believe that blogwars are more similar to organizational criticism in the past that remains largely private. They may not understand that even a single blogger or a small group of bloggers making common cause has more potential to cause harm than even some significant negative coverage in the mainstream media – for all the reasons identified above. It has been demonstrated in recent experience that management tends to take it seriously when the organization's business results show substantial impact that can be traced directly to blogwars. By that time, unfortunately, the horse has left the barn and you have to play catch-up.

The first step in responding is to start talking. How to talk and who to talk to are addressed in the next items. It can be very valuable talking directly to the bloggers. It can be very valuable setting up your own official organization blog. It can also be valuable, as Microsoft discovered, to allow and even encourage those within your organization to set up their own blogs without restrictions. You may consider sending a message throughout the organization that the widespread Internet conversation is carrying on without people within the organization participating. Without the perspective, factual information, and advocacy of those involved in the organization participating, it will be easy to see how casual observers may take what the critics have to say at face value. After all, lies or misinformation repeated often enough become the truth. Encouraging open communication by people within your organization adds to transparency, adds to the depth of conversation occurring on the Internet, and can significantly impact the way blog readers think about the organization.

4. Talk to the "Saveables"

When responding to critics, whether online critics or in the mainstream media, it is helpful to think about the tried and true separation of audiences. This idea simply says on any controversial issue where there is likely to be a clear difference of opinion, you can divide your audience into three categories: Saints, Sinners and Saveables. The Saints you have with you – they will support you regardless of what your opponents say. The Sinners are dyed-in-the-wool opponents. No amount of persuasion and presentation of evidence will convince them they are wrong. That leaves the Saveables, and these are the ones you want to, and need to, win over.

To be a Saveable, they have to be persuadable. They are largely undecided, but usually Saveables lean one way versus the other. It is helpful to think primarily about those who are leaning in the direction of your opponents. What is it in their experience that would give credence to your opponents? Why do they think your opponents may be right? What about your opponents' arguments do they find appealing?

To give validation to their inclinations is to start off on a ground they can respect and appreciate. And to address their concerns from a standpoint of simply not having all the facts and information they need to make a valid judgment avoids putting them on the defensive. To say, in effect, "Anyone who believes my organization could do anything wrong is either stupid or evil," is not very effective when appealing to Saveables. Works great with Saints, though, and that's why too often that kind of response is offered. It is very natural for us to have in mind Saints as our audience because it is so much easier and more pleasant talking to people who already fundamentally agree with everything you say and think. You are smart and honest. Saveables on the other hand are just not sure.

When talking to Saveables, give validity to their basic understandings, positions, concerns and questions. Address the factual issues that underlay the concerns. And above all, demonstrate that you are an honest, transparent and credible source of information in regard to the things that concern them.

Using the example of the non-profit organization under attack by critics, the Saveable-based response would say, "Given all the evidence of fraud and unethical conduct by many in the non-profit fundraising world, it is easy to understand why people would be easily convinced about the accusation against our representatives. It is also why our organization is very concerned about any evidence we receive about rule violations among our representatives and why we are vigilant in investigating and responding to any violations. The truth is, they do occur. But the truth also is, they are very rare. We have found three instances in the past five years...."

This approach grants them the basis for their concern and validates their underlying assumption, but then addresses the facts. Blog critics who fall into the reputation terrorist category typically do not do this and therefore tend to quickly lose their credibility among Saveables. They marginalize themselves by the venom, with their emotionally driven accusations and false information. But, often they need a little help in the process of destroying their own credibility.

5. Bolster Credibility

If there is a strong secondary theme in this book (after "move fast, it's an instant news world") it would be that credibility is the key to winning the reputation battle. Aristotle was right 2,500 years ago, as was discussed earlier. When it comes to blogwars, ultimately the battle will be won by the most credible.

Since this topic has been well covered in other chapters, we won't rehash it here. The same strategies apply when dealing with blog attacks. The first and obviously most important way of protecting your credibility is to always tell the truth. And telling the truth means in spirit as well as fact. No spinning. No twisting the facts to make them look different than they are. If there is bad news, talk about it and deal with it openly. If mistakes have been made, admit them, tell what you are doing about them and go on. If accusations are based on 10 percent truth and 90 percent nasty manipulation, recognize the 10 percent truth and then deal straightforwardly with the manipulation of the facts by the critics.

Sometimes, however, the damage to your credibility is so great that your opponents have the field without any effective response on your part. Finding individuals who have credibility with the Saveables (a much tougher job than finding individuals with credibility with the Saints) is necessary. "Borrowing" their credibility can re-establish your own.

One way of doing that is using Web sites that have been established simply to deal with the problem of who is to be believed on the Internet. A number of sites have now been established to investigate rumors, urban legends, "facts" presented on the Internet as truth, etc. Some of these sites have been particularly useful and effective in pointing out serious journalistic errors or frauds in the past few years. Like, "Consumer Reports," their entire future depends on being objective and completely truthful. If they demonstrate bias, sloppiness, or intentional deception, they are done for. Sites such as Snopes.com, ScamBusters.org and UrbanLegends.com can be extremely helpful in investigating and objectively pointing out false accusations against your organization.

Whatever you do and say, always keep in mind that ultimately the outcome of the battle you are in will be decided on by the Saveables and their primary criterion for deciding which direction to go will be based on who is most believable. It is virtually impossible for a Saveable to say, "I know what this person is telling me is the truth, but I am going to go with the other person anyway." For them to take that position, they are solidly in the Sinners camp.

6. Be Human

The wonderful thing about Internet publishing, and blogging in particular, is that it shows millions of people love to write and a great many of them are pretty good at it. There is great immediacy in blogging – only slightly less than email and instant messaging which is the height of keyboard-mediated immediacy. Thoughts flow freely, sometimes without much attention paid to spelling or grammar. There are logical jumps, rabbit trails, unsupported theses and flimsy argumentation. But there is frequently a strong personality that comes through clearly and compellingly in the postings.

Then comes the official corporate response as posted on the company Web site. Carefully constructed, formal, well-supported, concise and to the point. All hint of personality and character has been thoroughly scrubbed as it is "vetted" by senior executive after senior executive and the team of attorneys.

It doesn't work.

To talk to the millions who are part of the blogosphere, you need to talk in their language and meet their expectations. Certainly there are differences in style but that is related to the fact that people are very different, including bloggers. A corporate blog that does not convey a real person will most likely not have much credibility. Being human in part means admitting errors, revealing details that allow others to have an authentic peek into your life; expressing humor, outrage, bemusement and the thousands of other emotional reactions we are party to. Authenticity is essential. You will know, as you look back over the words you write whether or not they contain the truth and the whole truth. The challenge comes in when you have to (if you do) pass your corporate blog past the army of official approvers.

There is a strong sense in which any blog that has been approved loses credibility. It's one reason why Microsoft's thousands of bloggers have the credibility they do; it is well known that no company executive or lawyer reviews them or has assumed authority to modify them. Blogging is personal. To make it corporate is largely to destroy it.

7. Build Rapid Response Capability

Reputation terrorists operate at the speed of light. Their latest revelations make their way around the globe before you have time to dial the extension of your CEO. When facing a concerted effort to destroy or damage your organization's reputation by blogging or by building a network of the disgruntled, it is critical to create a rapid response team. It is very similar to being exposed to the risk of highly negative stories being published in this era of instant news – only faster.

Earlier, we discussed the "war room" concept that evolved in President Clinton's first campaign and how this was adopted by later campaigns. "Sentries" were posted at the opponent's campaign events and the first hint of a new attack was relayed back to the war room where a response was discussed. The agreed-upon message – a defensive correction or a counter-attack – was launched and before the new attack could generate any momentum in the press it was met with the counter-offensive.

A strike force of a communication manager, CEO or senior executive, an attorney or two, plus a support person or two should be formed to respond quickly. Pathways of involving all necessary decision makers should be clearly established. Ground rules should be set which make it clear what decisions can be made by the strike force and which should be elevated. An agreement should be made as to the expected response time of a major new blog attack as well as agreement as to the forms of the response: company Web site, blog sites, email distribution lists, response on blogger's discussions, mainstream media notifications, etc.

Major new accusations can roll quickly through the blogosphere and create momentum that is hard to quell if not slowed or stopped quickly. Blog reputation terrorists count on the speed of the Internet and the expected slow response of the target for their effectiveness. A quick response to even a relatively minor assault will convincingly show them that this strategy will not work in your case.

8. Take back the Search Returns

In a blogwar gone bad, any visitor using a search engine to find out more about your organization will have to wade through the dozens or thousands of negative sites in order to find yours. One way to distinguish between a casual blog critic and a dedicated blog reputation terrorist is to see how they attempt to build traffic to their site by leveraging the search of your name. They may very well take domain names that sound innocent enough and will lead the viewer to think they are selecting your organization's site. Then a barrage of venom and accusation greets the unsuspecting visitor.

As mentioned above, the way search engines work is by rewarding frequent posters and by scoring according to shared links. Bloggers have a natural advantage in search engine rankings. But many blog attackers leverage their often extensive knowledge of search engine optimization (now getting its own jargon: SEO) to make certain their blog gets a high ranking when visitors are searching for your organization. In the current terminology of the blog set, these bloggers know how to get "Google juice;" how to maximize the search returns for their site.

As company and organization leaders understand the increasing importance of search engines, they are getting more protective of their "real estate." They are grabbing more domain names to keep them out of the hands of those who would purchase them for the purpose of misusing. They are aggressively going after "cyber squatters," those individuals or companies who grab domain names for the purpose of profiting from the misdirection. It is illegal to cyber squat and a rather clear-cut process using a paid online mediator has been established to help resolve cyber squatting situations.

"Google bombing" is one term for intentionally manipulating Web sites to improve their google ranking. While it may be common for blog attackers to use such techniques, those in the blogosphere tend to consider it highly disturbing when companies or organizations – even those under attack or who have had their rightful names hijacked – use such techniques to re-establish search engine dominance. One company engaged in a heated online war had several articles written about it, including from a respected online journalism observer, about their attempts to minimize the damage by using search engine optimization techniques.

The hypocrisy of this position notwithstanding, in a blogwar the company or organization is at a serious disadvantage. It is not unlike a company responding to attacks from a citizen's group. The money raised by the citizen's group and used in the reputation attack is seen to be clean and honorable. The money used by the company to defend itself is frequently seen to be a disgusting example of the powerful using their ill-gotten earnings to maintain its power. Any effort to regain control of search engine rankings by the company will likely be the subject of many more blogs and used as an example of the company's unethical behavior. This does not mean you should not do it. It simply means you should be prepared for these kinds of attacks and be prepared to respond to them. The simplest response is to explain the tactics and methods that your attackers are using, how that can mislead people and why you think it is right and appropriate to provide people with access to full and complete information.

This brings us to the next question and that is legal action. At what point do you initiate legal action to silence the critics?

9. Move the Black Hat Carefully

As discussed earlier, when the black hat has been placed securely on your head, in this case by the blog critics, it must be moved. But there is considerable risk in moving this hat too heavy-handedly. Bloggers and blog readers tend to place a very high value on free speech. They do not take kindly to anyone interfering improperly or inappropriately to someone's right to express an opinion, no matter how inaccurate, unjustified or vicious that opinion might be. And no matter how much damage that opinion might be causing because it is broadcast via Internet to thousands or more.

That is why the very best response is to engage – not to remain silent. Win the credibility war by demonstrating your humanity, your humility, your dedication to honesty and the truth, and your commitment to protecting the rights of anyone to say what they want. And, if need be, enlist the help of others who have credibility with those you do not.

Remember that ultimately the outcome will be decided by Saveables who will base their decision on who is most credible, and to some degree who they like the best. So when it comes time to attempt to move the black hat from your head to the attackers, it is something to do carefully. You satisfy only yourself and the Saints if the outcome is to bloody your opponent without winning the hearts and minds of the Saveables. If the blog attacker fits in the reputation terrorist or activist category, it is likely that overheated statements or serious errors of facts have already been published on his or her blog. Any untruth, even the dangerous half-truths, needs to be quickly and aggressively challenged. When I say aggressively, I do not mean to make the correction personal. Assume honest mistakes. But make it very plain that errors have been made and then request a retraction and apology.

Taking this step of requesting and then demanding a retraction and apology is critically important, providing it is done in the context of respecting a person's right to express an opinion while denying them the right to intentionally post false or misleading information. Asking them to take action changes the field of battle by putting them on the defensive. Attackers love to attack. They do not normally enjoy being on the defensive. And as long as you are defending, it is hard to move the hat. Putting the attacker on the defensive without attacking them personally or mean-spiritedly is one of the most important elements in winning a blogwar. Once you have identified a clear error, misstatement, intentional exaggeration or other significant error on the part of the attacker, it is critical that you press this point. The blogger will come back with their attacks on you, but when you switch to try to respond to them, they win back the field of battle. You should respond to those by saying, "I will provide definitive answers to your questions about this after you have responded to my request for a full retraction and apology. If you are not willing to admit to your mistakes, there is not a lot of point of me continuing to try to correct your unending false claims."

This only is effective if the Saveables see that the information you have put forward is essentially indisputable. Someone who has made a mistake and refuses to own up to it is viewed by Saveables as untrustworthy. Sort of like a company who has messed up but will not admit it because attorneys are too concerned about the legal case. Nothing destroys credibility faster. That's why it is important to continue to press the issue of apology and retraction. Retraction is necessary because it removes the false information from the record, and apology is important because it is something that can be effectively used from then on to undermine the credibility of the attacker.

As effective as retraction and apology can be, there comes a time when stronger action is needed. When being pressed in this way, the blogger will almost always picture him or herself as the victim. "The big powerful company is trying to shut me down, they can't take the criticism and they will do anything to stop those who are just trying to expose the truth." Your attorneys, who should be involved in evaluating the situation, may be advising that the blogger has gone too far and broken the law. Again, there is a great risk in going after a blogger or a number of blog critics with legal action. It is almost impossible to avoid the appearance of attempting to shut off public discussion. That's why if that course is followed it is critically important to communicate about it. The discussion may very well turn to the actions your organization is taking, rather than the accusations against it. That has the benefit of shifting the field, but to a very dangerous one in terms of winning over Saveables. Since I view these battles as ultimately about winning over hearts and minds, I could only advise taking legal action if it is clearly demonstrated that it is necessary to protect the organization, and even then only if the actions can be openly discussed in the public forum including the Internet.

10. Never Stop Telling Your Story

It is quite easy to forget, in the heat of defending yourself or going on the offensive against your attackers, that you need to keep telling your story. By that I mean you need to continually remind the constantly changing audience how your company or organization is beneficial. In the non-profit agency we used as an example, there would be numerous examples of how people and villages or organizations benefited from the great work that was done and the generosity of the donors.

Obviously, one way of doing that is to use the blog you have launched to deal with the critics, not just for responding to critics, but to talk about the every day things that are going on in your organization. A quick review of Microsoft employee blogs reveals this is what happens. These fully unauthorized sites are not launched specifically to try to protect the company's reputation and defend against the multitude of blog attackers, but simply to reveal a little of their lives and thoughts as Microsoft employees.

From the perspective of the Saveable, fully understanding the value of your organization to the many people it serves is critical for them to make a positive decision about you. If they believe the blog critics but know your organization to do quality work, highly valued by your customers and employees, they will be conflicted. "They do good work, but are run by awful people who do bad things," they might conclude. Until you show them that those who are criticizing are not telling the truth and have motives of their own about damaging the good that is being done. Without reminding them of the overall picture, why your organization exists and why people benefit by the work your organization does, it will be considerably more difficult for them to tip in your direction.

Blogwars are not fundamentally different than other more traditional media-based reputation attacks and the response strategies are essentially the same. Like almost everything else having to do with the Internet, what makes blogwars dangerous is also what makes computer technology effective: activism is now better, faster and cheaper. Bloggers do not have to rely on compliant reporters to carry their message, nor do they have to depend on others with massive investments in communication infrastructure. Everything they need to bring your organization to its knees can be found in a small piece of metal and plastic they can put on their lap. That, and a simple, increasingly wireless connection to the entire world.

14.
The Ultimate Communicator

How will communications in the future be different than today? And what can we do today that will help us prepare for the communication challenges of tomorrow?

It is comforting to some degree to know, based on the record of human existence, that some things will likely never change. We will communicate. We will gather around common interests, needs and hopes and when we do, communication is how we will bond and how we will experience fellowship. When we form large groups, teams or organizations, we will designate some who have unique capabilities in communication to use their talents for the good of the group. We know that those communicators will have an instinctive understanding of their various important audiences and an empathy that enables them to see things and express ideas from their audience's perspective. We know that they will have the intelligence and skill to craft words in ways that convey knowledge, ideas, experience, emotion and meaning. And they will always keep their ears engaged, listening carefully and responding to what they hear and understand. Those things will likely never change.

We also know what will change: the technology of communication. Change has not always been the constant it is now. There were eras in human history when millennia passed with little to no variation in how our ancestors conducted their lives together. Our time is different.

I write this chapter about 17 years after two of the most significant events of our time occurred. On Nov. 9, 1989, the East German government announced that those wishing to cross the border from East Germany would not be stopped; a mass of East Germans in jubilation began to tear down the wall. As the wall was a symbol of the divided state of the world following World War II, the reduction of it to rubble was a potent symbol of the beginning of globalization.

As to the other event, we'll let Wikipedia, the Internet's new knowledge aggregator, explain:

> "In 1989, CERN was the largest Internet node in Europe, and Berners-Lee saw an opportunity to join hypertext with the Internet. In his words, 'I just had to take the hypertext idea and connect it to the TCP and DNS ideas and – ta-da! – the World Wide Web'."

CERN is the world's largest particle physics laboratory and is located in Switzerland. Tim Berners-Lee, now Sir Tim Berners-Lee, was a young scientist interested in this computer network that was being established to link scientists, educational institutions and major laboratories together. The creation of the World Wide Web and its application, not just to scientists and the military community (where the Internet was started), but to just about everyone in the universe, is about as history-changing as any event, at least in our time.

In 1989, globalization can be said to have truly begun, and in 1989 the Internet started on its path to becoming a powerful engine of globalization and a remarkable agent for change. For anyone uncertain of the role of the Internet in globalization, Thomas Friedman's The World is Flat will likely fill in the gaps.

Much has changed in the 17 years I mentioned. Globalization is rapidly changing the balance of power in the world, fundamentally altering nations, societies and people's lives. There is a growing sense that national borders do not mean what they once did, that ideas like laws, culture and mores are no longer applicable to simply the national or local level. There is also a sense that nothing much can be hidden. The destruction of the Soviet empire and the remarkable change in state control over the economy in Communist China was inevitable once communication broke the artificial barriers that were constructed. Freedom, liberty and the opportunity to advance through your own efforts are compelling motives for economic and political change.

From this vantage point in the still early years of the 21st century, it appears that change will continue apace in the general directions that have been laid out since 1989. Globalization appears to have achieved momentum that will make it stoppable only by a cataclysm of an almost unimaginable scale. And global communication based on the ever broadening and deepening Internet use will continue to change how people do business, how they build and maintain relationships, how they learn and change. It is useful to try to look ahead and see the trends that are forming now and what they might mean for communicators in the future.

Social Interaction

In retrospect, it should not be such a surprise that social networking is the true "killer app" of the Web today. This phenomenon, frequently referred to as "Web 2.0," describes the high level of interaction that Internet users are engaged in and particularly the ways in which the Web is used to build and maintain social connections. We are all part of communities: families, neighborhoods, work groups, church memberships, non-profit organizations, etc. Now the Internet is making possible the rapid development of communities without geographic limits. Communities focused on an unlimited number of shared special interests are being built around blog sites, community-based Web sites, organization and corporate Web sites and around specialty Web sites such as MySpace.com and Friendster.com.

Successful blogs need to be seen not just as the often cranky writing of someone hiding out in her bedroom with too much time on her hands, but as communities of readers and commentators gathered around either the special topics of focus or the personality of the writer.

Much focus in marketing and public relations work is now being placed on this social networking phenomenon. Companies and organizations well positioned to create and facilitate communities of customers and interested persons, but choose not to, will likely begin to lose their market position to those who aggressively pursue the community building opportunity. As discussed in the previous chapters, companies and organizations under attack from blogs and these communities absolutely need to participate, respond and create communities of their own if they are to maintain their reputation.

Building relationships and enjoying them will remain our chief source of joy and meaning in our lives – as it has been from the beginning. The Internet is simply the latest innovation to make that possible and it will continue to be used in expanding ways to meet this most basic human need.

Communicators of the future need to be fully prepared to participate in communities who are important to the organization. They also need to be able to develop those communities and provide leadership. In some cases, communities built through the Internet will be needed to counteract powerful communities built by the organization's detractors and opponents. Becoming aware of and using the rapidly increasing number of Web applications designed to facilitate community growth and communication will be an important skill in the very near future.

Video

Words less, pictures more. That may well be the mantra for the future. If I had any doubt about the validity of this observation it was erased when the Sept. 11 Commission Report was republished as a "graphic novel." The term graphic novel no longer refers to literature with over-the-top sex and violence described, it refers to a new phenomenon in publishing which blends comic books with fiction – or as in the case of the Sept. 11 Report, non-fiction. At this writing, it is unknown if the comic book version of the Sept. 11 Report will become a bestseller. But what is known is that major book retailers are establishing significant sections of their retail space specifically for this literature presented in comic illustrative form.

Words less, pictures more. The reasons are based in technology and globalization. While English appears to be becoming the language of international commerce and communication, language continues to remain a significant barrier to globalization. Images transcend language and are far more universal. If a story can be told or a message conveyed in pictures, no language barrier exists. Plus, the old saying stands:

a picture is worth a thousand words. Add motion and immediacy and you multiply that formula. Technology is making the capture, processing and distribution of still images and video much easier. The Internet, with rapidly advancing broadband access, makes distribution of video instantaneous and inexpensive.

Today's communicators who understand the rapid changes in our world are already using video to great advantage. The US Coast Guard, rapidly gaining a reputation as the best at communication of all federal agencies, uses video extensively in their media and public communication efforts. When former football star Larry Czonka was rescued from icy Alaskan waters the rescue was captured on video, placed on their communication system Web site, and when announced to the world via Sports Illustrated, thousands watched the rescue. In the tragic Selandang Ayu shipwreck in Alaska in late 2004, the Coast Guard posted video of the helicopter conducting rescue operations moments before its crash, which killed six of the rescued crewmembers.

Today's communicators who are not prepared to provide Webcasts of press conferences, virtually instant video uploads to their public information Web sites, and a steady stream of still images will soon find they are disappointing the expectations of the media and the public. When we can sit in our living rooms and view instantaneously what is happening on the ski slopes in the Olympics or the frontline of battle in the Mid-East, we will ask the question why we can't see what is going on with the oil spill that is ruining our precious waterways, or why we can't see into the meeting rooms of corporate leaders who are making decisions that are determining our lives.

Wireless and Portability

We have become accustomed to the idea that we live in a connected world. We are more connected than ever to our offices, our homes, and our relatives across town or across the globe. That connection we see as a plug that goes into our computers. But that physical connection is going away. Ubiquitous wireless connectivity combined with ever more portable devices is no longer a distant promise. To some degree, it is already here and coming with absolute certainty. "Getting away" will mean a conscious choice to disconnect as it already does for many.

Ubiquitous connectivity means that we will have the opportunity to maintain continual communication, and one of the principles of this book is that where there is the possibility there is demand. That means that CEOs will be expected to maintain constant communication. That the public will expect and demand virtually instant and continuous communication about events and consequences that affect them. There will be little to no tolerance for silence, not at the beginning, the middle or the end of a significant event. Those involved in rapid response communication need to be wired now for ubiquitous connectivity and need to understand that every day the expectations of audiences increase.

It remains to be seen whether ubiquitous connectivity will result in us having our brains and senses hard-wired to the Internet via implants, or even if we will evolve so that we are born with the connectivity we need. But what is all but certain is that the well-established pattern of wireless portability will result in 24/7 connectivity in ways that will be seamless with our everyday lives.

Speed

The primary message of this book is speed. Technology and social change have driven the need for speed in communication. With democracy comes the expectation of involvement, even control. That means that an ever-increasing number of people around the world have every expectation of being engaged in the decisions that affect them. Technology gives wings to these expectations meaning that if a butterfly flaps its wings in China and the impact on me will be great, I expect to hear about it fast and as close to the butterfly as I can.

There is no reason to believe that expectations about speed will diminish. There is every reason to believe that they will increase. Given that, there is no doubt that many businesses, corporate giants and organizations will find themselves offering too little too late. As we have seen in many examples, too little too late can often mean "too bad" for the organization.

Political and Legal Controls

Perhaps the greatest unknown in the further exploitation of the Internet and digital technology in communication is not on the technology innovation front, but on the political and legal front. The powerful have always tried to control information, recognizing that information is power. Understanding that, the American nation-makers made certain that a free press would help insure the continuing freedoms of Americans against a too-powerful government. The striking difference in the development of the press and the media in the US versus that of other nations and cultures around the world is wonderfully documented in Pulitzer Prize winning author Paul Starr's book The Creation of the Media: Political Origins of Modern Communication.

Google's controversial acquiescence in early 2006 to the Communist government of China is one example of political control squaring off against the realities of open communication on the Internet. The Chinese government was banning Google's search from accessing sensitive topics and banned Web sites and in order to secure government approval and greater access, Google agreed to censor search words and selected sites. This includes controversial and potentially damaging topics from the government's point of view such as Tiananmen Square and Falun Gong. A BBC Web site poll showed 80 percent of online voters disagreed with Google's position. Clearly, the ethos of the Internet is one of complete openness and full access and any attempt by any power, be it a corporate power or a political one, to control access is viewed dimly by today's information consumers.

Also in early 2006, Al Jazeera announced plans to launch an international news channel in English. The organization operates as the 24-hour news channel of the Arab world, but in the heated tensions of the war on terrorism and the Mid-East conflicts, Al Jazeera is known in the West for televising beheadings and broadcasting hostages begging for the their lives. Hardly ways to build loyalty and interest in the European and American markets, but this introduction highlights the role that communications can and need to play in bridging gaps and creating understanding.

Almost every day there are news stories relating to the ongoing interaction between our legal system and the increasingly open communication options. How far can online critics go in making statements about another person or company? What communication is discoverable and beyond the reach of opposing attorneys? How can intellectual property be protected in such a Wild West environment? Should there be no bounds on use of the Internet for behavior that most consider immoral or depraved?

While there is little doubt that the boundaries of technology-driven communication will continue to run into critical questions of law and politics, there is also little doubt that the current trend to ever more openness and access will also continue. The boundaries that are put in place by law and governments will continue to be pushed and, until there is a counter push of significant magnitude on the part of the general public, the pushing will likely result in further movement outward. The Chinese government's efforts to control access to information reveal it to be a relic of past tyrannies in today's frame of thinking. Relics are fine on the shelf to be looked at as curiosities but are not well accepted as a normal part of the contemporary world. Something has to give and it seems unlikely to give in the direction of tighter control and less freedom of information.

The Ultimate Communicator

With the need for virtually instantaneous and open communication with audiences who demand the straight facts directly from you, it would seem natural that organizations would delegate this increasingly important function to large staffs to manage. And that communication staffs would grow because of these increasing demands. Indeed, there is little doubt that corporate and organizational leaders will be spending more and more of their time on the important issues of stakeholder communication and that communication as a career will be an increasingly attractive option for intelligent and ambitious young people. But, increasing pressure will be put on the very few whose communication makes the greatest impact. And those few will become more directly involved in managing their own communication world.

The Ultimate Communicator is the person in your organization who everyone believes has their hands on the wheel, who makes the decisions that matter, who most directly impacts the lives of your organization's stakeholders. It is his or her personality and values and character that matter most to those who are affected by your organization. The natural result of the openness and transparency that has now become mandatory in the halls of business, government and non-profits is to focus on the few at the top and most usually, the person at the very top.

As goes the person at the top, so goes the organization. The tragic-comic episode of Michael Brown, head of FEMA during the early stages of Hurricane Katrina, provides a compelling example. The failures of a very complex organization during a time of extreme chaos were directly related to his own failings as an individual. His weakness as a communicator, his obvious discomfort in facing the harsh criticism, and his questionable credentials all played into the story of abject failure reported by the media. Rudy Giuliani on the other hand, the Mayor of New York during the Sept. 11 attacks, came to represent all that was good, strong, effective and compassionate about the police and fire agencies of New York who responded. Certainly the case can be made that the respective failure and success of the agencies mentioned was more important in determining public sentiment than the leaders. Yet, how can you separate the two? Can we really imagine FEMA suffering the same loss of public confidence if Rudy Giuliani had been the director during Katrina? No, because we sense that he would have been on the ground, up to his waist in flood waters, holding African-American children in his arms as he appeared to be personally directing the efforts of his over-taxed staff.

The instant news world places a high premium on personal, direct, involved leadership. It also places a premium on men and women of exceptional character. At a time in which personal morals have largely lost their historic underpinnings in faith and godliness, the public now places a very high value on leaders who are fundamentally honest, good-hearted, courageous and unselfish. We want leaders who are not only effective, but who are good.

As the communications world becomes ever more technology-dependent, it would be a natural assumption that the organization leaders would become further and further removed from the mechanics of communication. It will be, we tend to think, the staff people who will push the buttons that will get the messages out to the stakeholders eager to hear. But an intriguing passage in Thomas Friedman's The World is Flat suggests that just the opposite may be true. Perhaps the Ultimate

Communicator will become more and more his or her own master when it comes to planning, managing and executing the most vital communications at the moment of crisis.

The passage is worth quoting at length:

> "Before Colin Powell stepped down as secretary of state, I went in for an interview which was also attended by two of his press advisers, in his seventh floor State Department suite. I could not resist asking him about where he was when he realized the world had gone flat. He answered with one word: 'Google.' Powell said that when he took over as secretary of state in 2001, and he needed some bit of information – say, the text of a UN resolution – he would call an aid and have to wait for minutes or even hours for someone to dig it up for him.
>
> 'Now I just type into Google "UNSC Resolution 242" and up comes the text,' he said. Powell explained that with each passing year, he found himself doing more and more of his own research, at which point one of his press advisers remarked, 'Yes, now he no longer comes asking for information. He comes asking for action.'"

Friedman goes on to explain how Powell maintained a constant instant messaging relationship with Britain's foreign secretary, Jack Straw at summit meetings. And how, when he wanted to contact the Russian foreign minister, he tracked him down by cell phone in Laos. Powell commented, "We have everyone's cell number," referring to his fellow foreign ministers.

Friedman makes the critical point: "The point I take away from all this is that when the world goes flat, hierarchies are not being leveled just by little people being able to act big. They are also being leveled by big people being able to act really small – in the sense that they are enabled to do many more things on their own."

As I contemplated the implications of this insight, I happened to have lunch with a client using the virtual communications technology referred to earlier. He is the fire chief in Bellingham and I first met him when he was serving as the first Information Officer of the Olympic Pipeline accident. The conversation turned to his use of the virtual communication center and he commented that that morning he had put out a press release. I didn't think twice about it at first and then, suddenly, I wondered and asked if it was normal for the fire chief to put out his own press release? No, he answered. Normally it would be done by the communication manager, but she was busy on other tasks for the City and so he did it himself.

Without this Web application, would he have gone through the process of getting the release out to his list of local reporters? No, he would have waited. But because he had the power in his hands to draft, edit, approve, distribute, post to his Web site and whatever other form of communication he wanted to engage in, it changed his behavior and he did it himself. Knowing he can easily operate the machinery that will enable him to communicate to the world gives this fire chief a greater level of confidence in his ability to do his job with the community of 85,000 whom he serves to protect.

One of the critical tasks the Ultimate Communicators will do on their own is communicate. Michael Chertoff, the current head of the Department of Homeland Security, using the same virtual communications technology, could instantly command the communication resources of every state and local police, fire and emergency response organization in the nation. He could be awoken at 2:30 a.m. and find the nation in a deep crisis. He could use his laptop or home office computer to take immediate control of every first responder organization. He could access the individual contact lists of their communication control centers and send email messages to every reporter working for every local radio station and the smallest dailies. He could use the text-to-voice capability to phone messages to critical team members or reporters. He could post his urgent and personal message that would instantly appear on the "New Updates" section of every small police and fire Web site across the country. He could do it himself without the help of a single aid or a single IT manager. Furthermore, he could call 1600 Pennsylvania Avenue and have his role as Ultimate Communicator pre-empted by the Ultimate Communicator living in that grand house. And that person could also easily push the buttons him or herself that would enable instantaneous access through all the agencies and offices under his or her control.

That is not a fictional dream world in terms of technology. It exists today and increasing numbers of Fortune 100 corporations, universities, federal agencies, emergency management agencies, and many others are currently employing it. It is not just for the large and vulnerable. Instant news world communication capability is needed regardless of the size of the organization or the number of stakeholders impacted. Whether or not it is employed is not a matter of size as it is a matter of understanding the nature of today's communication environment and the need for speed.

For those readers who are CEOs, you already have an understanding of the critical role that communication plays in your future and the health and welfare of the organization you lead. You are concerned about what you need to do to prepare to meet communication challenges in the most extreme conditions. You would not be reading these words otherwise. To you I say, remember that it is ultimately who you are as a person that will be measured. There is little room to hide and, hopefully, little reason to. The mass of faces out there, for the most part, are human too and remarkably willing to forgive and to accept weakness and failure, but only if failings are acknowledged. They want to see and know and respect the real you. How you go, so goes your organization. Credibility, ultimately, is a terrible thing to waste.

For those who are not CEOs or Ultimate Communicators, but whose task is to help protect the organization and prepare it to meet the accelerating demands of stakeholders, the media and the public, to you I say, you have the most exciting job in the world. But your job is not to be the focus of attention but to be the window by which those who care about your organization can see it operating. Not all is pretty or as it should be. But those things we wish to push into dark closets need to be cleaned up because in this world, even the closets have windows. Ultimately your task is to help prepare those who represent the organization to the world and who will face their scrutiny in times of great trial. It is your privilege to prepare them to be authentic and honest and forthcoming. To understand that hiding and covering up and "spinning" is deadly in this new world of instant and open communication. To know that their strength and goodness and right action is desperately needed and needed to be seen in words and in pictures.

Index

A

B

T

U

V

W